Amazigh Politics in the Wake of the Arab Spring

Amazigh Politics in the Wake of the Arab Spring

BRUCE MADDY-WEITZMAN

University of Texas Press ◆ Austin

Copyright © 2022 by the University of Texas Press
All rights reserved
Printed in the United States of America
First edition, 2022

Requests for permission to reproduce material from this work should be sent to:
  Permissions
  University of Texas Press
  P.O. Box 7819
  Austin, TX 78713-7819
  utpress.utexas.edu/rp-form

♾ The paper used in this book meets the minimum requirements of ANSI/NISO Z39.48-1992 (R1997) (Permanence of Paper).

Library of Congress Cataloging-in-Publication Data

Names: Maddy-Weitzman, Bruce, author.
Title: Amazigh politics in the wake of the Arab Spring / Bruce Maddy-Weitzman.
Description: First edition. | Austin : University of Texas Press, 2022. | Includes bibliographical references and index.
Identifiers: LCCN 2021024487 (print) | LCCN 2021024488 (e-book)
ISBN 978-1-4773-2482-0 (hardcover)
ISBN 978-1-4773-2483-7 (PDF e-book)
ISBN 978-1-4773-2484-4 (ePub e-book)
Subjects: LCSH: Berbers—Political activity—Africa, North—History—21st century. | Arab Spring, 2010– | Berbers—Ethnic identity. | National characteristics, African. | Berbers—Africa, North—Social conditions—History. | Africa, North—Politics and government—History—21st century. | Africa, North—Ethnic relations—History.
Classification: LCC DT193.5.B45 M3268 2022 (print) | LCC DT193.5.B45 (e-book) | DDC 960.3/312—dc23
LC record available at https://lccn.loc.gov/2021024487
LC e-book record available at https://lccn.loc.gov/2021024488

doi:10.7560/324820

For Maya, Ilai, and Lavi.
May you help make the world a better place.

Contents

List of Maps **ix**
Acknowledgments **xi**

Introduction **1**

1. Toward a Second Republic? Algeria and the Amazigh Question **21**
2. Obscure No Longer: Libyan Imazighen in a Fractured Polity **55**
3. Azawad: The Abortive Republic **87**
4. Tunisia: The Amazigh Factor Enters the Realm **105**
5. Moroccan Imazighen and the *Makhzen*: From Recognition to Malaise **125**

Conclusion **157**

Notes **163**
Index **199**

List of Maps

0.1 Amazigh-speaking groups **8**
0.2 Tamazgha **12**
1.1 Amazigh-speaking regions in Algeria **24**
1.2 Mzab-Wargala Amazigh-speaking region **42**
2.1 Ethnic groups in Libya **59**
3.1 Azawad **88**
4.1 Amazigh-speaking concentrations in Tunisia **107**
5.1 Amazigh-speaking regions in Morocco **128**

Acknowledgments

As all scholars and writers know, writing is a supremely solitary enterprise, all the more so during COVID-19. Nevertheless, we also know that our projects cannot be accomplished successfully without the input, assistance, cooperation, and support of any number of individuals and institutions. I benefited greatly for a decade from the opportunities to participate in several high-level academic conferences and panels in Morocco, Italy, Turkey, and the United States on subjects related to the Amazigh issue and state-minority dynamics in general. My thanks go out to the various organizers: Will Kymlicka and Eva Pföestl (in Rome), Katherine E. Hoffman and Jane Goodman (Tangier), Bill Lawrence (Washington, DC), Thierry Desrues and Mohand Tilmatine (Ankara), Anna Maria Di Tolla (Naples), Habiba Boumlik and Lucy McNair (New York), and Moha Ennaji (Fez). Many people have generously provided feedback, shared their own writings, forwarded documents and other materials, consented to answer my questions and meet for conversations, and connected me with additional persons. For all of that and more, I extend my thanks to Massin Aaouid, Ahmed Arrehmouch, Ahmed Assid, Soubeika Bahri, Anna Baldinetti, Abdellah Benhssi, Fathi Benkhalifa, Kawtare Bihya, Abdelilah Bouasria, Ahmed Boukous, Habiba Boumlik, Nadir Bouhmouch, Madghis Buzakhar, Mazigh Buzakhar, Maya Charrad, Mohamed Chtatou, Meryam Demnati, Anna Maria Di Tolla, Moha Ennaji, Omar Fasstaoui, Ricard González, Maha Jouini, Mounir Kejji, Asma Khalifa, Bill Lawrence, Elhabib Louai, Belkacem Lounes, Zorg Madi, Michelle Medina, Wail Moammer, Samir Nefzu, Lahcen Oulhaj, Boubker Outaadit, Mohamed El Ouazguiti, Emily Parker, Rachid Raha, Moha Tawaja, Amazigh Tazaghart, Mohand Tilmatine, Baha Udawd, Omar Uxabassu, Omar Zanifi, and an anonymous Libyan Amazigh activist. I apologize if I have inadvertently left anyone off the list. Paul Silverstein and Mohamed Daadaoui offered valuable constructive criticism on the entire manuscript. Moreover, I have benefited greatly from their own scholarship and discussions with them over the years. Naturally, I am responsible for any remaining shortcomings.

Special thanks go to Jim Burr, senior editor at the University of Texas Press, for all of his support and goodwill and for shepherding this project to fruition together with Editing, Design & Production Manager Robert Kimzey and the rest of their team. I have never encountered a more professional operation in the academic publishing world. Elena Kuznetzov of Tel Aviv University's Moshe Dayan Center for Middle Eastern and African Studies prepared the maps in her usual excellent fashion, together with UT Press. Jon Howard did an expert copyediting job, Jeff Georgeson was a careful proofreader, and Peter Brigaitis and Marie Nuchols were meticulous indexers. Thanks also to Ayelet Levy, Sarah Hassnaoui, and Rachel Shafer for their assistance in gathering materials, as well as to the Inter-Library Loan staff at Tel Aviv University's Sourasky Library, which provided invaluable assistance in overcoming the obstacles posed by the coronavirus pandemic. So did Marion Gliksberg, Librarian of the Dayan Center. The Dayan Center, together with the Department of Middle Eastern and African History, have been my professional home for four decades, and I am extremely grateful for the supportive and congenial environment.

Finally, a heartfelt thanks to my wife and life partner, Edie Maddy-Weitzman, not only for her unstinting support but also for speaking up at just the right moment, telling me to go and write this book.

Introduction

It is now a decade since Mohamed Bouazizi, a despairing twenty-six-year-old vegetable peddler in a dusty Tunisian provincial town, set himself aflame and triggered a tsunami of popular protest that cascaded back and forth across the Arab Middle East and North Africa. The storm that he unknowingly unleashed toppled four long-serving autocratic rulers—Tunisia's Zine El Abidine Ben Ali, Egypt's Husni Mubarak, Libya's Muammar Qaddafi, and Yemen's Ali Abdallah Salih; fractured three states—Syria, Libya, and Yemen; contributed to the rise of a global jihadist movement (the Islamic State, or ISIS) and the expansion of a pan-Kurdish space that challenged, separately and together, the post–World War I territorial order that was fashioned out of former Ottoman lands in the Levant and Mesopotamia; and impacted the regional geopolitics and beyond. The diminution of *haybat al-sulta* ("fear of the regime") was integral to the renewal of active contentious politics in the region, coming after decades of relative stability and domination of societies by authoritarian regimes.[1] Thus, even in the countries where the protests did not reach a critical mass to threaten the regimes—the Gulf monarchies (apart from Bahrain), Jordan, Morocco, Algeria, and Lebanon—the authorities there could hardly carry on without regard to their societies' increased readiness to challenge the status quo.

There have been numerous studies of the uprisings and their consequences over the course of the decade-plus since Mohamed Bouazizi's dramatic act of protest. The political scientist Marc Lynch, who coined the term "Arab Spring" to describe the budding protests in January 2011,[2] had already suggested that a new kind of pan-Arab identity shaped heavily by the rise of satellite television broadcasts and the internet was driving a second "Arab Awakening" that heralded a brighter future for populations living under decades of repressive authoritarian rule.[3] Fawaz Gerges emphasized the protesters' rejection of al-Qaeda's radical jihadist ideology and demands for democracy and accountability of their governments.[4] For many, the protests heralded a new democratic wave, following the so-called third wave two decades earlier in Latin America and elsewhere.[5] But the resultant success of Islamist movements and political parties in Tunisia and Morocco—and most importantly Egypt, where the Muslim Brotherhood ascended to power— gave pause, for Islamists in general had a more limited, instrumentalist view toward democratic process. Years earlier, political scientist Amr Hamzawy had cautioned against the view that increased political openness in the region would ultimately result in secular forces replacing authoritarian regimes. Islamists, he emphasized, were embedded in the social fabric of Arab societies and thus did well in competitive elections.[6] To be sure, Islamist movements were not all of one stripe, as was shown, for example, by the Ennahda Party's acceptance of democratic rules of the game in the new, post–Ben Ali Tunisia. Still, the electoral successes of Ennahda and Islamist parties in Morocco and Egypt, combined with the ongoing chaos in Syria, Libya, and Yemen, disappointed those who hoped that the inspiring scenes of masses of peaceful protesters on Tunis's Avenue Habib Bourguiba and in Cairo's Tahrir Square were harbingers of a new liberal democratic order. References to an "Arab Winter" and, alternatively, an "Islamic Winter" now entered the lexicon.[7]

From a different angle, the Saudi-led counterrevolution designed to prop up like-minded regimes—in Bahrain, Egypt (apart from the 2012–2013 Muslim Brotherhood–led government), and the Jordanian and Moroccan monarchies—indicated that the long-dominant authoritarian order was not fading away.[8] Hovering over everything was Syria's descent into horrific violence, which resulted in the deaths of hundreds of thousands of people and injured millions, uprooted half of its twenty-five million population, and caused untold property damage. The Syrian regime's loss of control over much of its territory, along with similar developments in neighboring Iraq, opened the door to both the jihadist ISIS and ethnonational Kurdish groups, suggesting— incorrectly as it turned out—that post–World War I territorial arrangements were being overturned.[9] In any case, existing sectarian, tribal, and religio-communal affiliations were even more salient, posing additional challenges to the Arab state system's ruling elites.

From the perspective of more than a decade, it is clear that Tunisia, the inspiring exemplar of the 2011 uprisings, constituted the exception among countries in the Arab Middle East and North Africa: it was the only country that successfully transitioned to a democratic, pluralist regime, however fragile and vulnerable it might continue to be. The authoritarian model of governance, which had dominated the Middle East–North Africa region in previous decades, made a comeback after having been buried (prematurely, as it turned out) during the initial euphoria amid the Arab Spring. This was certainly the case in the Maghreb, as shown in *The Lure of Authoritarianism: The Maghreb After the Arab Spring*, a fine collection of essays published in 2019.[10] And yet, at the very moment of its publication, there was a new outbreak of protests and challenges to governing elites in Sudan, Iraq, Lebanon, and Algeria, resulting in talk of an "Arab Spring 2.0."[11]

Clearly, the 2011 upheavals had not been simply a blip on the screen. Everywhere in the region, politics had become more contentious, even if the preponderance of power remained in the hands of authoritarian rulers and allied elites. In an essay published in 2019, political scientists Larbi Sadiki and Layla Saleh seemed to anticipate the renewal of protests in the late 2010s. The 2011 uprisings had ruptured the status quo, they wrote, as those on the political margin had "rekindled the practice of speaking back (dissent and protest) or striking back (with physical force)."[12] The new reality was one in which "peoplehood" (*hirak*) expressed its "moral outrage" against the coercive state (*dawlat al-iqrah*). Their usage and redefinition of *hirak* as "peoplehood" (generally translated as "movement") were prompted by the large-scale sustained protests of the same name in 2016–2017 in Morocco's northern Rifian Amazigh region. It was also prescient: soon, the term would be applied to the yearlong massive countrywide antiregime protests in Algeria that began in February 2019.

To be sure, lumping all the protests—violent and peaceful, the Islamic State, and Tunisia's Revolution of Dignity—into a single category exposes analytical shortcomings. Wisely, though, Sadiki and Saleh avoided predictions of outcomes and restated the obvious, namely, that the circumstances of contentious state-society relations vary from place to place. Still, it remains to be seen whether their belief that these relations were being permanently reconfigured to the benefit of society—resulting in less authoritarian, more pluralist, and democratic politics—will be proven correct. In any case, their focus on the continuing tensions between center and periphery (i.e., those who are of, or benefit from, the state and those who are marginalized and left out) and the resulting "return of the periphery to politics in challenging the authoritarian state" provides a useful perspective.[13] Frederic Volpi's 2017 study elaborates on these ongoing tensions and unsettled issues in North Africa.[14]

The Amazigh Identity Movement

Highlighting the Rifian *Hirak* brings us to the subject of this study: the Amazigh[15] identity movement[16] and its place within the larger picture depicting the Arab Spring and succeeding decade. It is a subject that has flown well under the radar of most analyses, as neither Morocco nor Algeria, the two main Amazigh population centers, experienced serious threats in 2011 to the existing order. Another reason, though, may have stemmed from the tendency to downplay the salience of Amazigh elements in what are generally defined as "Arab" states. One important exception is found in *The Lure of Authoritarianism*. The Amazigh movement, as well as the movement for women's rights, the editors stated, were the notable exceptions to the deepening of the overall trend toward greater authoritarianism in North Africa, as their "grassroots activism" on behalf of their agendas has been more successful than that of any other social groups.[17]

To be sure, this success was relative and differed from place to place. Moreover, differences within the Amazigh circles over strategy and tactics often hampered its efforts. Nonetheless, the decade-plus since 2011 was a formative period for Amazighité (lit., "Amazighity") and thus for North African states and societies as a whole. The central argument of this volume is that the increasingly visible and assertive Amazigh movement shifted its emphasis from being primarily ethnocultural to one that was more explicitly political and socioeconomic. Several common themes characterized this shift, even as the specifics varied from country to country:

1. In both Morocco and Algeria, in the formal, constitutional sphere, Tamazight was recognized as an official state language, along with "*Amazighiyya*" as a component of their respective national identities; in Libya, intensive efforts to achieve similar recognition fell short of the mark but remained an area of contention; in Tunisia, by contrast, the efforts by activists and sympathetic non-Amazigh liberals did not bear fruit.
2. The territorial dimension was increasingly salient. In Algeria, the concept of self-determination, whether within a federal and consociational democratic Algeria or even complete independence, was now part of the Kabyle political lexicon. "Autonomy" and "self-determination" entered into the lexicon of Libyan Amazigh as well, even if their meanings remained vague and organically linked to the Libyan state and nation as a whole. In Morocco, Amazigh intellectuals spoke of the need for genuine regionalization, and the large-scale Rifian *Hirak* protests clearly had an ethnopolitical and territorial dimension. And in northern Mali, Azawad, an independent Tuareg-led state, was briefly established but lacked the capacity to survive.
3. Socioeconomic marginalization, including discrimination and willful neglect by state authorities against Amazigh populations in peripheral regions, was increasingly central to the Amazigh movement's discourse, and protests over specific grievances abounded. Insistence on their rights was

framed as being commensurate with their status as the indigenous people of their lands, in line with the 2007 UN Declaration on the Rights of Indigenous Peoples.
4. Formidable obstacles remained extant. One in particular was the difficulty in building durable alliances with other elements in society that would help the Amazigh advance toward their strategic, long-term goals of refashioning the fundamentals of their countries' national identities.
5. The increasing salience of trans-state ties between Amazigh organizations across North Africa and in the Amazigh diaspora was noticeable. Moreover, diaspora-based organizations and communities played significant roles in bringing the Amazigh agenda to the attention of the international community. Social media was an ever more important tool for mobilizing on behalf of the Amazigh cause, helping to sharpen the collective consciousness of the Amazigh in both the imagined homeland of Tamazgha and the diaspora. This transnational sharpening was also accompanied by the further articulation and elaboration of more local identities, particularly among Libyan, Rifian, and Kabylian Amazigh.

This overall shift toward explicitly political issues further refined the Amazigh movement's rejection of the hegemonic postcolonial narratives that had consigned Amazigh communities to subordinate status within independent Arab nation-states. Hence, the Amazigh question, in all of its varieties, constituted an integral part of North Africa's increasingly contested politics during the Arab Spring decade. As surviving regimes struggled to recover their fraying legitimacy, and new ones sought to ensure it, they could no longer ignore Amazigh demands, even as their strategies ranged from partial acknowledgment and co-optation to overt repression. The unfolding of these multivectored, multidimensional developments in Morocco, Algeria, Libya, Tunisia, and the Sahel region form the heart of this volume.

This detailed study of the Amazigh question is situated within the larger sets of questions related to the status of minority groups in their societies. A recent collected volume on minorities in the Middle East focused on "the lives of minorities as subjects in their own right, and not only as objects of larger political movements," as well as the importance of "exposing the way in which minorities interact and influence their own plural societies as 'informed social agents.'" One question addressed in the volume is: "How do minority populations integrate into their host societies, both as a function of their own internal choices and as a response to majoritarian consensus on their status?"[18]

It is a relevant question for the Amazigh case, as much for what it doesn't ask as for what it does. Although Amazigh speakers are a minority in every state in which they reside, Amazigh activists reject the very idea of "minority" status on both historical and practical grounds. The pan-Amazigh discourse insists that the large majority of North Africans are of Amazigh, and not Arabian–Middle Eastern, origin. Indeed, recent genetic studies tend to confirm that the Arab contribution to the northwestern African gene pool is small.[19] These findings undermine the traditional Arab-Islamic narrative that North Africa's Berbers are of Eastern-Semitic origin and that their Arabization and Islamization was, in essence, a reunification with long-lost cousins under the enlightened banner of Islam. It also calls into question the insistence of nationalist movements and postindependent ruling elites that North African states are Arab. Of course, this doesn't resolve the question regarding where the Amazigh actually come from. But it does suggest that, between 2500–1200 BC, the bulk of North Africa's population can be categorized as "proto-Berber."[20] Amazigh groups everywhere have embraced the discourse of indigeneity and its attendant rights and protections. Unlike nearly all other cases of indigenous groups, however, the Amazigh discourse rejects the conflation of "minority" with "indigeneity" out of an understandable belief that being in a minority will inevitably enshrine subordinate status. Increasingly, Amazigh activists advocate a combination of genuine democratization and decentralization to ensure Amazigh continuity and development. Among Algeria's Kabyles, there is a growing emphasis on their distinct nationhood and territorial homeland—requiring a legal status akin to Canada's Quebec or Spain's Catalonia—within a transformed Algerian polity. Rifian autonomists speak a similar language. Some Kabyles and Rifians go even further and advocate a complete divorce from the state. In 2012, a Tuareg movement in Mali tried and failed to achieve just that.

Background and Context: Who Are the Amazigh?

North Africa's Tamazight-speaking peoples have been central to the mix of factors that shaped the region's history for millennia. Having constituted a majority of the population in Morocco at the beginning of the twentieth century, their current numbers are commonly estimated to be 40–45 percent of Morocco's thirty-seven million persons, 20–25 percent of Algeria's forty-four million, 6–10 percent of Libya's seven million, and 1–2 percent of Tunisia's 11.8 million.[21] Another two million persons of Berber origin can be found in the diaspora, primarily in Western Europe; approximately three million Tuareg Berbers live in the Sahel-Sahara regions, primarily Mali, Niger, and Burkina

Faso; 25,000 Imazighen populate the Siwa Oasis in Egypt's Western Desert; and a sprinkling are in Mauritania.

Language is generally a defining feature of an ethnic group, and that is certainly the case here. Imazighen speak various dialects—three main ones in Morocco, four in Algeria—of what is accepted to be a common language, Tamazight, that belongs to the Afro-Asian (formerly Hamito-Semitic) category. Up until the middle of the twentieth century, their language was almost exclusively oral and their social organization tribal. Clan and tribal ties remain significant for many, even though they have lost most of their primary functions.

The Greek and Latin words for "barbarian" were often applied to the peoples encountered by the Hellenizing empires during the Classical Age, and the Arabic *barbar* was applied to a variety of populations west of the Arabian Peninsula, including those just across the water in East Africa.[22] North Africans west of the Nile were known by a variety of other terms, including "Africans," "Numidians," and "Moors" or various tribal-related terms. Berbers became a "named" collective during and after their conquest by Arab-Islamic forces beginning in the late seventh century. They were almost entirely Islamicized during the ensuing centuries and by the fourteenth century had been elevated to the status of a "great nation" by the most famous of all Arab Muslim historians, Ibn Khaldun. Their degree of self-awareness as Berbers, and how they even came to be called "Berbers," are open for debate. A 2019 study of medieval Arabic-language sources probes the ideological and historical contexts in which "Berberization" took place and challenges the application of the term by most scholars to the more remote pre-Islamic past.[23]

During the sixteenth to eighteenth centuries, whether in the Ottoman North African domains—the regencies of Tunis, Tripoli, and Algiers—or the Moroccan sultanate, Berber populations were increasingly marginalized from the centers of power and faded gradually from view as a named collective. Ironically, it was the European powers that preserved a version of the name—"Barbary," in its English version. This was salient in the context of the centuries-long battles with corsairs ("pirates," in the European lexicon) based along the "Barbary coast" that preyed on European shipping. (The reverse was true as well.)

The revival and ultimate reification of "Berbers," as juxtaposed to "Arabs," by the French colonial project—first in Algeria in the mid-nineteenth century, then in Morocco in the first decades of the twentieth—have been well documented.[24] French colonialism and the accompanying linkage of North Africa to the global economic system, along with the penetration and dissemination

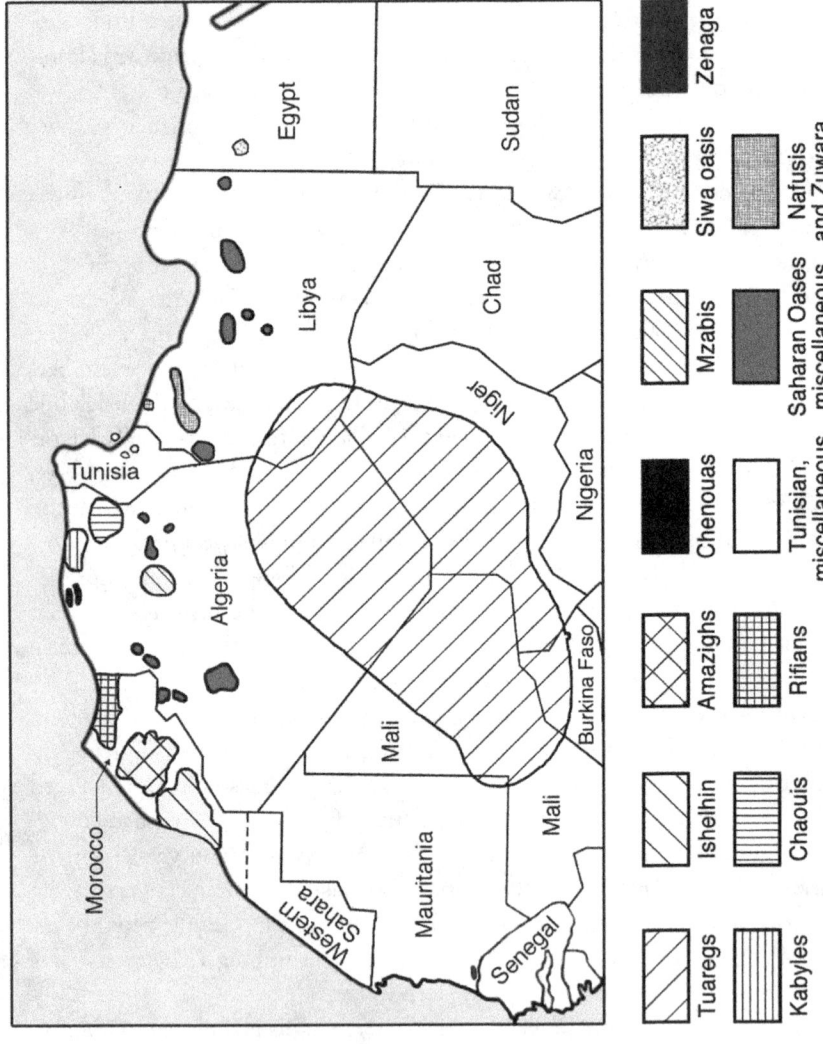

Map 0.1 Amazigh-speaking groups

of European culture, had as profound an impact on North African states and societies as the Islamic conquests wrought more than a millennium earlier. Berber populations, much like the rest of society, were affected in myriad and contradictory ways. Even as they were sometimes singled out for preferential treatment, owing to their allegedly higher place on the scale of civilization than Arabs, the various forms of colonial violence inflicted on them were no less harsh than on other segments of Muslim society. Nationalist anticolonial movements in Algeria and Morocco, which began to emerge in the late 1920s and gathered steam in the 1930s and 1940s, left little room for Berber specificity, partly because of their opposition to pro-Berber French policies, but also because of extant differences. In Morocco, for example, the mix of disdain and fear felt by urban Arabophone elites toward rural, primarily Berber, tribal sectors overlapped with ethnic differences. The overarching Algerian nationalist doctrine emphasized Islam and Arabness, including the Arabic language, as exclusive markers of national identity. Notwithstanding this problematic environment, Berbers were very much a part of both countries' national movements.

The Independence Era

Given these circumstances, it was only natural that newly independent nation-states (Libya in 1951, Morocco and Tunisia in 1956, Algeria in 1962) left little or no space—discursive or concrete—for legitimate expressions of Berber collective identity. This didn't seem to matter to scholars, who tended to downplay or even disregard the salience of Berber ethnicity regardless of circumstances. No less an intellectual luminary than Ernest Gellner, for example, dismissed the idea that tribally based Berbers could develop a more all-embracing type of ethnopolitical identity, writing that "in his heart, the Berber knows that God speaks Arabic and modernity speaks French."[25]

As for the ruling elites, they were determined to contain and subsume their Berber populations under the rubric of an overarching nationalist ideology that gave preeminence to Arabness and Islam. In Morocco, this formula was directly linked to the king's status as a direct descendent of the Prophet and "Commander of the Faithful" (*Amir al-Mu'minin*), both spiritually and temporally.[26] The conflated primacy of Islam and the king meant that Berbers could be full members of the Moroccan nation but that their language would naturally be subordinated to Arabic, the sacred language of the Qur'an. In Algeria, the independence movement's mantra "Islam is my religion, Arabic is my language, Algeria is my country" was formulated to challenge French colonial rule, which insisted that Algerian Muslims had no common past or common identity and remained in force. Both countries put down uprisings in Berber regions shortly after achieving independence and seemed secure for years afterward in the knowledge that their Berber populations would not pose any further serious challenges to the established sociopolitical order. Similarly, in Tunisia, founding president Habib Bourguiba was dismissive of the country's small remaining number of Amazigh speakers. In Libya, King Idris, although being congenitally opposed to establishing a strong central government, adopted policies that favored Arab tribes over their Amazigh neighbors, while Qaddafi's strident Arabism and personality cult required the erasure of any manifestations of Amazigh identity from public life.

However, matters developed differently. The impact on societies of complex processes of economic and political penetration by outside forces, national integration, and state-building have never been uniform and often reinforced existing communal affiliations even as their nature and content are substantially altered.[27] Although Berbers were steadily drawn into the wider national orbit over the ensuing decades, the state-building and nation-building formulas of both Algeria and Morocco proved to be inadequate in addressing the specific Berber components of their societies. As a result, a new kind of "imagining," in the Andersonian sense,[28] began to emerge. Algeria's Kabyle Berber community led the way in acquiring attributes of what Anthony Smith calls a modern *ethnie*—"a named unit of population with common ancestry myths and historical memories, elements of shared culture, some links with a historic territory and some measure of solidarity at least among [its] elites."[29] In line with the Hrochian model of the crucial initial role played by intellectuals of nondominant ethnic groups in fostering nationalist sentiment,[30] Paris-based Kabyle intellectuals, beginning in the mid-1960s, articulated a coherent narrative of Kabyle and Berber history and culture that laid the foundation for the modern Berber identity movement. Kabyle ethnic consciousness, distinctive from and opposed to the dominant Arab-Islamic mantra, was raised during the 1970s via work in the cultural and educational spheres and vocally manifested itself in football (soccer) stadiums as well. Although the specific context was very much Algerian, the larger context was the weakening after 1967 of the radical pan-Arab idea embodied by Egypt's charismatic leader Gamal Abdel Nasser and the pan-Arab Ba`th Party.[31] The increasingly charged nature of Kabyle–state relations eventually resulted in a six-week shutdown of many public services and institutions in Kabylia in March–April 1980. Known as the "Berber Spring" (*Tafsut Imazighen*), this "episode of contention" was the first substantive challenge to the Algerian regime since the early years of independence and was a harbinger of things to come.[32]

In Morocco, Berber–state relations were less charged than in Algeria, and important Berber rural elites and leading army officers were aligned with the Palace. Thereafter, the new Berber imagining and the resulting challenges that were posed to the official national narrative and accompanying policies developed more slowly. But there, too, urban intellectuals took the lead in advancing ethnocultural themes that paralleled and complemented the work being undertaken in Paris and Algeria. At the same time, Berbers were stigmatized because of two failed military coups in the early 1970s that had a distinct Berber "coloring," and many Berber activists in leftist groups and their families were left with deep scars by the state's brutal repression of all dissent during the 1960s and 1970s. Known as the "Years of Lead" (*les années du plomb*), it was a dark period in Moroccan history.[33]

By the early 1990s, the various strands of Berber activism had sufficiently crystalized into what can only be called an "identity movement," a development that fit neatly into the increased centrality of "identity politics" worldwide.[34] Amorphous, leaderless, and multivectored, with both country-specific and trans-state aspects, it had one clear core demand: the recognition by North African state authorities of the existence of the Amazigh people as a collective and of the historical and cultural Amazighité of North Africa. To that end, the movement's first action item was that Tamazight be made an official language alongside of and equal to Arabic, with all the attendant implications for the educational system and public sphere. Equalization also required a redressing of what movement activists viewed as the systematic economic and social neglect of the heavily Amazigh peripheral regions of North African states.

The Amazigh grand narrative rebrands all of North Africa and the Sahel as the land of "Tamazgha," belonging to the Amazigh from time immemorial. Its boundaries extend from the Egyptian Western Desert oasis of Siwa westward to the Canary Islands, 100 kilometers off the coast of the Western Sahara, where the Guanches, a Tamazight-speaking aborigine population, lived before eventually disappearing under the weight of Spanish colonial conquests at the end of the fifteenth century. This notion cannot be accepted uncritically.

Ramzi Roughi contends that the concept of North Africa as being a Berber land is something that emerged among Arab and Muslim writers during the fourteenth to sixteenth centuries and was refashioned by French colonial rulers for their own ideological purposes.[35] The latter are in fact often blamed for fabricating Berberism in order to promote a divide-and-rule policy. But this, too, is essentially an ideological argument that denies the existence of Berber agency and Berber specificity. From a different angle, the essentialism often displayed by Berber identity agents is not substantially different from

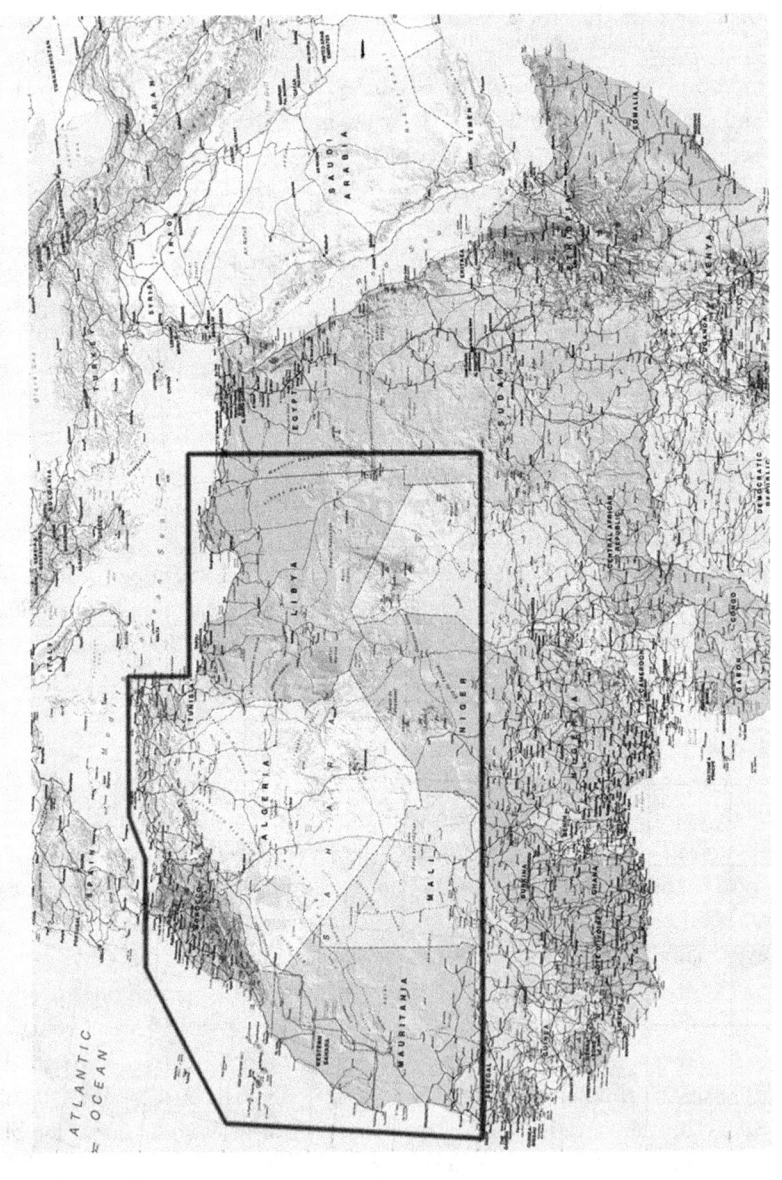

Map 0.2 Tamazgha

the Arab-Islamic nationalists whom they oppose. Of course, they are in good company: all social identities are constructed, and ethnonational movements have always been selective in choosing what they want to remember and what they want to forget.[36]

In any case, the sprouting of modern Berber identity proved to be a durable phenomenon. Berberism gradually but steadily became part of the larger contentious landscape of North African states and societies during the decades preceding the Arab Spring. To be sure, this landscape varied greatly. In Algeria, a sudden and chaotic democratic explosion in 1989–1991 was followed by a descent into horrific conflict between the Algerian military–led regime and radical Islamist groups that lasted for much of the rest of the decade. Throughout, its Kabyle Berber community forged an increasingly assertive counterpoint to both the regime and the Islamist opposition. In the midst of the regime's fight for survival, a massive, months-long school boycott in Kabylia during 1994–1995 produced the regime's first-ever concessions, as it recognized the Amazigh component of Algeria's national identity and pledged to introduce the teaching of Tamazight in Algeria's schools. Six years later, and twenty-one years after the iconic Berber Spring, a second and angrier confrontation with the authorities, sparked by the death of an eighteen-year-old in police custody following his arrest the previous evening, left 126 Kabyles dead. Known among Kabyles as the "Black Spring" (*Tafsut Taberkant*), it appeared momentarily that the Kabyles were on the cusp of leading a larger civic movement on behalf of a genuine democratic Algeria, but this possibility was quickly checked. Kabylia, however, remained in a state of civil revolt that lasted for years before receding. As in 1995, the regime offered a symbolic concession, amending the Algerian constitution to make Tamazight a "national" language, and Algeria's President Abdelaziz Bouteflika went so far as to declare in a 2004 campaign poster "WE ARE ARAB AMAZIGH."[37] For Kabyles, these episodes pushed them toward what is known in the social movement literature as "threshold crossings," that is to say, some type of cognitive conversion into a more self-conscious and mobilized political community.[38] They also radiated outward, in both directions, toward the Rif and Libya's Nafusa Amazigh, in particular. Amazigh militancy was less widespread among Algeria's other Berber communities but was no longer entirely dormant.

Morocco, Algeria's neighbor and longtime geopolitical and ideological rival,[39] has always kept a close eye on developments there. The 1980 Berber Spring events had prompted firm action by Moroccan authorities to clamp down hard on nascent Berberist activities. But developments at the end of the decade and into the 1990s prompted an opposite response. The regime now began a cautious process of political liberalization in order to bolster its legitimacy and to ensure Western economic aid. It was an approach that dovetailed with the need to build an effective counterweight to the kind of confrontational Islamist politics that was mushrooming in Algeria and elsewhere in the region. With those considerations in mind, the Amazigh movement now had a part to play, and it was tentatively encouraged to do so. But this was not only a top-down process. Amazigh associations began to mushroom, and activists and intellectuals fashioned a coherent platform outlining the movement's overall narrative and demands. The arrest and conviction of Amazigh activists in spring 1994 created considerable controversy and led to the king's intervention. Not only were they pardoned; King Hasan II publicly legitimized the "dialects," namely, the Amazigh component of Moroccan identity, for the first time, and instructed Moroccan schools to begin teaching Tamazight and the media to begin broadcasting news bulletins in the country's three main Amazigh dialects. Although implementation of the directive to teach Tamazight would come only nine years later, Hassan's action provided important initial legitimization for the Amazigh movement's activities.

These efforts received a major boost following the ascent of Mohamed VI to the Moroccan throne in July 1999 after his father's passing. Successive steps by the new king between 1999–2003 raised significantly the status of the Amazigh language and culture, which the king repeatedly declared was an integral part of the national patrimony. He also extended conciliatory gestures to the long-neglected Rif region, where his father had brutally put down an uprising in 1959. Amazigh intellectual and cultural production began to flourish, and hundreds of intellectuals signed a lengthy manifesto laying out their grand narrative of the past and demands for the present. Activism among first-generation students, particularly in the heavily Amazigh southeast, also manifested itself.

Toward the Arab Spring: An Amazigh Balance Sheet

As the first decade of the twenty-first century concluded, the balance sheet was decidedly mixed. The Algerian *pouvoir* (literally, "power," i.e, the regime)[40] had outlasted the years-long citizens' movement in Kabylia, creating a real malaise among Kabyle activists, whose energy appeared to be spent. Having survived the "dark decade" of the 1990s, and awash in petrodollars and Western backing for the "war on terror," the regime seemed firmly ensconced and was of no mind to address Amazigh grievances seriously. In Morocco, severe limitations on the Amazigh movement's ability to advance its agenda remained, notwithstanding the important steps taken by the king. His overall strategy remained one of co-optation and containment, while potential allies in other sectors of Moroccan society had limited influence, and hostility to the Amazigh agenda both in the bureaucracy and among Islamist and Arab nationalist circles was extant. So, too, were the yawning social and economic disparities between the heavily Amazigh periphery and the country's main centers. Libya's Amazigh activists had sufficiently emerged so as to trigger a brief charm offensive by the regime before it returned to its traditional hostile stance. And in Mali, repeated efforts to fashion a modus vivendi between the regime and its Tuareg communities after Tuareg revolts in the mid-1990s and in 2005 failed, leaving many Tuaregs sullen and potentially rebellious.

As nondominant ethnonational groups became increasingly assertive around the world, Amazigh activists often drew parallels with the Kurds—the other main ethnolinguistic community in the Greater Middle East that lacked statehood and self-determination. Kurdish flags were even waved at Amazigh demonstrations. They also viewed the Catalans of Spain as a model of emulation and inspiration. In turn, the Catalonia regional government provided some financial and moral support to Amazigh groups. But apart from similar ethnonational agendas, the Amazigh movement was light-years behind the Kurds and Catalans when it came to tallying achievements. Moreover, the movement's agenda was still far from being universally accepted by the Amazigh populaces themselves. In fact, Berbers could be found all across the political spectrum, including the upper echelons of the ruling elites and radical Islamist elements. Of course, this also is a familiar phenomenon in the history of ethnonational movements—in which the activists' first task typically has been to persuade members of the "nation" to prioritize membership in the collective and work for its success. Bringing about a conceptual revolution that would make being Berber "matter" on a grand scale, even as it very much mattered in different ways to individual Berbers,[41] was no small task, and the obstacles to success were many.

Still, from the perspective of more than a half-century since the end of colonial rule, the Amazigh movement had achieved considerable success. Its intellectual, cultural, and political efforts raised fundamental questions for North African states and societies regarding their pasts and their futures. Ruling elites in North African states had been compelled to sit up and take notice of the movement's existence and to offer concessions. They did so against the background of their own acute needs for "recontracting" with their societies and relegitimizing their own rules in the face of myriad challenges, first and foremost those posed by vibrant Islamist movements offering their own solutions to the countries' obvious social, economic, and political shortcomings.

Farther afield, the new Berberism had by this time also begun to reverberate in Libya and even among the Tuareg of Niger and Mali. Diaspora-based activism was a vital source of support, culturally and materially, with social media becoming a vital part of their toolbox. The new Berberism had by this point fashioned a coherent historical narrative, commemorative rituals marking seminal events, and cultural markers that transcended state boundaries. Examples include the Yennayer New Year festival and the Berber Spring, a calendar, a flag, a revived and modified ancient script, and iconic artists and songs. One song, "Ekker a Mmis Umazigh" ("Rise Up Son of Amazigh"), written in 1945 by a Kabyle Algerian nationalist, was translated into Tashelhit, the dialect of Morocco's largest Amazigh community, and was included in a 2009 album of the well-known Moroccan Amazigh band Saghru, with appropriate changes to the text so as to expand its context beyond Algeria. A previous album included the song "Ulaç Smah" ("No Forgiveness"), a long-standing mantra of militant Kabyles. Both provided evidence of the trans-state aspects of modern Berberism.[42] And even without the modifications to "Ekker a Mmis Umazigh," the song had a pan-Amazigh quality to it, greeting "our brothers, from Rio de Oro [in what is today the Western Sahara][43] to Siwa [the Egyptian Amazigh oasis]; Children, the same blood unites us."[44] On the institutional level, pan-Berber sentiment and solidarity were given expression by the establishment of the Paris-based World Amazigh Congress in 1997, whose members represented associations from across the Amazigh universe, and the smaller, Brussels-based World Amazigh Assembly, established in 2011.

The Amazigh movement, much like minority movements elsewhere, placed great emphasis on the values of democracy and human rights, along with a Western-inspired liberal-humanist discourse. Other civil society elements, including groups battling for women's rights, the rule of law, and the liberalization of political life, shared their concerns. Still, as with the Amazigh themselves, these elements were in the minority. Entering the second decade of the twenty-first century, the various branches of the Amazigh movement confronted entrenched regimes and considerable opposition within their societies, guaranteeing that their struggles would continue to be uphill and lengthy.

Structure of the Study

As already noted, the political dimension of the Amazigh question became pressing across the region between 2011–2020. Neither did Amazigh-regime dynamics play out in North African states in isolation from one another. Moreover, diaspora-based pan-Amazigh organizations and expanding social media platforms reinforced the transnational and deterritorializing aspects of the Amazigh movement, strengthening the belonging to Tamazgha, the imagined Amazigh homeland.[45] Concrete assistance, particularly educational materials, were shared across state boundaries, and material sustenance was tendered to Libyan Amazigh who found refuge from the fighting in Tunisian Amazigh communities. Nonetheless, the Amazigh story since 2011 varied considerably from state to state, justifying this volume's analysis of developments specifically in Algeria, Libya, Mali, Tunisia, and Morocco.

In chapter 1, I focus on Algeria, especially the highly charged nature of Kabyle-state relations. As with much of Algerian society, Kabyles were deeply alienated from the regime, and the discourse of Kabyle ethnonationalism with explicitly political demands was sharpened accordingly. These ideas also spread beyond the bounds of Kabylia and helped shape the escalating interethnic tensions in the Mzab region. The Algerian *pouvoir* was sufficiently concerned with Amazigh militancy in 2016 that it made a previously unimaginable concession: recognizing Tamazight as an official language. However, most Algerian Amazigh were extremely cynical about the move and skeptical that it would be implemented. Kabyles played central roles in the 2019 *Hirak* protests, and the country's rulers targeted the waving of the Amazigh flag at demonstrations, hoping to divide and weaken the protests. At the same time, *Hirak* leaders refrained from substantive discussion about a federal framework for a future Second Republic, which would provide Kabyles with a measure of control over their own territory. The COVID-19 crisis put a halt to the protests, but it was clear that the future trajectory of state-society relations, and even the very nature of the Algerian state, would be determined in no small part by the way in which the "Kabyle question" was addressed.

In chapter 2, I analyze the emergence on the public stage of Libya's formerly ignored Amazigh community, beginning with its participation in the armed uprising against Qaddafi's regime in February 2011. Its contribution to the battle was a formative moment for the community, as the death of hundreds of fighters sharpened the Libyan Amazigh self-view as an ethnopolitical collective and provided them with a degree of legitimacy for advancing demands in the post-Qaddafi era. These demands, which paralleled those in other parts of Tamazgha, were both ethnocultural and political: Libya's national identity should be redefined to include the Amazigh and other minority groups; the new constitution should recognize Tamazight as an official language; and the new Libya should be a democratic state for all of its citizens, including safeguards for linguistic and cultural rights and religious freedom. The draft constitution that was finally completed in 2017 went only partially in this direction. However, on the ground, the fractured nature of post-Qaddafi Libya enabled the Libyan Amazigh to establish rudimentary institutions of their own and achieve a measure of agency in certain spheres. Terms such as "autonomy" and "self-determination" were now being used by Amazigh activists, even if their meanings remained vague. With the country divided between competing factions, Libyan Amazigh focused on consolidating their achievements, opposing the Benghazi-based forces of General Khalid Haftar, and continued lobbying regarding the desired nature of the country while waiting for the dust to settle.

In chapter 3, I extend the analysis to the Tuareg of the Sahel region, particularly Mali. The establishment of the breakaway state of Azawad in April 2012 was the culmination of events triggered by the Libyan rebellion. It was also the latest iteration of Tuareg opposition to the colonial-determined order. For Amazigh partisans in North Africa and the diaspora, Azawad's proclamation of independence seemed to be nothing less than a great leap forward, and the new state's commitment to democracy, ethnic pluralism, and secularism fit hand-in-glove with the overall Amazigh agenda. But the moment was brief, owing to the lack of state-building capacity, opposition by the international community, and, most importantly, the swift takeover of the region by local and international jihadists. French intervention restored the fragile status quo ante, and the proponents of an independent Azawad abandoned their demands for independence in 2015. Five years on, however, the same underlying conditions that had led to the Azawad secession episode were still very much present. The need for a reformed Malian state to address Tuareg grievances was a variation on the theme of Amazigh–state relations throughout North Africa. In addition, the whole episode sheds light not only on the Tuareg predicament but also on the strengthened place of an evolving Tuareg community within the wider, and increasingly politicized, Amazigh milieu.

In chapter 4, I unpack the depth of Tunisia's Amazighness while analyzing the ways in which the country's Amazigh dimension slowly crept into the public sphere after the 2011 revolution. With long-term survival as an ethnolinguistic group at risk, activists seized on the sudden demise of the repressive Ben Ali regime, demanding recognition and protection of their language and culture. They received considerable support from the Amazigh diaspora and sympathetic UN forums. Although the 2014 Tunisian constitution failed to acknowledge the country's Amazigh dimension, their ongoing debates over the nature of Tunisian democracy and the country's national identity offered some possibilities for Amazigh activists to become part of the conversation and to be supported by those favoring a celebration of the country's diversity. The contested place of the Amazigh community in Tunisia's evolving polity is thus also part of the larger Amazigh story. In addition, the unattractiveness of Arab nationalist ideas for Tunisians not affiliated with the Islamist current made "being Amazigh" a potential alternative pole of identification for Arabized Imazighen, one that could be blended with other elements. Such a formula carried relevance for Amazigh communities elsewhere as well.

In chapter 5, preceding the conclusion, I examine the myriad aspects of the Amazigh issue in Morocco, home of the largest numbers of Imazighen in the world. The country's public sphere was increasingly contested, and Morocco's diverse Amazigh communities were integral participants, from the large-scale national protests of 2011 to the overtly regional-ethnic ones in the Rif in 2016–2017. A major achievement was registered with the constitutional recognition of Tamazight as an official language of the state, and Amazigh associations and local communities were ever-more assertive regarding their social and economic rights, particularly on land issues and the state's neglect of basic needs in the country's peripheral regions. After interminable delays, an Organic Law laying out the timetable for implementing the incorporation of Tamazight in all spheres of public life was finally adopted in 2019. At the same time, Morocco's "deep state" apparatus retained a preponderance of power, the Rifian *Hirak* had been crushed, and Amazigh movement activists were divided on how to proceed and pessimistic about the future. What seemed certain was that Morocco's governing class, much like their counterparts across the region, would have to contend with the Amazigh factor as part of a larger need to renew its legitimacy in the eyes of an increasingly alienated and youthful population.

CHAPTER 1

Toward a Second Republic?
Algeria and the Amazigh Question

Unlike neighboring Tunisia and Libya and, of course, Egypt, Algeria did not experience a serious regime challenge during the tumultuous months of mass protest that swept through the region at the end of 2010 and early 2011. Even Morocco—its neighbor and rival to the west—witnessed more sustained and coordinated protests. A major challenge to the Algerian *pouvoir* would burst forth only at the very end of the decade, part of the renewed antigovernment activism across the region that included Sudan, Lebanon, and Iraq.

The absence of a major threat to the Algerian political status quo in 2011 requires explanation. The underlying social, economic, and political grievances that fueled the overthrow of the Tunisian and Egyptian presidents, sparked a civil war that ultimately toppled Libya's Qaddafi, and posed the first significant challenge to the Moroccan status quo in decades, were very much present in Algeria as well. Overall unemployment officially stood at 10 percent, with youth unemployment (below age 25) at 21.5 percent and a similar percentage of unemployed among university graduates; the gross national income per capita for the country's 36.6 million persons was $8,320, a figure that concealed huge differences between rural and urban sectors. Twenty-three percent of the population earned less than $2 per day. Algeria at the time was ranked number 84 on the UN's Human Development Index, just behind Tunisia and Jordan. Most important, the country's ruling elites were viewed as being interested in lining their pockets at the expense of delivering vital public services, as evidenced by Algeria's poor ranking on Transparency International's 2011 "Corruption Perception Index": number 112 out of 184 countries—tied with Egypt, Kosovo, and three other countries and considerably worse than Tunisia and Morocco.[1] Three years earlier, US ambassador to Algeria Robert Ford had characterized Algeria as an "unhappy country," with its populace well aware that the riches being generated by oil and natural gas exports were not being directed to solve an acute housing shortage, high unemployment rate, and deficient infrastructure. The public's resulting alienation from an indifferent and unresponsive authoritarian regime was obvious.[2] Protests, sometimes violent, were a regular part of the Algerian landscape for a decade starting in 2000. Much of the public was, according to Hugh Roberts, "in a permanent state of moral revolt"—not for the purpose of overthrowing the existing order but to attract the attention of the authorities to address their grievances.[3]

This dynamic reached a different order of magnitude at the beginning of 2011. In early January, authorities instituted large price increases in basic foodstuffs. It was a case of bad timing. The move touched off more sustained protests in multiple areas, which were further inspired by the rising tide of antigovernment demonstrations in neighboring Tunisia and then in Egypt. At least four persons followed the example of Tunisia's Mohamed Bouazizi—who had literally lit the spark of the Arab Spring protests—and fatally set themselves ablaze. Government buildings, particularly town halls, were among the targets of the demonstrations and riots, which included a fair degree of looting and burning.[4] Their focus was on socioeconomic issues: a lack of affordable housing, rising food prices, failing educational health systems, and nepotism and corruption in government. However, the protests never took on an overt political character with concrete demands.[5]

Worried about a possible spillover effect from Algeria's neighbors, the regime moved quickly to contain the unrest. Even as police clashed with protesters, the government agreed on January 8 to a temporary cut in taxes and duties on sugar and cooking oil; the state of emergency, officially in force since January 1992, was formally abolished (it was a symbolic and largely meaningless gesture); and on April 15, Algerian president Abdelaziz Bouteflika broke a three-month silence, promising a series of constitutional and other reforms to a nationwide television audience.[6] In doing so, he was following a similar script laid out by Morocco's King Mohamed VI a month earlier. Bouteflika's move was widely viewed as a ploy, but the initial energy of the protests had already dissipated. It would be three years before the promised package of constitutional reforms would be tendered and almost another two before being adopted with little discernible impact.

The failure of the disparate protests to coalesce into a broader challenge to the regime can be ascribed, at least in part, to the fresh memory of the horrific violence in the 1990s that pitted an armed Islamist insurgency against the Algerian military; a measure of credit went to Bouteflika for restoring stability to the country following his ascent to the presidency in 1999. Azzedine Layachi stated succinctly that "most Algerians were just not up for another fight in the early weeks of 2011."[7] The deteriorating situations in Libya and Syria reinforced this reluctance. As one activist explained: "The regime played the card of fear ... an old theme ... so, we fell back into our torpor because the images of Libya and Syria evoked the nightmare of the '90s terrorism."[8] A widespread belief that the military wouldn't hesitate to employ brute force to repress any movement that threatened the country's overall stability also contributed to the public's wariness.[9] The lack of credibility and massive following among the opposition political parties didn't help either. This was made apparent by the short-lived attempt in mid-February to organize a more overtly political protest spearheaded by the militantly Kabyle and secular party, the Rassemblement pour la Culture et la Démocratie (RCD), headed by Dr. Saïd Sadi. Its narrow constituency—not to mention Sadi's problematic status as a supporter of the military's cancellation of the 1992 elections and subsequent wholesale crackdown against the Islamist opposition—limited the possibility of mobilizing key organized sectors, such as the country's major labor union, behind the protest. In any case, the police were deployed in large numbers to block it.[10]

The Amazigh Factor

The RCD's desultory effort leads to broader questions that stand at the heart of this chapter: Where did the Amazigh communities, in particular its Kabyle component, fit into this overall picture of alienation and protest? And what of the lack of sustained action and sullen acquiescence to the status quo? What were the major developments and trends within the Algerian Amazigh milieu? And how did relations between Algeria's Amazigh communities and the regime evolve over the course of the decade? Before addressing these questions, it's necessary to provide some background and context.

Algeria's Imazighen, often estimated to be 20–25 percent of the country's total population (44.5 million as of May 2021), comprise five distinct ethnolinguistic communities concentrated in five regions: the Kabyles, whose traditional bastion is the Kabylian mountains east of Algiers, are usually said to constitute approximately two-thirds of the total;[11] the Chaouis, in the Aures Mountains, are somewhat less than one-third; the remaining belong either to the Mzabi-Ibadi community in the southern Mzab Valley, the Saharan Tuareg, and the Chenoua in the mountains west of Algiers.

Almost from the outset of France's decades-long conquest of Algeria, part of its colonial project had been to reify extant differences between Berber-Kabyle and Arab communities, promoting a pseudo-scientific notion of hierarchy that ranked the Kabyles higher on the "civilization" scale than Arabs and thus candidates for eventual assimilation, or at least association with Algérie

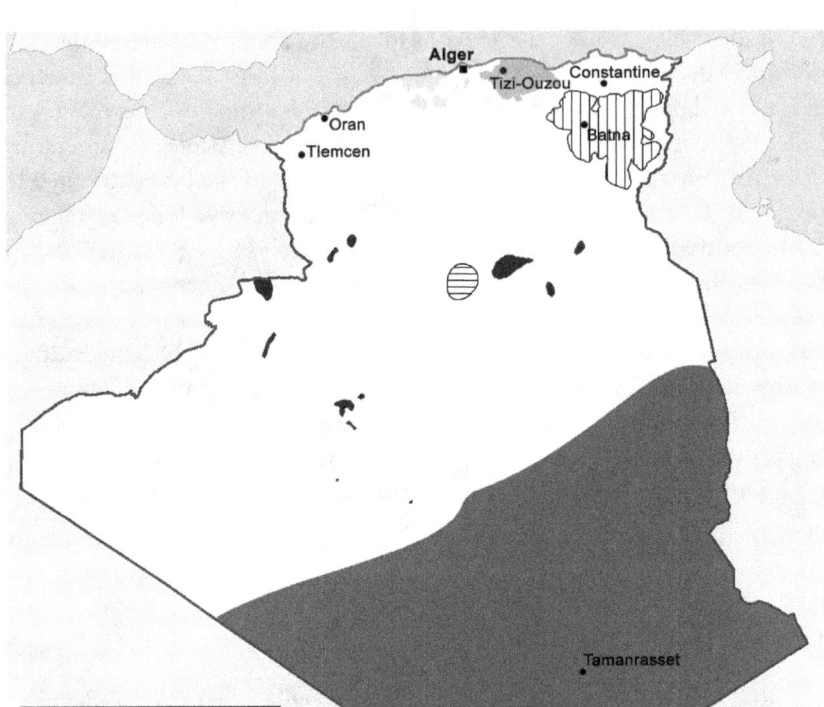

Map 1.1 Amazigh-speaking regions in Algeria, based on https://www.wikiwand.com/en/Languages_of_Algeria

Francaise.[12] To be sure, French policies to prioritize Kabyles in this "civilizing project" were applied in a desultory fashion,[13] and Kabyles would play a central role, both as individuals and as a community, in Algeria's war of independence (1954–1962). Still, French officials and scholars were not wrong in identifying Kabyle specificity, not only regarding language but also in social organization, religious praxis, and even political culture.[14] Along with the profound impact of French colonialism, these preexisting elements would form some of the essential building blocks for what would eventually become a modern *ethnie*. Thus, from the moment of independence, the place of the Kabyles—as a specific ethnolinguistic community within the Algerian nation and as to their relationship with the regime—would be problematic. The same was true for the much smaller Mzabi community.[15] The Kabyles' increasingly sharpened self-definition and politicization, facilitated greatly by Paris-based Kabyle intellectuals, would gradually radiate outward and influence Berberist discourse and practice throughout the Amazigh universe.

Two important challenges to the monism of the Algerian state, occurring twenty years apart, were formative experiences in the evolution of modern Kabyle identity and the fraught relationship between the Kabyle region and the central state: the iconic Berber Spring of March–April 1980 and the angrier (and more fatal) Black Spring of 2001. Crucial developments in the twenty-year interim laid the foundation for the events of 2001, which marked another stage in the politicization of collective Kabyle identity.[16]

The Berber Spring was a six-week-long strike in 1980 initiated by university students angry over the authorities' abrupt cancellation of a scheduled lecture on Berber poetry by the most important Kabyle intellectual luminary, Mouloud Mammeri, leaving an audience of more than a thousand persons empty-handed. The strike spread quickly to factories, hospitals, schools, and businesses, displaying the depth of anger over what was widely seen as the repression of Kabylian culture by a regime ideologically committed to the Arabization of Algerian life. Evoking the 1968 Prague Spring, the strike was the first significant challenge to the regime's authority since it had forcefully suppressed a Kabylia-based opposition in 1963–1964. Moreover, the regime's crackdown on the strikers—which included numerous arrests, trials, and convictions—had the opposite effect, contributing to the Kabyles' sense of difference and alienation from the state and creating a marker for the newly emerging pan-Berber commemorative calendar.

The coalescing of Kabyle collective identity during the 1980s became apparent when the country underwent a sudden, albeit brief, democratic experiment between 1989–1991 following a violent, weeklong explosion of anger in October 1988 that was put down by security forces with more than 500 dead. Within months of the liberalization of political and social life, more than 150 cultural institutions had sprung up in Kabylia; additional ones were established in Algeria's other Berberophone regions and among Berbers in Algeria's major cities. By 1994, the number of cultural institutions would increase to 528 within Kabylia's two primary provinces and additional ones in the Aures.[17] Cultural festivals, colloquiums, and publications proliferated. In the official political sphere, two Kabyle-based parties surfaced. The older and larger of the two, the Front des Forces Socialistes (FFS), was headed by Hocine Aït Ahmed, one of the nine historic "chiefs" of the Front de Libération Nationale (FLN) that had achieved independence for Algeria in 1962 after a brutal eight-year struggle. Aït Ahmed had unsuccessfully led a challenge to the ruling FLN faction in 1963–1964 and spent the next decades in exile. The FFS posited a national democratic agenda but drew its support almost exclusively from Kabyles.[18] The newer—and more militantly Kabyle and secular—party, the RCD, drew on younger activists in the Berber Culture Movement that had planted roots in the 1970s and 1980s. Together, the two parties captured the lion's share of the Kabyle region's votes in municipal elections (June 1990) and parliamentary elections (first round in December 1991), providing alternatives to the despised ruling FLN and its primary challenger, the newly formed Islamic Salvation Front (FIS). Indeed, it was the only region that failed to give FIS candidates decisive victories.

Algeria's ensuing descent into horrific violence (the 1990s, in common parlance, are known as the "Dark Decade") had myriad consequences for the Kabyle community, as it frequently seemed to be caught between the hammer of radical Islamist terrorism and the anvil of a military regime hostile to the Kabyle-Berberist agenda. Even as the FFS and RCD differed on tactics and strategy throughout the years of crisis, the ethnolinguistic demands of modern Berberism now began crowding onto the national stage. An extended and massive school strike between September 1994 and March 1995 demanding official recognition of the Tamazight language illustrated the mobilizational power of Kabyle-Berber identity demands. On the official political side, eight Algerian opposition groups, including the FFS (but not the RCD), met in Rome in January 1995 in an attempt to end the violence and restore democracy and the rule of law. Their final statement included a declaration that "the components of the Algerian character are Islam, Arabism, Tamazight, and the two cultures and languages contributing to the development of that character. They should have their place and should be strengthened in the institutions, without any exclusion or marginalization."[19]

Three months later, and within days of large-scale commemorations in Kabylia of the fifteenth anniversary of the Berber Spring, the Algerian authorities for the first time officially acknowledged the legitimacy of the Amazigh component of Algerian national identity. An announcement emanating from the president's office proclaimed the establishment of the Haut Commissariat à l'Amazighité (HCA), which would be "charged with the rehabilitation of Tamazight [culture] . . . one of the foundations of the national identity, and the introduction of the Tamazight language in the systems of education and communication."[20] This was mainly a tactical step, outpacing a tentative commitment taken by Morocco's King Hasan II the previous year to inaugurate the teaching of "dialects" in primary schools. Both were designed to contain the Amazigh current while also establishing a counterweight to Islamist forces. In Algeria, this included support for self-defense militias in Kabylian villages.

The regime also undertook steps previously unthinkable, including introducing the teaching of Tamazight in Kabylian areas beginning in the 4th grade, as well as a constitutional amendment recognizing the Amazigh component of Algerian national identity alongside Arab and Islamic ones. Over the next twenty years, reluctant Algerian authorities would periodically be dragged into making further concessions. However, these had little or no ameliorating impact on its increasingly alienated and defiant Kabyle population.

The depth of alienation and anger was put on full display in June 1998 at the funeral of the singer and activist Lounès Matoub, a militant Kabyle icon equally hostile to the Islamists and the regime. Although he had apparently been assassinated by a radical Islamist faction, the 100,000-plus people attending his funeral turned the event into a demonstration against the regime, its alleged complicity with the murderers, and its newly proclaimed Arabization measures. Protests would continue for several weeks.[21]

By the end of the 1990s, the Islamist insurgency had been defeated for the most part, even if the violence had not ceased entirely. A modicum of civilian rule was restored with the 1999 election of the military's preferred candidate, former foreign minister Abdelaziz Bouteflika, to the presidency. The foreordained results had caused the six other candidates to withdraw prior to the vote. Officially, the voter turnout was 61 percent, although the real figure was probably far lower. In Kabylia, it was only 5 percent. During a campaign appearance there, Bouteflika was greeted with insults, and stones were thrown at his car. Commenting angrily on the episode, he said: "I thought I would find giants there but I found gnomes!" Kabyles, he advised, should "go out from Kabylia and discover the rest of Algeria." In any case, he emphasized that "the Berber language will never, never be an official language in Algeria."[22] It would be Bouteflika's last visit to the region.

Even as life slowly returned to normal, much of the Algerian population remained estranged from the ruling elite. In April 2001, the special nature of Kabylian alienation was put on full display, as the death of an eighteen-year-old secondary-school student while in police custody touched off what the International Crisis Group called "the most protracted rioting in Algerian history." Le Printemps Noir (the "Black Spring," or *Tafsut Taberkant*) resulted in the death of 126 and many more injured at the hands of security forces, which employed indiscriminate violence, including torture and extrajudicial killings.[23] As was true in the October 1988 riots, there was evidence of a hidden hand behind the violence—namely, a faction within the regime seeking to manipulate the situation. In any case, rioters attacked not only symbols of state authority but also the offices of the Kabyle political parties. Moreover, efforts were undertaken outside established party channels to translate the protests into something more sustained. Numerous local grassroots groups rallied under the umbrella of the Coordination Inter-wilayas des 'Aarch, Daïras et Communes (CIADC), more commonly known as the "Citizens' Movement" or the `aarsh ("tribes"). The hybrid nature of this body was apparent in form and content: As a citizens' movement, it called for the transfer of state authority to democratically elected institutions; as `aarsh, whose social and cultural basis was rooted in Kabylian villages, it called for recognition of Tamazight as an official language of the state and an emergency plan for the social and economic development of Kabylia and the country as a whole.

Mass demonstrations, highlighted by the June 14, 2001, March for Democracy on Algiers by hundreds of thousands, indicated the passion that the new coordinating body was generating. Marchers were met by *agents provocateurs* (undercover troublemakers) who incited deadly clashes in order to discredit the movement in the eyes of the Algerian public, and they were unable to repeat the event. Kabylia would be in a state of civil revolt for years afterward, characterized by strikes and boycotts of municipal and parliamentary elections. The CIADC itself proved to be unwieldy and failed to assemble a recognized leadership with a coherent program; the authorities engaged in their time-honored practices of co-optation, manipulation, and fostering internal divisions within the CIADC. By 2007, authorities had regained control on the ground, and the unprecedented grassroots movement faded away.

While refusing to accede to CIADC's demand for the withdrawal of the hated gendarmerie from Kabylia, Bouteflika did make a constitutional concession, as had been done in 1995. In April 2002, the National Assembly approved without debate a constitutional amendment designating Tamazight as a national language. The move had little practical consequence, falling far short of the CIADC's demand that it be made "official" and equal in status with Arabic, with the appropriate accompanying resources for its dissemination. Bouteflika himself confirmed that this was not in the cards. While acknowledging the Amazigh origins of most Algerians, he also reiterated the classic Arab-Islamic narrative stipulating the Arab origin of the Amazigh.[24] Still, it marked another official step toward acknowledging the legitimacy of the Amazigh language and culture—including Imazighen—as a collective within the Algerian nation.

To be sure, the language issue remained contentious. A decade after Tamazight classes had been inaugurated, it was being taught in only eleven out of forty-eight provinces, with 90 percent of the 100,000 participating students being in the four Kabyle-dominated provinces.[25] Moreover, proficiency was not being achieved. According to one activist: "The reality is quite bitter: there are no students who can suitably read, write, recite or conjugate any Amazigh verb . . . !"[26] The script issue was also highly charged. To the dismay of Kabyle intellectuals and activists, Algerian authorities encouraged writing Tamazight in Arabic characters, even though the Latin script, with appropriate notation, had been developed decades earlier and was already widely used. The same issue was extant in Morocco, where the king decided in 2003 on compromise: Tamazight would be written with a modified version of the ancient Tifingah script.

In Algeria, conversely, a multiplicity of actors and approaches shaped by ideological divisions and regional differences made it impossible to develop a coherent approach to promoting the language. Existing institutions designed for that purpose lacked legitimacy and leadership, teachers were unprepared and operated intuitively, and methodologies were "appalling."[27] School manuals were prepared in all five varieties of Tamazight in use in Algeria—Kabyle, Shawi, Chenoua, Mzabi, and Tamashek (the Tuareg dialect)—and in three different scripts. Teachers who used the Latin script exclusively viewed the advancement of other scripts as both antipedagogic and designed to undermine the Berber culture movement's attempt to link promotion of Tamazight to the creation of an opening to Western culture and modernity. In 2010, the whole issue burst forth in heated exchanges between Arabophone and Berberophone academics when two of the former advised Berbers to adopt the Arabic script.[28]

Another indication that the modern Kabyle project was reaching critical mass was the surfacing in Kabyle public discourse of the concept of "autonomy." It was an imprecise but highly charged idea, widely dreaded by many postcolonial states struggling to fashion a cohesive and coherent national identity and political system. Even before the Black Spring events, Kabyle intellectuals and artists had already begun raising demands for linguistic and cultural autonomy within a reformed and democratic Algeria. In its aftermath, an overtly political dimension was added, with the proclamation in June 2001 of the Mouvement pour le Autonomie de la Kabylie (MAK), headed by the longtime poet, singer, and activist Ferhat Mehenni. While advocating universal Western values, following the French *laïcité* model, Mehenni and his supporters were assiduously Kabyle in orientation. The crisis that had shaken Algeria since independence was rooted in the regime's efforts to dilute Kabylian identity and subordinate it to an Arab one, he said. Federalism may be the answer to Algeria's Jacobin-style, heavy-handed, centralized state, but Kayblia was no longer willing to wait for the country's other regions before moving forward. Denying separatist intentions, he declared that an autonomous Kabylia, modeled on the large-scale autonomy of regions in Spain, Canada, and Quebec, would actually open a new era of cooperation between Kabylia and the central government in Algiers, one in which the scourge of Islamist terrorism could be combated successfully. Kabylia's flag would be flown in public places alongside the Algerian national flag.²⁹

Many Kabyles may have instinctively favored the idea of autonomy. However, there was no immediate, discernible impact on the ground. Mehenni himself was viewed with opprobrium by the authorities—and perhaps worse. He firmly believed that the murder of his eldest son, Améziane, in 2004 outside a Paris nightclub was a hit job ordered by Major General Mohamed "Toufik" Médiene, the longtime head of the Algerian government's powerful intelligence service (the DRS).³⁰ Undeterred, and perhaps spurred by these events, Mehenni continued his Paris-based activities. In 2007, MAK formally issued a document outlining the autonomy project, which was to be decided via referendum in Kabylia in coordination with Algerian authorities.³¹ The following year, Mehenni issued a provocative request for autonomy for Kabylia to the Algerian authorities, with copies going to a slew of international organizations, including the United Nations, the European Union, the International Federation for Human Rights, Human Rights Watch, and the Mediterranean Union Summit in Paris in July 2008, as well as to Nelson Mandela. Two years later, Mehenni went further, proclaiming the establishment of the Provisional Government of Kabylia (GPK, or Anavad), designed to be the executive arm of the MAK. Its proclamation carried more than a whiff of the next step to come.

A Fragile Stability—2011–2018

As already noted, the widespread protests in early 2011 failed to crystallize into a sustained and coherent challenge to the existing sociopolitical order. The uneasy stasis in state-society relations resurfaced in 2014 against the backdrop of a 50 percent drop in oil and gas revenues—which restricted the regime's ability to address social and economic issues—in addition to increasing lawlessness and radical Islamist violence. In an election whose results were again foreordained, the increasingly infirm President Abdelaziz Bouteflika, confined to a wheelchair following a 2013 stroke, was reelected overwhelmingly for a fourth term. To be sure, the official turnout rate (51.7 percent) was far lower than it had been in the previous 2009 election (75 percent), perhaps due in part to the protests organized by the short-lived Barakat ("Enough") movement, which had quickly organized in anger over Bouteflika's refusal to step down after promising to do so. Even though the movement's organizers were explicitly reformist and were not seeking the destruction of state institutions, they were nonetheless vilified by the regime: among other accusations hurled at them was that they were "Kabyles" (some, but not all, in fact were), an indication of how the Kabyles continued to be the internal and dangerous "Other" for many Algerians.[32] Some of Algeria's opposition political parties also called for a boycott. However, the low turnout was most likely because the elections were essentially meaningless.[33] For many Algerians, continuity, combined with passivity, remained the only available option—at least for the time being.

What was the nature and essence of the Algerian *pouvoir*, which was seemingly impervious to challenges to its hegemonic status? Understanding the inner workings of Algerian decision-making has never been easy. Yet, despite its opacity, the system's outlines are clear. Yahia Zoubir characterized the regime as "neo-sultanic" or "neopatrimonial," marked by personal rulership with little regard for any underlying ideology or values. Although the army had essentially brought Bouteflika to power, he gradually forced senior officers into retirement and succeeded in reducing the military's role in politics. Underscoring this was his 2015 removal of the powerful DRS head, General Médiene. There was no move to strengthen Algeria's formal governing institutions (parliament, the judiciary) or tackle the country's endemic corruption: Algeria ranked 106, out of 180 countries, on the 2019 Transparency Index (a negligible improvement since the beginning of the decade). Instead, Bouteflika surrounded himself with family members, led by his younger brother Saïd, friends and individuals from his home region of Tlemcen, and business associates.[34] Rachid Tlemcani complemented the picture, pointing to structures of power "shaped by relations of loyalty" that compete for security and energy revenues. The actors in this complex web of interlocking and competing networks of groups and families, approximately thirty-five in number, are "the military and security hierarchy, the presidential clan, and the corps of high-ranking civil servants but also ... political parties, the general trade union (UGTA), the media and 'captains of industry.'" Thus, even as Bouteflika's health deteriorated further during his fourth term, and even as oil revenues declined by half, the system continued to operate, with the military and security services budgets unaffected by the drop in revenues.[35]

Kabylian Radicalization and Divisions

The general stasis in the country's politics led Kabylian intellectuals and activists to redouble their efforts to shape and promote a Kabylian ethnonational agenda. Their debates and proposals contained a range of ideas directed at altering fundamentally the country's centralized governing structure and bringing about genuine democracy. Indicating awareness of where the political winds were blowing, FFS and RCD officials spoke more consistently of the need for "regionalism" and "decentralization" and even local or regional "autonomy" (and not only for Kabylia but for the whole country). The MAK, for its part, was focused on Kabylia, refusing to wait for the idea to achieve a critical mass in other regions.[36] The idea of autonomy—belittled and marginal when Ferhat Mehenni first raised it in 2001—was penetrating deeper into Kabylian discourse. FFS officials, in turn, accused the government of supporting the MAK to create what the Algerian sociologist Fatma Oussedik calls "dangerous classes" that imperiled an imagined "national unity." By doing so, their thinking went, they could contain and isolate Kabylia, justify repressive policies, and maintain power.[37]

Projet pour un état Kabyle (Project for a Kabyle State)

MAK's establishment of a "provisional government" in 2010 was followed in 2011 by its declaration that "self-determination" was a "strategic objective." Self-determination is a simple concept and thus resonates among politically self-conscious ethnonational communities. According to international law, self-determination does not rule out options other than complete independence. However, in practice, it is generally understood as a means to achieve it. Three years later, in 2014, what had been implicit was now made explicit: notwithstanding regime efforts to block its convening, an MAK executive meeting in Semaoun, located in the Soumman Valley[38] in Béjaïa Province, declared that its goal was to achieve independence for Kabylia. MAK's third general conference, held in the village of Aït Zellal in February 2016, confirmed this, endorsing the Projet pour un état Kabyle.[39]

This latest iteration of a document first formulated in 2014 laid out the ideological underpinnings of the project and a mechanism for implementing it. Regardless of what the future might bring, it is likely to continue serving as a foundational reference point for Kabylian ethnonationalism, as it lays out a coherent narrative of the Kabyle people's collective existence. Kabyles, it declares, have a particular identity and personality, a common history, territory, and sociopolitical organization that has been shaped over centuries by a common language, culture, and civilization as part of the larger Amazigh nation. Its explicit appeal to Western societies and governments (and implicit appeal to world Jewry and even the State of Israel)[40] was apparent. The values of the Kabyle nation, the document says, are those of "democracy, freedom, secularism, and solidarity with other peoples," which are "in perfect harmony with the Amazigh identity foundations" grounded in the *longue durée* of Amazigh history. Not only have the Kabyle people contributed to the "universal cultural heritage"; they also contributed to "the liberation of Europe against Nazism and Fascism" while concurrently opposing "the anti-Semitic policies of the Vichy government."

The document enumerates a story of continuous struggle by Kabyles over the past 150 years, initially against French colonial conquests, then a century later in the vanguard in the war of independence, and finally against a repressive and racist Algerian state guided by an exclusive Arab-Islamic ideology bent on erasing Kabylia's existence. The legitimacy of the Kabyle Project, the document states, also derives from numerous international treaties and conventions, from the UN Charter and Universal Declaration of Human Rights to the 2007 UN Declaration on the Rights of Indigenous Peoples.

What would the Kabylian state look like? It would be "democratic, republican and pluralist," with the exact relationship among the various governing institutions to be decided in the future. Among those institutions would be Kabylia's traditional sociopolitical units, "the `Aarchs and Confederations of the `Aarchs, dissolved by the French colonial regime after the uprising of 1871"; the colonial regime established its own forms of ruling over the indigenous population that the Algerian regime built on. This was a central theme of the Kabyle movement's alternative historical narrative: precolonial Kabyles governed themselves, and postcolonial Algeria's efforts to destroy any semblance of Kabyle agency were a direct continuation of colonial policies.

As envisaged in the Kabyle Project, each village, the basic institution of Kabylian society, "will be represented in proportion to the number of its inhabitants through democratically elected representatives by its basic bodies, the *Agraw* [assembly of all adult villagers] and *Tajmaat* [council of representatives of each clan]." One explicit aspect of the plan was the insistence on the complete separation of religion and state, with a guarantee of freedom of conscience and worship, with religion to remain in the private and individual domain. Here, too, deep-rooted sociocultural notions were invoked to emphasize the commitment to secularism, including the ancestral precept *"Jmaɛ Liman"* (lit., "all beliefs/religions"). The phrase is often employed when making "a solemn statement or promise undertaking to do something or affirming that something is the case." Swearing an oath in the name of all beliefs or religions is said to serve as evidence of the tolerance and openness of Kabylian culture.[41] Given the centrality that Islam plays in Algerian public life and its enshrinement in the country's constitution, this emphasis on the need for freedom of religion, separation of religion and state, and secularism shows the truly revolutionary nature of the Kabyle political project. Three points are worth noting in this regard:

1. Although less than 1 percent of Algeria's 44.5 million citizens are Christians, Kabylians make up a disproportionate number of them, owing to the Catholic Church's proselytizing efforts during the colonial era.[42] More recently, Protestant Evangelicals have established a presence. US State Department reports on international religious freedom document all kinds of obstacles and harassment, official and unofficial, of both Christians and Ahmedi Muslims engaged in the practice and promotion of their faiths.[43] Thus, the call for secularism and the privatization of religion carried practical significance.
2. Traditional Kabyle religious praxis was Sufi in nature, centering on spiritual matters through the identification of saints and brotherhoods. The penetration of official, state-inspired Islam—which included the 1967 abrogation of customary law in matters of personal status, the subsequent decline in stature of local imams and eventual replacement by state functionaries, and the corresponding decline of local brotherhoods and marabouts—dealt powerful blows to Kabyle religious autonomy.[44] Although many Kabyle militants were avowedly nonpracticing Muslims, the valorizing of Kabyle traditional praxis served to legitimize their transformative vision.[45]
3. The Grenada-based scholar Carmen Garratón Mateu pointed to a new threat to traditional Kabyle Islam: the religious radicalization of certain sectors of Kabyle society via the penetration of Salafism. Frederick Wehrey and Anouar Boukhars also provide evidence of state promotion of the Salafi current in Kabylia. Salafis reportedly had taken over several mosques, or even built their own, as happened in Beni Douala, a town in Tizi Ouzou Province.[46] The *Manifeste Kabylie*, issued in 2014, made the same point (see below). However, there has also been pushback by local councils against Salafi imams. For his part, the knowledgeable scholar Mohand Tilmatine contends that the threat is exaggerated, owing to the deep roots of secularism and opposition to Salafi Islam in the region.[47]

Unlike the MAK's earlier autonomy project, whose confirmatory referendum was to have been coordinated with the Algerian government, the proposed referendum on establishing a sovereign Kabylian state was to be internationally supervised. If necessary, international supervision and accompaniment during a transition period was also envisaged, owing to the need to neutralize possible actions by the Algerian authorities to thwart the Kabylian state's establishment.

Manifeste Kabylie

MAK's open advocacy of a complete divorce from the Algerian state was controversial, to say the least. Many among the activist Kabyle community even believed that it was a bridge too far. Just months after the 2014 MAK leadership meeting, an alternative approach "addressed to all Algerians, whether they are ordinary citizens, political actors of the opposition or holders of power," was tendered by scores of Kabyle intellectuals, many of whom had been affiliated with the RCD, and even with the MAK, and who justifiably believed that they expressed "a strong tendency of the current Kabyle opinion." Their *Manifeste Kabylie* called for the establishment of a new social contract through the reformation of the Algerian state, whose "hyper-centralized nation-state model, inherited from the French Jacobin model, based on the unicist idea of the nation, is outdated and unsuitable for multicultural societies like ours." Algeria, it declared, should be transformed into a consociational democracy, one in which the Kabylia region would have a defined and territorially demarcated status, as did Quebec and Catalonia, and share power with other communities in a democratic Algeria.[48]

Similar to MAK's Kabyle Project, the *Manifeste* provides a marker for the understanding and shaping of the Kabylian ethnonational movement. There is no daylight between the documents regarding the foundations of Kabylian identity and the historical narrative that had unfolded, indicating the high degree of consensus among Kabylian intellectuals and activists.

Ongoing interethnic tensions in Algeria's southern Mzab region (for details, see below) constituted further material for Algeria's ongoing debates over Islam, pluralism, and ethnicity; as such, they were also addressed in the *Manifeste*. Were the state to have a genuinely plural character—in which communities could preserve their particularity and integrity through appropriate institutions—then the endemic crisis there would have ended and future tragedies elsewhere would have been forestalled. In this case, the document referred to the need for the state to recognize "the specificities of the Ibadi confessional rite" (most Kabyles and other Amazigh communities are Sunni Muslims), the Mzabis' "cultural, linguistic and organizational differences," and its "territoriality." It was the state's "support for the Wahhabi doctrine, which was hostile and intolerant of any other form of religious expression in Islam," the *Manifeste* emphasized, that had fueled the hostilities and resulted in the loss of life.

This was even more the case, it declared, in Kabylia, which was being subject to an "ethnocidal policy." During the preceding decade, Kabylia had experienced a state-directed "invasion of all spaces by the official culture and language [Arabic], by a supervised and funded Wahhabism that targets the heart of the villages by [promoting] widespread corruption, in particular [among] a fringe of the political, cultural and sporting elite." The objective of the regime's various manipulations and instrumentalizations was clear: "dekabylization." The results, said the *Manifeste*, were already grim:

> The Kabyles' linguistic territory has shrunk dramatically, especially in urban areas, the management of their land heritage is no longer within their competence, their desperate youth are sadly showing a record suicide rate, and insecurity reigns in the region with the persistence of terrorist pockets and the proliferation of banditry, preventing any social progress and any economic development.

Kabylia's existing political elite, the document declared, was not bereft of responsibility for this dire situation.

Given the heterogeneous nature of Algerian society, the *Manifeste* declared, there needed to be a "paradigm shift," one that would move away from an unjust "majority rules" form of democracy to a power-sharing "consociational" democracy that "allows for a balance of power and will avoid any form of exclusion or underestimation of regional populations." Talk of a specific political status for Kabylia, the document's authors knew, would surely be met with charges of separatism, as had already been leveled at the MAK over the years, even prior to its shift toward self-determination and independence. In response, they reversed the charges: failure to resolve the political impasse as suggested might well result in the violence and chaos that characterize postcolonial states elsewhere. In other words, they positioned themselves, and their ideas, as the last line of defense from a potentially violent breakup of the Algerian state.

Nine months after the government's March 2016 adoption of a new constitution (see below), the *Manifeste* group convened a political convention and issued another detailed statement that, like its previous one and the MAK's Kabyle Project, sharpened the Kabylian ethnonational discourse and strategy—"the deconstruction of the nation-state" as it is currently constituted. The purpose of the meeting, it stated, was designed to fashion a political body that had a "credible, thoughtful and achievable project" (unlike Mehenni's advocacy of independence) and also differed from the established Kabylian political parties' more limited vision.

The goal of the project was a consociational democracy, one that conferred sovereignty on its various communities through regional parliaments, which was the best way to address different interests while maintaining national cohesion and comity. Achieving this goal, the document's authors acknowledged, was a long-term project. But it should start with the gradual and sustained emancipation of Kabyle society "from the grip of the rentier and patrimonial system." The challenges were manifold and came from two different directions: the corrupt and authoritarian regime, and "the Islamist current, which is insidiously settling in clientelist networks and the associative fabric, under the guise of charitable action."

The path forward, declared the statement, would be three pronged: (1) sustained promotion among the public of the idea of autonomy; (2) the mobilization of all the energies and skills, inside and outside Kabylia, to fashion and implement concrete development projects; and (3) the involvement of citizens at the village level to improve their living conditions, preserve their culture and the environment, and enhance social solidarity.[49]

The response of one prominent MAK supporter, the exiled artist and journalist Djaffar Benmesbah, was quick—and withering. Was this a "credible, thoughtful and achievable project"? The autonomous entity being proposed would be nothing more than a "vassal state," he declared, forever dominated by an Arab-Islamist regime guided by Wahhabi ideology. Moreover, he claimed, the program being advocated was an elite project that did not reflect the will of the people: "Any elite that replaces its people is deeply reactionary."[50]

The mutual bitterness and recriminations within the Kabyle movement were palpable and did not bode well for the future. Nonetheless, the consociationalists continued to develop their project. The next stage of their efforts came a year later. Meeting in February 2017 in the commune of Aït Oumalou,[51] in Tizi Ouzou Province, activists announced the establishment of a political movement, the Rassemblement pour la Kabylie (RPK), which would be devoted to advancing the principles laid out above. Although its priority was Kabylia, the announcement stated that the RPK would campaign for democracy, modernity, and human rights throughout Algeria. Its first challenge was to obtain legal standing from the state, which was in no hurry to grant it.[52] But one close observer of the Kabylian scene was of the view that the RPK would benefit from the GPK/MAK choice of secession and "inherit" the latter's formidable mobilizational work done over the preceding fifteen years.[53]

The Funeral of Hocine Aït Ahmed

Any doubts about the resonance among wide sectors of society regarding the militancy and assertiveness being expressed in Kabyle intellectual circles should have already been put to rest at the end of 2014: on December 23,

Hocine Aït Ahmed died at age eighty-nine. One of the nine *chefs historiques de la révolution* and the founder and longtime unquestioned head of the FFS, he passed away in his home in Lausanne, Switzerland, where he had lived much of his life since going into exile in 1966. The events serve as a case study in the politics of memory and commemoration, and the popular response to his death and funeral provided clear evidence of the militancy and sense of alienation among Kabylian youth.

The Algerian regime had recently taken several steps to expand the officially sanctioned narrative regarding the history of the war of independence and its immediate aftermath. Historical figures who had been marginalized, or murdered and erased from the history books, were now publicly acknowledged in a variety of ways.[54] Aït Ahmed, it will be recalled, had led a failed uprising in 1963–1964, leading to his imprisonment and even the imposition of a death sentence, before being allowed to leave for Europe. His return to Algeria in 1989, and his efforts to challenge the status quo in the subsequent tumultuous decade, did not bear fruit, and he returned to his home in Switzerland. In line with the Algerian authorities' new, more inclusive approach toward the past—and undoubtedly aware of Aït Ahmed's standing within Kabylia—they sought to retool and appropriate Aït Ahmed's legacy. Accordingly, the Algerian national press was fulsome in its praise of Aït Ahmed and his contribution to the independence struggle. An FLN official declared that "we have been unfair, and ungrateful" to Aït Ahmed. An eight-day mourning period was declared, and the entire government, led by Prime Minister Abdelmalek Sellal, gathered at the airport to greet the plane bearing his coffin. The plan was to hold a state funeral for Aït Ahmed, in which his body would be interred in Algiers's El-Alia cemetery, the traditional resting place for heroes of the war of independence.

However, his family would have none of it and even refused to interact publicly with government officials at the airport. In line with Aït Ahmed's wishes, they transported his coffin to his native hamlet that bears the family name, in the mountains of Kabylia, where he was buried next to his mother.

Not surprisingly, the regime's gestures also fell flat with much of the Kabylian public. The fact that Aït Ahmed's agenda had always been "national," and not ethnocentric, and that his legacy had begun to be questioned by Kabylian writers in recent years,[55] did not matter to the tens of thousands of people (if not more) who thronged the hillside village and noisily negotiated the narrow steep terrain to the burial site, many waving Amazigh and MAK flags alongside the Algerian national flag. At this visceral moment, whatever criticisms there were of Aït Ahmed's often controversial actions during his long career did not matter. For them, he was a heroic leader and a militant son of Kabylia who had stood consistently in opposition to a corrupt regime. Moreover, as Roberts astutely pointed out, Aït Ahmed's lofty status was also grounded in Kabylian culture: His ancestral village was one of Sufi sheikhs who played crucial mediating functions between rival clans and tribes, and he himself was of important saintly lineage. Being buried in a maraboutic village alongside his ancestors indicated a desire to maintain his unrivaled standing posthumously.[56]

Constitutional Upgrade

In February 2016, the Algerian parliament adopted the package of constitutional reforms that President Bouteflika had first spoken about five years earlier. A prime motivation for adopting the package was concern over the 2014 protests that had accompanied his election to a fourth term. Thus, a two-term limit was reintroduced, after having been removed before the 2009 election so as to enable Bouteflika to stand for a third term. The new constitution solemnly promised to ensure "the separation of powers [between the three branches of government], the independence of the judiciary, the legal protection and the monitoring of public authorities' performance in a society where legitimacy shall be prevalent and man shall prosper in all aspects of life." As it happened, the gap between the text and the actual nature of regime-society relations remained unchanged, as the reforms amounted to a refurbishment of the existing semiauthoritarian system.[57]

One change in the new reforms did stand out: with an eye on the deepening alienation and increased activism in Kabylia, Tamazight was now upgraded to being an "official" language of the state and not just a "national" one (as it had been since 2002). What had been unfathomable at Algeria's birth—and twenty years after the state's first formal acknowledgment of the country's Amazighité and commitment to introduce the teaching of Tamazight in the country's schools—was now accepted by the state, however reluctantly. In doing so, Algeria was belatedly following Morocco's official recognition of Tamazight five years earlier.

To be sure, it was clear from the outset that the Algerian authorities were even less committed than their Moroccan counterparts to translating the text into substance. Salem Chaker, the France-based Kabylian scholar and unofficial dean of Berber studies, quickly pointed out that Tamazight, even with its official status, remained constitutionally subordinate to Arabic, which remained the "national and official language" and the "official language of the state" (Article 3). Moreover, the constitution also reemphasized the regime's core ideology of promoting the Arabization of Algerian life, mandating for that purpose the establishment of a Supreme Council of the Arabic Language, attached to the president's office.[58] While the Preamble to the constitution reiterated the existing description of the basic components of Algeria's identity as being "Islam, Arabness (`uruba) and *Amazighiyya*," it also defined Algeria as an "Arab land" (*ard `arabiyya*) and an "inseparable part of the Greater Arab Maghrib" (*al-maghrib al-`arabi al-kabir*), along with being a Mediterranean and African land (*wa-bilad mutawatisiyya wa-ifriqiyya*). In this context, it is worth mentioning that the official French translation (and unofficial English one) of the constitution does not separate "Arab" from "Mediterranean and African" ("*pays arabe, méditerranéen et africain*"), and removes "*Arabe*" from "*du Grand Maghreb*."[59] By contrast, on this point there is no difference between the Arabic and French versions of the 2011 Moroccan constitution, which is more in line with the Amazigh movement's discourse, referring to Morocco as being part of the "Greater Maghrib," thereby implying that it is not purely an "Arab" region.[60]

In pointing out Tamazight's subordination—"Tamazight is also a national and official language" (Article 4)—Chaker also noted that the constitution required several measures needed to lend concrete content to Tamazight's official status. These included the creation of a language academy to oversee its development, with emphasis on "all its linguistic varieties in use on the national territory" (i.e., there would be no standardization of the language); and the drafting of an "Organic Law," which would determine the modalities of implementation. Such an academy was supposed to have been established almost a decade earlier, and the Haut Commissariat à l'Amazighité to promote the language had already been established in 1995. If the Moroccan example was any guide, then the required Organic Law would not be drafted and approved in the near future—if at all. As Chaker also noted, the recognition of Tamazight in 2002 as a national language had had no practical effect, as Arabic remained the exclusive language of institutional and public spaces. The new upgrade was done for the same reason—to try to neutralize the Kabyle opposition, without genuine commitment.[61] Undertaken in October 2018, a widespread and vocal boycott of Arabic-language classes in Kabylian schools indicated the Kabylian public's belief that the regime wasn't serious about upgrading Tamazight's status.[62]

An additional gesture by the regime came at the end of 2017, with the decision that henceforth Yennayer, the Amazigh New Year, would be recognized as a national holiday on January 12. Amazigh activists in both Morocco and Algeria had repeatedly called for such action, and Libyan Amazigh had now joined them as well. In recent years, Yennayer had made its way onto the Amazigh commemorative calendar, marked by celebrations and, in Kabylia, large-scale demonstrations spearheaded by MAK. As with so much else of the Berberist agenda, Islamist groups opposed valorizing Yennayer. In fact, Salafist preachers defied government instructions to refer favorably to the holiday in their Friday sermons, and a prominent Salafist even issued a fatwa forbidding the celebration of this "pagan" holiday.[63]

The announcement recognizing Yennayer also stated that President Bouteflika had "urged the government to spare no effort to generalize the teaching and use of Tamazight, in accordance with the Constitution" and instructed it to accelerate preparations for the creation of an Algerian Academy of the Amazigh Language.[64] At the same time, security forces continued to harass and detain MAK activists and made extensive use of social media to spread disinformation. In June 2018, Mehenni called for the establishment of a Kabyle security force to replace those of the state. The RPK's executive bureau characterized his call as "extremely grave," indicating again the deep split between the two groups over how best to advance the Kabyle cause.[65] On the ground, though, Kabylian militancy continued to deepen.

Troubles in the Mzab

Far from the center of Algeria's ongoing sociopolitical stasis, the Mzab region, 600 kilometers south of Algiers, had been the scene of periodic bouts of intercommunal tension and violence for more than a decade. The context was very much specific to that region but was nonetheless also part of the larger story of Algeria's malaise, including its Amazigh dimension.

Historically, the Mzab Valley's five fortified towns have been home to one of the smallest—albeit the most distinctive and cohesive—of all Amazigh communities. Speakers of the Tumzabt dialect (which is related to other Saharan Amazigh dialects), the community's distinguishing feature is its adherence to the Ibadi creed of Islam. (The other main Ibadi Berber communities are those in the Jebel Nafusa region in Libya and in Djerba, Tunisia.) By contrast, the vast majority of North Africa's Muslims, Berbers and Arabs alike, belong to the Sunni Maliki school of jurisprudence and practice. Consequently, the "official" Islam of all North African states is presupposed to be Maliki. However, by not specifying this, Ibadi Islam is accorded a "hushed recognition," albeit not one anchored in law.[66] Deeply rooted in the area since the early centuries of Islam, this insular Ibadi Mzabi community, numbering approximately 30,000 persons during the 1950s, preserved its social and cultural cohesion and economic and social dominance of the surrounding Arab tribes right through the colonial era.[67]

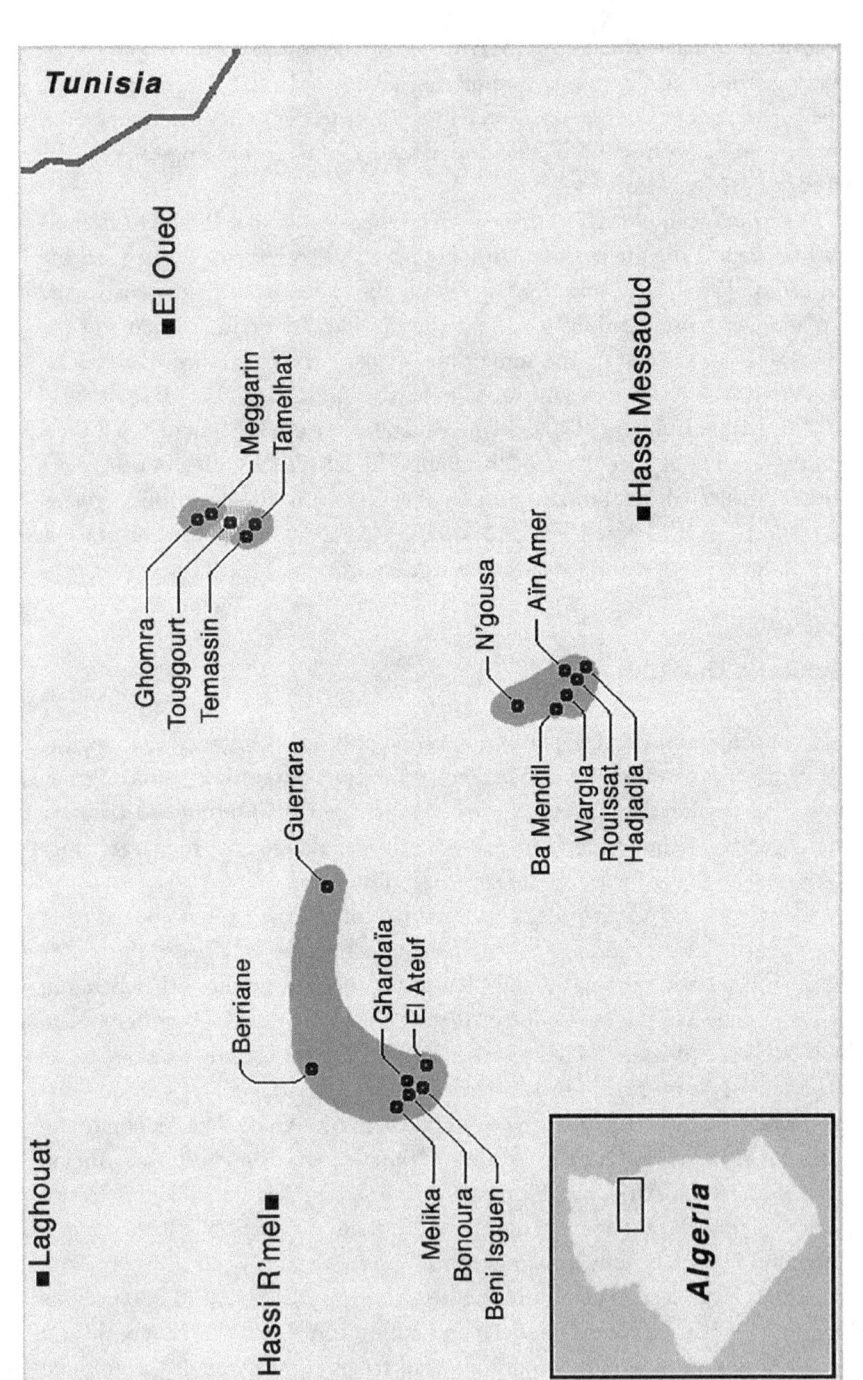

Map 1.2 Mzab-Wargala Amazigh-speaking region, https://www.wikiwand.com/en/Mozabite_language

But the era of independence brought new and difficult challenges. The country's hegemonic discourse and fundamental documents (e.g., the 1976 National Charter) rejected completely any notion of regional, ethnic, or linguistic differentiation.[68] On the ground, the Mzab region now experienced a more intrusive state apparatus, with the town of Ghardaïa being made capital of the *wilaya* ("province") of the same name in 1985. Economic changes accompanied by an influx of people from outside the region occured thanks to the development of the Hassi Messaoud oil field, located approximately 400 kilometers to the southeast. There was a rapid rise in the rates of population growth and urbanization, in line with countrywide trends, as well as the settling of nomadic or seminomadic Arab tribes, who were often squeezed off of their traditional pasture lands by state development projects. The results were manifold: by 2010, the Ghardaïa wilaya (covering 86,000 square kilometers) had a population of 375,000, which included people from all over the country and neighboring ones as well. Mzabi Berbers, now numbering less than 200,000, had lost their previously unquestioned demographic and economic predominance. According to an International Crisis Group analysis: "Official administrative posts were filled primarily by Arabs and deepened class tensions, pitting relatively wealthy urban Mzabis against poor Bedouin Arabs who used the Arab national parties and their influence for social mobility."[69] As in Kabylia, the regime instrumentalized the so-called quietist Salafi current in the south. Doing so had nefarious implications for the Mzabis, as Saudi-trained Salafi preachers exploited the tensions to brand Ibadis as "enemies of Allah" and "Shia apostates," thereby justifying violent attacks on them.[70]

In this new lived reality, conflicts over land and property rights and other local, even neighborhood, issues escalated periodically into spasms of violence, dating back to 1985. These quickly took on an intercommunal/ethnoreligious character: Mzabi Ibadi Berbers versus Chaamba (Arabic: "Sha`anba") Sunni Arabs.[71] Fifteen persons, mostly Mzabis, died in November–December 2013, and at least ten others may have been tortured by security forces. During the next two years of intermittent violence, Ghardaïa's mixed neighborhoods self-segregated; Mzabis formed self-defense groups and disseminated videos of police sheltering Arab protesters. In one, they claimed to identify the wilaya's security chief desecrating a cemetery, including the mausoleum of a Mzabi sheikh, designated as a UNESCO World Heritage Site. The peak episode occurred between July 7–10, 2015, leaving dozens killed, hundreds injured (mostly by gunfire), and thousands of homes and businesses burned. The Mzabis believed, not without reason, that the government apparatus, particularly security forces, were siding against them and even enabling "hooded men" to take the law into their own hands.[72] Of course, this violence should not be seen as proof of the existence of innate and unchanging ethnic or sectarian hostilities between the two communities. But it does prove that in times of social, economic, political, and cultural conflicts, particularly during periods of rapid change, preexisting communal affiliations often become more salient.

What, if anything, was the wider meaning of this local conflict? As Fatma Oussedik noted, the country's official national narrative has never provided space for cultural, ethnic, religious, or linguistic differences, and its clientalist, rentier-based policies left little room for autonomous economic and political activities. Thus, any challenge to that worldview and the methods of control posed an inherent threat to national unity and needed to be repressed. In this regard, the festering tensions in Ghardaïa Province contained echoes of Kabylian-state relations and provided yet another measure of the state's ongoing crisis and the regime's declining legitimacy.[73]

Given these dynamics, it is hardly surprising that the Kabyle-Amazigh discourse and praxis filtered into the Mzab. The two "Kabyle" political parties—the FFS and the RCD—had already established a presence there, and expressions of solidarity from Kabylia became more frequent as the violence escalated. At the center of the new Mzabi militancy, and in opposition to Mzabi's traditional tight-knit elites, who had "lost traction with the community's youth,"[74] stood Dr. Kemal Eddine Fekhar. He was an activist physician, former head of the regional branch of the Algerian League for the Defense of Human Rights (an organization founded in the mid-1980s with a heavy Kabyle representation), former member of the FFS party, and an open admirer of Ferhat Mehenni. In late 2013, he established the Movement for Autonomy of the Mzab; its ideological underpinning was identical to that of the MAK, as was its willingness to internationalize the issue. In this, he was supported by Amazigh organizations elsewhere. For example, in January 2014, the World Amazigh Congress (Congres Mondial Amazigh, or CMA) called on the UN Special Representative on the Rights of Indigenous Peoples to visit Algeria as soon as possible to report on the situation, and on the United Nations and European Union to ensure that Algeria lived up to its international obligations to honor individual and collective rights and freedoms.[75]

The violence in June and early July 2015 brought matters to a head. On July 2, just days before the peak of the Ghardaïa clashes, Fekhar appealed to Secretary-General Ban Ki-moon requesting UN intervention to stop the Algerian government's "apartheid and ethnic cleansing" policies. On July 9, the authorities arrested Fekhar and twenty-four others, charging them with committing terrorism and incitement to hatred; distributing material harmful to the national interest; and defamation of state institutions. The CMA immediately called for international action, including by the United Nations, to protect the Mzabi Berbers from "persistent attacks on their physical security and the systematic destruction of their property and culture."[76]

Some of Fekhar's codefendants, whose numbers increased to forty over the next year and a half, were also accused of forming a criminal gang to commit crimes and premeditated murder. Mzabi activists have even been branded as traitors for allegedly collaborating with Imazighen beyond Algeria's borders. Moreover, the fact that Fekhar had had contact with Moroccan officials in the past made him a natural target for Algerian authorities keen on blaming Morocco for the unrest.[77] These charges, which mirror the Moroccan authorities' suspicions that some of their own Amazigh militants were in contact with Algerian authorities,[78] were specious. But Amazigh activist circles in Morocco and the diaspora did campaign for his release and established personal ties with him. After two years in detention without being brought to trial, and following his lengthy hunger strike and a joint appeal by Amnesty International, Human Rights Watch, EuroMed Rights, and Front Line Defenders, Fekhar was released from prison without charges.[79]

However, on March 31, 2019, Fekhar was rearrested on the ground of "incitement of racial hatred," owing to his accusations on social media of discrimination by local officials against Ibadis.[80] He, together with a detained associate, immediately launched another hunger strike in protest. This time, however, the results were tragically different: His condition deteriorated rapidly, and on May 28 Fekhar died after being transferred to a hospital. His lawyer suggested that inadequate medical care and the indifference of judges to his health condition indicated that the death was "planned," coming as it did during the massive ongoing protests in the country, with the hope that it would go unnoticed. As it happened, thousands attended his funeral, protesters in the streets of Algiers observed a minute of silence in his memory, and Amnesty International criticized sharply the regime's detention policies that had led to his death.[81]

Taking It to the Streets: The End of the Bouteflika Era

Suddenly, in February 2019, the Algerian *pouvoir* was confronted with a massive peaceful protest movement unlike any experienced before. The trigger was the announcement that Bouteflika would stand for a fifth term as president in the election scheduled to be held in April, even though he was virtually incapacitated and hadn't spoken in public for years. Unlike in 2011—when the authorities were able to deflect popular protests without much difficulty and thereby avoid the fate of many other Arab regimes—this time the power in the streets created a new dynamic that rocked the political system to its foundations.

As noted earlier, the public's deep-rooted sense of alienation and anger toward a corrupt ruling oligarchy lacking in democratic legitimacy had been a given for many years. It was expressed in "complete apathy toward public affairs, strikes, riots, absenteeism, lack of civism, disrespect for state symbols, brain-drain, and illegal and legal migration of the youth."[82] The sharp downturn, beginning in 2014, in oil and gas revenues that accounted for about 60 percent of the country's GDP and 97 percent of its export income, plus the resulting free fall in foreign currency reserves and skyrocketing budget deficits,[83] pointed to a possible (if not inevitable) unraveling of the "ruling bargain" between the regime and society at some point.

Details of the decision-making process that led to Bouteflika's renewed candidacy are lacking. However, one can assume that the presidential clan, led by his powerful brother Saïd, and allied senior officers, bureaucrats, politicians, and labor union leaders decided that their interests would best be protected by maintaining him at the symbolic top of the pyramid of power, regardless of his incapacitation.[84]

Their decision was stunningly contemptuous of the public and backfired spectacularly. On February 10, a statement signed by Bouteflika was released announcing his intention to run for a fifth term: it triggered widespread, ever-multiplying protests that crystallized into the *Hirak al-Sha`bi* ("People's Movement"), which was carrying out a peaceful and often good-humored *Thawrat al-Ibtisam* ("Smile Revolution"). The initial demand of the protests was simple: "*Makach al-Khamsa ya Bouteflika*" ("There is no fifth [mandate] Bouteflika"); the protesters frequently referred to him as *la momie* ("mummy") or, alternatively, as *poupiya* ("doll/puppet"). Often, they created a couplet, adding *jibou l'BRI wo zidou sa`ika* ("bring [we do not fear] the BRI and Sa`ika [police and army forces]").[85] Their initial demand soon evolved into a larger, amorphous but powerful demand: *Système, Dégage!* or, in the Algerian dialect, *Yetnaḥāw gāʿ* ("they [the entire ruling `asaba ("gang")] shall all be removed").[86] In other words, the Algerian state should be remade into a genuine democracy. The protests were quintessentially Algerian, claiming legitimacy as the true heirs of the Algerian War of Liberation from French colonialism, whose fundamental values the *pouvoir* had betrayed. The participation of a heroic icon from that war, the eighty-three-year-old Djamila Bouhired, directly connected the young generation of protesters to that time, lending them credence and contributing to their mobilization abilities. Weekly peaceful marches brought millions into the streets, leaving the authorities scrambling to respond.

On April 2, following repeated unsuccessful attempts to tamp down the protests through placating gestures, Bouteflika resigned. The key player in bringing about the resignation was Chief of the Armed Forces Ahmed Gaïd Salah. One week later, parliament confirmed Bouteflika's interim successor, Abdelkader Bensalah (another member of the old guard), until new presidential elections could be held. The new president was quickly dubbed "Ibn Salah" by the protesters (i.e., he was controlled by Gaïd Salah).[87] The whole episode up to this point closely resembled the dynamics surrounding Egyptian president Husni Mubarak's removal from power in February 2011, with the army taking the self-designated role as guardian of the state.

Over the next year, Algerian civil society sought to maintain the momentum of its extraordinary mobilization, holding weekly mass demonstrations demanding the dismantling of the entire system of power, accompanied by the tendering of numerous plans for a gradual transition to a genuine democratic system. The *pouvoir*, for its part, sought to contain and eventually wear down the *Hirak* through a combination of tactics. Prominent figures of the ruling elite were sacrificed, including Saïd Bouteflika, who received a fifteen-year prison sentence for conspiring against the state and undermining the authority of the army (plotting to overthrow Ahmed Ben Salah); two former prime ministers, Ahmed Ouyahia and Abdelmalek Sellal, who received fifteen- and twelve-year sentences for corruption-related offenses; as well as several other ministers and well-connected businessmen. Former DRS strongman Médeine, who had been removed from power officially in 2015; Louisa Hanoune, the secretary-general of the Workers' Party; and another senior former official in the security services were convicted of the same charges as Saïd Bouteflika and also received fifteen-year sentences. Former police chief Abdelghani Hamel received a similar sentence in March 2020, along with stiff sentences for his four children and wife, for illegally amassing immense wealth and numerous homes.[88]

Proposals for a regime-led national dialogue were also tendered but drew little response. The regime's tactics also included use of brute force against demonstrators, arrests of *Hirak* activists, and attempts to sow internal divisions among the protesters by playing the Kabyle card (see below). The culminating point for the regime was the holding of presidential elections on December 12 despite strong opposition, enabling it to claim that the country was getting back to business as usual. Five establishment politicians put forth their candidacies, with former prime minister Abdelmadjid Tebboune winning easily. Less than 40 percent of eligible voters participated, according to official figures (which were probably inflated), indicating that much of the public remained unwilling to bring the *Hirak* protests to an end. Eleven days later, Gaïd Salah died suddenly of a heart attack. He was replaced as interim Army Chief of Staff by a close associate, the seventy-four-year-old Saïd Chengriha, introducing yet another level of uncertainty to the situation.

The standoff between the regime and the *Hirak* continued into 2020. So did the weekly protests until they were suspended in late March 2020 owing to the COVID-19 emergency. As was the case with other regimes around the world, the *pouvoir* viewed the crisis as an opportunity to crack down even more on everything associated with the protests. On March 25, an Algiers court convicted the journalist Khaled Drareni, a reporter for Reporters sans Frontières and cofounder of the news website *Casbah Tribune*, whose Twitter feed covering the protests had 140,000 followers, on charges of incitement and committing an "attack on national unity"; his sentence was left unspecified. The internationally renowned Committee to Protect Journalists branded the authorities' action "ludicrous" and called for his immediate release. One prominent *Hirak* leader and opposition member of parliament, Karim Tabbou, who had been held in solitary confinement since September, received a one-year sentence for "incitement to violence" and "harming national security" resulting from a speech criticizing the role of the army in politics. The sentence was roundly condemned by Amnesty International.[89] Concurrently, Tebboune pardoned more than 5,000 prisoners but failed to include the dozens of *Hirak* activists in that amnesty.[90]

True to form, Tebboune sought to placate the public and reinforce his legitimacy by appointing a committee of experts to draft additional constitutional changes, which included presidential term limits and new powers for the parliament and judiciary. The preamble of the new text even made favorable reference to the *Hirak*'s peaceful efforts to promote social transformation and build a new Algeria.[91] The new constitution was approved by a national referendum on November 1, 2020. However, voter turnout was less than 25 percent, thanks in part to a boycott led by the *Hirak*. Tebboune himself had been flown to Germany for treatment for COVID-19, where he remained for more than two months, leaving the country in an extended state of uncertainty. Few if any persons believed that the new constitution was anything more than window dressing.

The Kabyle-Amazigh Dimension of the *Hirak*

Although Karim Tabbou's agenda was national and not Kabyle-centered, his background as a protégé of Aït Ahmed made his antiregime militancy and resultant prominence in the *Hirak* another chapter in the Kabyle story.[92] And not surprisingly, given the depth of alienation in Kabylia, the very first demonstrations against Bouteflika's planned candidacy occurred in two Kabylian towns: Bordj Bou Arréridjis, 150 kilometers east of Algiers, and Kherrata, 150 kilometers farther east. An additional protest then took place in Khenchela, in the Aures Mountains, in the region of the Chaoui, Algeria's second-largest Amazigh community. Khenchela was close to where a local association, sixteen years earlier, had erected a statue of the Kahina, the mythical Berber queen, who had resisted Arab Islamic invaders in the late seventh century and was purportedly from the region.[93] Protesters ascended to the roof of the town hall to remove a giant portrait of Bouteflika that adjoined the national flag. Kherrata carried its own special symbolism, having been one of the sites of France's brutal retaliation following the May 8, 1945, outbreak of violence in the town of Setif (50 kilometers south), a seminal episode in the history of colonial Algeria.[94] To be sure, these protests were not specifically Amazigh or Kabyle in content; in fact, one could argue that they were explicitly national. Indeed, they set the stage for the first mass protest in Algiers, on February 22, 2019, that launched the *Hirak*.

Nonetheless, as the movement gathered strength, an Amazigh-Kabyle dimension surfaced, highlighting once again the unique status that Kabylia and Kabyles have played in the history and politics of modern Algeria. At the center of things was a symbol: the Amazigh flag, a tricolor with the letter Z in Tifingah script, symbolizing the Amazigh ("free man") in the center. Created by Mohand Arav Bessaoud, the Kabyle militant and cofounder in 1966 of the Académie Berbère in Paris, the flag was adopted at the founding meeting of the World Amazigh Congress, convened in the Canary Islands in 1997, and is now displayed widely among Amazigh communities in North Africa and the diaspora. While the Algerian national flag was waved ubiquitously and displayed at every *Hirak* protest, the Amazigh flag was also displayed, sometimes together with the national flag, sometimes alone.

The Amazigh flag's presence quickly became the subject of debate within the Amazigh community and beyond. Some Imazighen feared that displaying the flag would be seen as overly provocative and used against the community. Indeed, Islamist-leaning elements called on their Kabyle brothers to display only the national flag, and to write their slogans in Arabic, so as not to undermine national unity. Opponents of the Kabyle-Amazigh belittled the flag as the "flag with a fork" (*rayat al-farchitta*) that represented "separatists"; the accusation of a "foreign hand" being behind the Amazigh cause resurfaced, including reference to Mehenni's favorable view of Israel.[95] The Mehenni/GPA critique was the opposite: conjoining the national flag with Amazigh symbols was naive at best and a betrayal of Kabyle national aspirations at worst. On the ground, however, the Amazigh flag continued to be displayed at protests. MAK flags were waved more discreetly, and only during protest marches in Kabylian cities.

On June 19, Gaïd Salah decided to play the Amazigh card in an attempt to weaken the *Hirak*. Waving the Amazigh flag, he declared, was an insult to the national flag, "a unique emblem that represents the symbol of Algeria's sovereignty, its independence, its territorial integrity and its popular unity." Those seeking to "manipulate" people's sentiments by employing symbols other than the national flag would be arrested, he said. Scores were subsequently detained for doing so, even though there was no legal basis for the arrests. Salah's emphasis on the singularity of the national flag, "a flag for which millions of people have fallen to their deaths as martyrs," constituted a desultory response to the *Hirak*'s claim to be the legitimate heirs of the Algerian revolution.[96] On the tactical level, it was reminiscent of the regime's ultimately successful efforts to prevent the 2001 Kabylian protests from taking on a larger, national dimension.

Unlike that earlier episode, however, there was a good degree of pushback. In addition to continuing to wave the flag, Amazigh student activists also donned traditional Kabyle and Tuareg robes in protest against Salah's edict. Moreover, the bulk of non-Amazigh *Hirak* protesters recognized the Amazigh flag for what it was and embraced it as an additional symbol of their identity, representing the country's millennial-old cultural substrata[97] as well as being a clear symbol of opposition to the hated *pouvoir*. Amazigh flags were seen at protests in places where no Amazigh resided, and the chant *Qbāyel, 'arab . . . Khawa, Khawa w l'Gaid Salah ma' l'Khawana* ("Kabyle, Arab—Brothers; and Gaid Salah Is with the Traitors") became part of the lexicon of protest slogans. The traditional Kabyle protest slogan *Ulaç Smah Ulaç'* ("No forgiveness, none") took on an additional connotation beyond the Amazigh cause.[98]

To be sure, one could not yet speak of a broad new consensus that recognized Kabyle specificity within a gestating "Second Republic." Elements loyal to the regime continued to play the Amazigh card, particularly through social media, with Kabyles being labeled "Zouaves," a derogatory reference to auxiliary (mostly Kabyle) troops recruited by the French colonial authorities. Islamists on social media accused Kabyles of celebrating Gaïd Salah's death, as did the leader of a small Islamist party and member of parliament, who called the Kabyles "dogs" and "the worst kind of Jews."[99] All of this indicated that the debate regarding the appropriate symbols and identity references of the Algerian republic was acquiring new saliency.

Kabylia and the Presidential Election

Voter turnout for elections in the Kabylia region during the preceding two decades was the lowest in the country. This was again the case on December 12, 2019, when the long-delayed presidential election was held in the face of the *Hirak*'s opposition. In Kabylia, the resistance to the election was broad. More than fifty mayors had already declared in September their unwillingness to cooperate in the preparations needed for the elections. As the election date approached, the brick became the symbol of their opposition, with activists erecting brick walls at the entrances to Tizi Ouzou and to government buildings there to prevent distribution of election materials. Only two of the five presidential candidates even ventured briefly into the region to campaign, where they were met with hostility.[100] Election Day itself was highly charged everywhere in Algeria, but especially in Kabylia, with some polling stations being ransacked and others blockaded. Many were never opened. As previously noted, the national turnout was officially reported to be just under 40 percent, a figure that is probably inflated. In Kabylia's two provinces, however, there was no possibility of inflating the numbers, as the boycott in its two primary provinces was nearly total: The official participation rate in Wilayat Tizi Ouzou was 0.04 percent; in Wilayat Béjaïa it was 0.18 percent.[101] Nearly two decades after the Black Spring and ensuing years of civil revolt, Kabylian Amazigh were more alienated than ever from the *pouvoir*, providing potentially fertile ground for the far-reaching proposals of Kabyle intellectuals and activists.

Conclusion

After having avoided the 2011 Arab Spring upheavals roiling so many other states, the Algerian regime ended the decade facing a broad, nonviolent movement for fundamental political change. Although the COVID-19 crisis gave the regime an advantage over the *Hirak*, the collapse of the oil and gas market seemed to guarantee that the regime's ability to regain its previously unchallenged domination over society would be minimal. The struggle over the fundamental contours of the Algerian polity that had burst forth in 2019 appeared sure to continue in one form or another.

Kabyles, and Kabylia, have always been Algeria's most well-defined "Other," even as Kabyles played key roles in the independence movement and among independent Algeria's intellectual, professional, and political elites. Over the course of Algeria's first half-century, the combination of an overcentralized authoritarian system, rigid ideological principles, endemic corruption, and a failure to address the material needs of an expanding young population had undermined the regime's legitimacy. Coupled with the two seminal episodes of confrontation in 1980 and 2001, this mix of factors produced an evolving and dynamic ethnonational consciousness that by 2010 penetrated into a considerable portion of Kabylian society. This process continued apace throughout the ensuing decade.

Together with the rest of Algerian society, Kabyles shared a high degree of alienation toward the *pouvoir*. This was expressed in very public and vocal protests on important dates in the Kabyle-Amazigh commemorative calendar and particularly at Aït Ahmed's funeral. More generally, civil society pursued a policy of what Hadj-Moussa and Tilmatine call "patrimonialization," a "collective assignment of meaning" resulting in the strengthening of shared values that center on "the recovery, conservation or restoration of a space, property or practices related to culture and the Kabyle language." Examples abound. They include a new wave of young singers and the rediscovery of old ones; the reemergence of local festivals and traditions; and the "reberberization" of toponyms and writing in Latin or Tifinagh script on roads and in public spaces, often with the Arabic crossed out.[102]

Whereas the idea of autonomy had seemed at the time of the MAK's 2001 founding to be little more than the creed of a few utopianists, by the middle of the next decade it seemed to have touched a respondent chord among many Kabyles, who were now openly defiant of the regime. The discourse of Kabyle ethnonationalism had been sharpened and expanded: self-determination, whether within a completely reorganized federal and consociational democratic Algeria or an independent state, was now part of the political lexicon, even if the ability to translate ideas into action was beyond reach. These ideas also spread beyond the bounds of the region, becoming part of the highly charged situation in the Mzab.

To be sure, the *pouvoir* still had the upper hand. But its recognition of the depth of Kabyle self-conscious "Otherness" and alienation led it in 2016 to make what was previously an unimaginable concession: the recognition of Tamazight as an official language, along with a commitment to promote and develop its usage. It was an act with considerable symbolic significance, constituting another achievement in the efforts by the Kabyle-Amazigh movement to be valorized as a collective and laying down a baseline going forward. Not without reason, Kabyles were mostly cynical about the move. Their skepticism of the official commitment to promoting Tamazight was confirmed anew in March 2020, when the regime closed down the first daily newspaper to be published exclusively in Tamazight after only four issues, the official reason being that it was using the Latin script and not Arabic or Tifingah.[103]

The *Hirak* protests exemplified the unique status of Kabylia and the strength of Kabyle collective identity within Algeria. The first significant protests occurred in Kabylian towns; some of its prominent leaders were Kabyles; and, of course, the Amazigh flag was prominently displayed in the protests alongside the Algerian national one. Within Kabylia, the MAK flag was also displayed at protests in a clear act of defiance. Of course, public display of the Amazigh flag was not universally accepted, and Gaïd Salah sought to use it as a way to sow division among the *Hirak*. However, it was a tactic that didn't appear to gain traction. At the same time, regardless of the preliminary discussions among *Hirak* leaders about the desired contours of the future "Second Republic" that they hoped to build, they didn't appear to have touched on the ideas put forth by Kabyle intellectuals for a consociational democracy with a defined territorial governing status for Kabylia. How things would play out—nationally and regarding the Kabyle dimension—remained to be seen. But Kabyle-Amazigh ethnonationalism had sunk deep roots, notwithstanding the internal differences regarding tactics and strategy. Hence it seemed clear that the future trajectory of state-society relations in Algeria—and even the very nature of the Algerian state—would be determined by the way in which the Kabyle question was addressed, and by the behavior of Kabyle actors themselves.

CHAPTER 2

Obscure No Longer: Libyan Imazighen in a Fractured Polity

The story of Libya's "Arab Spring" stands apart from its North African neighbors. Whereas the 2011 protests in Morocco and Algeria did not constitute serious challenges to the regimes' grips on power, in Libya, as in Tunisia and Egypt, they resulted in regime change. But unlike in Tunisia and Egypt, where mass peaceful protests toppled Zine El Abidine Ben Ali and Hosni Mubarak within a matter of weeks, Libya experienced a prolonged and bloody armed conflict between forces loyal to Libyan leader Muammar Qaddafi and a loose coalition of opposition elements under the umbrella of a hastily constituted National Transitional Council (NTC). The NTC was backed by a NATO-led air campaign and international legitimacy conferred by the United Nations. Qaddafi was brutally put to death on October 20, 2011, forty-two years after leading a military coup d'état against the monarchy that had governed Libya since achieving independence in 1951.

Over the ensuing nine years, Tunisia established a pluralist democratic political system that, however fragile, stood out as the success story of the Arab Spring; Egypt experienced prolonged instability, multiple elections, and a year of Muslim Brotherhood–led government before the military-led restoration in July of the old authoritarian order, led by Abd al-Fatah al-Sisi. Libya, by contrast, neither established viable new governing institutions nor restored the old dictatorial order. Rather, it was a chaotic arena of conflict and political dispute, involving multiple societal actors and agendas and compounded by the involvement of other countries pursuing their own geopolitical interests. Moreover, the fracturing of the state had destabilizing effects all over the region, from the Sahel to the Sinai: Radical jihadists gained a foothold in the country; Tuareg migrants from Mali and Niger, many of whom had served in Qaddafi's army, streamed back home and turned Mali into a conflict zone; and traffickers in arms, drugs, and would-be migrants to Europe from sub-

Saharan Africa ran rampant. Repeated efforts to fashion a workable, constitutionally based political order in Libya foundered, as did numerous efforts by the United Nations and neighboring states to mediate between the warring parties. By summer 2020, the country was divided between the Tripoli-based, UN-recognized Government of National Accord (GNA), which was receiving crucial support from Turkey and Qatar, and the Benghazi-based Libyan National Army, headed by General Khalid Haftar and supported by Russia, the United Arab Emirates (UAE), and Egypt. Neither side was able to achieve a decisive military advantage.

Many factors account for these wildly diverging outcomes, including Qaddafi's especially brutal rule, the lure of Libya's oil riches, the huge amount of weapons stores that became available for the taking, and the country's strategic location astride the central Mediterranean region. One element centers on the notion of "stateness." Introduced in 1968 by the British scholar J. P. Nettl, it has become "the most prominent concept in state-centred, empirical research on democratic transition and stability."[1] Sometimes slippery but nonetheless useful, the concept of stateness focuses on the intertwining elements of an entity's administrative effectiveness, the degree to which it has a monopoly on violence, and a political-cultural element (i.e., the degree to which there is agreement on who is a member of the community and what constitutes its territory). States that have higher degrees of stateness tend to have correspondingly higher degrees of social cohesion, although this doesn't automatically translate into regime legitimacy. In applying this broad definition to North African states, it is clear that Egypt and Tunisia have comparatively high degrees of stateness, with clearly defined territorial cores and histories of centralized bureaucracies over the *longue durée*, and well-defined social identities linked to their territories.[2] Although the outcomes of the Arab Spring protests were very different from one another, their comparatively high degree of stateness underpinned both.

Libya, by contrast, arrived at independence with a very low level of stateness, having been cobbled together out of three distinct regions (Tripolitania, Cyrenaica, and Fezzan) that, apart from their opposition to Italian colonialism, had little to bind them together. Efforts by Libyan exiles during the colonial period to imagine and fashion a modern integrated national identity did not take root inside the country at the moment of independence.[3] Indeed, the first (and only) king of independent Libya, Idris I, whose legitimacy derived from his status as head of the Cyrenaica-based Sanusi religious order, was a "reluctant monarch" who preferred a federal system with a weak central government; thus he explicitly opposed the state-building and nation-building efforts typical of newly independent governing elites.[4] But the discovery of rich oil fields in the country in 1959 introduced a new factor into the equation, generating long-term socioeconomic changes and intensified demands among an increasingly urban, educated, and youthful society.

A bloodless coup by a coterie of junior officers, led by Qaddafi, toppled the monarchy on September 1, 1969. His role model—Egypt's president Gamal Abdel Nasser—had led a similar coup in 1952, and Qaddafi promoted himself as the heir to Nasser's pan-Arab leadership. His 1973 nationalization of the majority of the country's oil assets was a revolutionary act; that act gave him the material tools by which he could build a power base, crush all opponents, and exert influence beyond Libya's borders. One may argue that a modern Libyan national consciousness more fully crystallized during Qaddafi's long tenure. So far, however, that has not translated into the kind of social cohesion and comity needed to forge a workable consensus on how to govern the country.

To the astonishment of many, the rebellion against Qaddafi had an Amazigh component. Almost overnight, Libya's Imazighen went from being a repressed and marginalized minority to one that played a meaningful role in the fighting. Accompanying their military mobilization was a cultural one: after having long been forbidden, teaching of the Amazigh language and cultural activities suddenly flourished in areas vacated by Qaddafi's officials. This paralleled developments in Syria's Kurdish regions. Similar to Syria's Kurds, who drew on the ideological and material support from Kurdish nationalists in other parts of the pan-Kurdish universe, Libyan Amazigh were assisted in the educational sphere by Algerian and Moroccan Amazigh teachers and materials. They had a clear political agenda as well: the new Libya, they insisted, must be multicultural and democratic, a country that respected the rights of all ethnolinguistic communities—Amazigh, Tuareg (considered by Libyan Amazigh activists to be a distinct subset of the Amazigh community), and Tebu, as well as Arab. They advocated repeatedly for constitutional recognition of their language and culture, similar to their counterparts in Morocco and Algeria, albeit with less success. In response, and in light of the absence of a cohesive state authority, the Imazighen declared that, in their areas at least, Tamazight would be an official language. As of 2020, the main task was to consolidate their achievements in order to cope with whatever the future would hold. The unfolding of these developments, in the context of an ongoing armed conflict and fractured polity, forms the heart of this chapter.

Libya's Amazigh Communities—Background and Context

The territory of modern Libya is an integral part of the Amazigh movement's *imaginaire*. The name "Libya" (*libyè*) was coined by the ancient Greeks, referring to the region west of the Nile Valley; the "Libu" were a prominent tribe in the region. Moreover, the Amazigh calendar, developed in the 1960s by the Paris-based Académie Berbère, dates Year One as 950 BC, the approximate beginning of the Libyan Pharaonic Dynasties in Egypt, under Shoshenq I (the biblical Shishak).

Libya's population, as of mid-2020, was approximately seven million. Out of that, its Amazigh population is commonly estimated between 6–10 percent (400,000–700,000), although a report tendered to the UN Committee on the Elimination of Racial Discrimination in 2004 by the Paris-based Tamazgha claimed far higher numbers (1.5 million, or 26 percent).[5] As in Morocco, Algeria, and Tunisia, Libyan Amazigh activists insist that the bulk of the country's population is of Amazigh origin, whether Arabized or not. Their core territorial area is Jabal Nafusa (Adrar n Infusen), in the country's northwest, near the border with Tunisia. In addition to the main towns of the region—Yefren, Jadu, and Nalut—other Amazigh communities in the west range from the coastal town of Zuwara to the oasis of Ghadames, 462 kilometers southwest of the country's capital, Tripoli, near the common border with Algeria and Tunisia.

Several Arab towns are also part of the Nafusa region, the most prominent being Zintan, 60 kilometers southwest of Yefren. The Zuwara area had included forty to forty-five villages populated mainly by the Aït Willut tribe, but the last of these had emptied out by the mid-1950s. Similarly, many young Nafusa Amazigh had migrated in recent decades to Tripoli and other coastal cities in the Tripolitanian region. According to one activist, fully half of all Libyan Imazighen now live in Tripoli.[6] There is also a cluster of three Amazigh enclaves among the eastern oases. In addition, Libya has a native population of 20,000 Tamashek/Tamaheq-speaking Tuareg, known as Kel Ajjer, traditionally based in the far southwest of the country, whom Qaddafi referred to fondly as "free sons of the Arab nation," owing to their nomadic lifestyle.[7] As with the Mzabi Amazigh community in Algeria and the Ibadi community in Djerba, Tunisia, the Ibadi creed predominated among Nafusa Imazighen, although the depth of religious knowledge and praxis was shallower than in the Mzab, thanks partly to discriminatory practices by Qaddafi's regime.

Up until the 2011 rebellion, Western analysts tended not to pay attention to Libya's Amazigh community or even distinguish them from the numerically dominant Arab population. Even the 2020 edition of the CIA's *World Factbook* implicitly highlighted the country's perceived homogeneity, stating that 97 percent of the population is ethnically "Arab and Berber." To be sure, factional divisions in the region traditionally crossed ethnic lines, and the common Arab-Berber jihad of 1912–1918 against the Italian invaders identified Tripolitania as a common homeland (*watan*) worth fighting for.[8] Still, ethnic

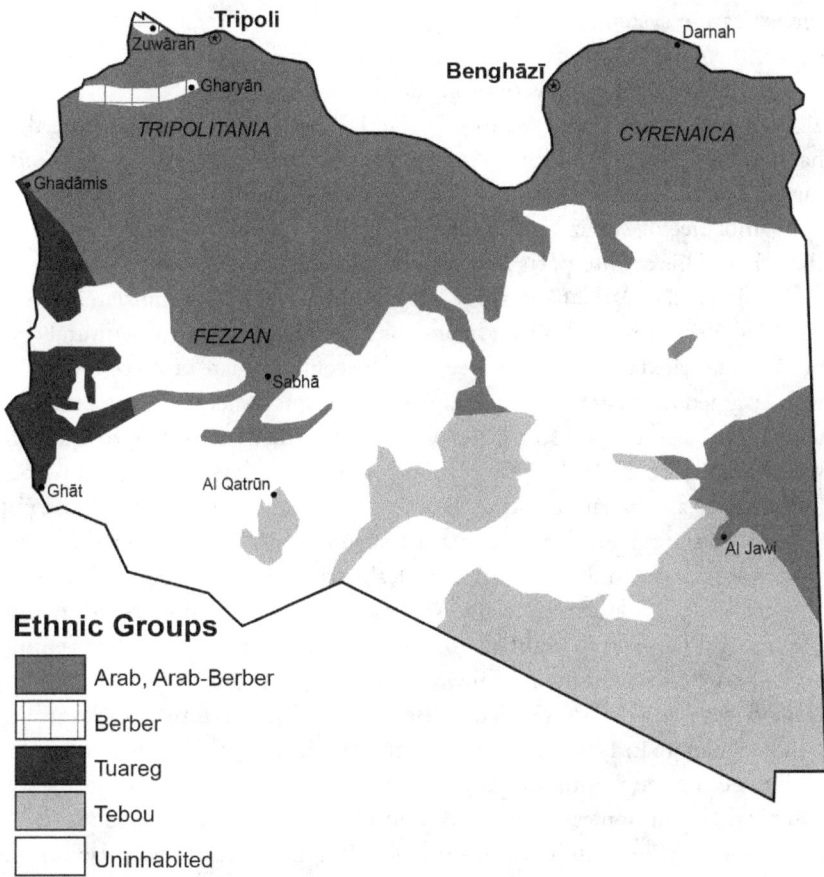

Map 2.1 Ethnic groups in Libya, abbreviated version of https://commons.wikimedia
.org/w/index.php?search=Libya+ amazigh+maps&title=Special:Search&profile
=advanced&fulltext=1&advancedSear ch-current=%7B%7D&ns0=1&ns6=1&ns12
=1&ns14=1&ns100=1&ns106=1#/media/File:Libya_ethnic.svg

distinctions mattered at times, and armed conflict between Berbers and Arabs did sometimes occur in the past. Italy exploited these divisions to help subdue and occupy Tripolitania in the early 1920s.[9] As part of efforts to increase the "legibility" of the native population,[10] the 1936 colonial census recorded 78 percent (ca. 600,000) of the population being "Arab" and "Arab-Berber," 9.3 percent (70,000) "Berber," and 4.7 percent (35,000) "Turk-Berber."[11]

Libya's official national narrative, emphasizing the Arab identity of the country, did not differ in substance from that of postindependent Algeria. Libya, Algeria, and Morocco all promoted the Arabization of public life and the education system. Similarly, longer-term processes, including the expansion of formal education, economic integration, and increased social mobility, adversely affected the levels of proficiency in Tamazight among Libya's Imazighen, just as they did in Morocco, Algeria, and Tunisia as well. Those that had moved to larger urban areas were prone to assimilation into the surrounding Arab and Islamic milieu. But Qaddafi's denial, dismissal, and repression of any semblance of Amazigh specificity were of a different order of magnitude than that of his counterparts in neighboring states.

Ideologically, Qaddafi's mantra "we are all Libyans" was translated into a complete negation of ethnic and religious pluralism. Libya's own cultural revolution, launched by a Qaddafi speech in the central square of Zuwara in 1973, was designed to created a completely homogeneous society: Arab in ethnicity and language and Sunni Muslim in religion.[12] Berbers, according to Qaddafi, were Semitic tribes who had migrated in antiquity to North Africa, and Berber identity was a colonial invention designed to balkanize the region. As he put it in a 1985 statement: "If your mother transmits you this language, she nourishes you with the milk of the colonialist, she feeds you their poison."[13] In this, Qaddafi was on ground trodden by Arab nationalists throughout North Africa. He did give his own special twist of a history lesson, however: "We [Semitic Arabs] set out from Yemen until we came here [to Libya]. We went by land, by land [*barr barr*], so they called us 'Berbers.'... Libya is for the Libyans. We will not tolerate in Libya any ethnic zealotry [*shu`ubiyya*]."[14] On another occasion, he warned community leaders: "You can call yourselves whatever you want inside your homes—Berbers, Children of Satan, whatever—but you are only Libyans when you leave your homes."[15] Tribal identity was also on the forbidden list, although he was well aware of its centrality in Libyan society and used it for his own ends.[16] In the Nafusa region, land expropriation measures benefited certain landless Arab tribes, breaking up an old alliance with their Imazighen neighbors and creating conflicts that would continue to unfold during the post-2011 period.[17] Well aware of the widespread opposition of Amazigh families to having their children marry Arabs, the regime sought to counter this by transferring Amazigh workers to predominantly Arabophone areas to promote their assimilation.[18]

Qaddafi's highly trumpeted Arab Socialist *jamahiriya* ("polity of the masses") and insistence that he had no formal role in governing the country masked a brutal dictatorial regime with an extreme personality cult that negated all individuality and difference. Libya's Berbers were among those on the receiving end of these discriminatory and repressive policies. The Berber language was banned from use outside the home; Berbers were erased from the country's history; cultural associations and festivals were banned; and even giving Berber names to one's children was made illegal. Children with non-Arab names were not registered with the state and thus denied education. Most, being Ibadis, suffered religious discrimination as well. Collective discrimination included the closure of the region's only hospital in Zuwara, as well as the failure to extend to the Nafusa region the water supplied to Tripoli by the Great Man Made River project. Even the name of the Jabal Nafusa region was officially erased, being replaced with Jabal al-Gharbi ("Western Mountain"). Berbers had previously played important roles in the professional officer corps, but their ranks were sharply reduced. Those remaining in their position were viewed with suspicion and often assigned difficult tasks in the far south. The resentment, which only increased official suspicion and repression, was palpable.[19]

Chilling accounts of the arrest, torture, and murder of several activists, writers, and scholars during the 1970s and 1980s—some of whom had founded Libya's first Amazigh association, the Rabita Shamal Ifriqiya (North African League)—indicated that Qaddafi's cultural policies were being met with resistance.[20] In fact, the combination of Qaddafi's repression and the ethnocultural flourishing in Kabylia, next door in Algeria, had a galvanizing effect on many young Libyan Imazighen. Such a dynamic calls to mind the rise of Kurdish militancy in Turkey in opposition to the state's "extreme makeover" policies,[21] and the influence of Kurdish ethnonationalism emanating from next-door Iraq.[22] The iconic 1980 Kabylian Berber Spring (*Tafsut n Imazighen*) was particularly inspiring to Libyan Amazigh activists: under its influence, an activist from Jadu wrote a well-known poem in the early 1980s ("*U Salet Idnegh Tefsut*," or "Together We Raise Up Spring").[23]

Not surprisingly, the regime viewed Amazigh communities as opposition strongholds. As was the case in Morocco during the 1960s and 1970s, Amazigh activists were represented prominently in the broader Libyan opposition. Following the discovery of a 1984 plot to overthrow Qaddafi by the National Front for the Salvation of Libya, the houses of some Imazighen members were destroyed, and two members were hung in Nalut.[24]

One especially prominent individual, who is considered emblematic of Libyan Amazighté, was the poet and scholar Saïd El Mahroug, known as "Sifaw." A member of the Libyan Writers Union, his poetry, in both Arabic and Tamazight, was a "crime" that he was willing to commit. Dedicated to recovering and renewing the Amazigh collective memory and language, he published several studies on the Amazigh language, grammar, and mythology. Repeatedly harassed by the authorities, he eventually was paralyzed from a car accident that was probably caused deliberately. In 1994, he died in a Tunisian hospital.[25]

The first years of the twenty-first century witnessed the beginnings of what

Anna Baldinetti called a "nascent Amazigh civil society" among Libyan Imazighen, beginning with the internet-based activities of exiles who were increasingly plugged in to an emerging global civil society. Concurrently, the Qaddafi regime moved to normalize its international relations after many years of isolation.[26] As part of its efforts to bolster its image abroad, and to neutralize criticism of international human rights bodies, the regime's unwavering hostility toward anything Amazigh was modified by occasional gestures of acknowledgment and conciliation overtures, led by Qaddafi's son and heir apparent Sayf al-Islam.[27] Over the course of the decade, regime-Amazigh dynamics fluctuated considerably, occasionally raising hopes for real change that in the end did not materialize.

Meeting in London in 2000, some of those exiles established the Libyan T'mazight Congress (Agraw a'Libi n'Tmazight). Its founding manifesto presented several guiding principles and an agenda that was situated in the Amazigh movement's universe—one in which ethnocultural and national aspects were intertwined. Just as Moroccan Amazigh intellectuals had laid out in their detailed *Manifeste* some months earlier,[28] their Libyan counterparts called for a fundamental redefinition of Libyan national identity, anchored in the country's constitution, to include the country's Amazigh component. Tamazight, they demanded, should be recognized as a national and official language, alongside Arabic, with the requisite support for educational institutions, governmental and public offices, media, and public use that would translate such recognition into reality. In addition, the document enumerated concrete demands that painted a picture of the discrimination and repression that they faced:

> The immediate cancellation of all suppressive orders and actions against the Amazigh and their rights, such as forfeiting of land, hindering civil and regional administrative rights, oppressing the right to practice religious faith, prohibiting the establishment of cultural organisations and civil rights organisations, misrepresenting Libyan history and effacing of cultural and geographical features and landmarks; and the immediate terminations of all forms of abuse against the rights of Tamazight scholars and activities, and rehabilitation of those affected by this abuse.[29]

The following year, Mohamed (Madghis) Umadi, a young exiled activist who had first discovered his Amazigh heritage while studying in the United States, established the website *Tawalt* ("Word"), which quickly became a repository for Libyan Berber history and culture. One knowledgeable writer called it "the main cultural and political conduit for Libyan Berbers."[30] The site was suddenly closed in early 2009,[31] following a threatening demonstration of 300 regime supporters outside the Umadi family house in Yefren. His brother, Abderrazaq Madi, was one of four Libyan members of the World Amazigh Congress's Federal Council; in 2005 he had participated in a CMA meeting in Nador, Morocco, and since then had been barred from traveling abroad. As a result, his father, Salem Madi, a longtime activist who had spent years in Qaddafi's prisons, went in his son's stead to the 2008 CMA meeting in Meknes, Morocco, provoking the demonstration. His daughter, Zorgh, then a teenager, was in the house at the time and related her palpable fear as the mob threw rocks, painted slogans on the walls of the house, and shouted menacing slogans. The real reason for the demonstration was anger over a statement Salem Madi had made to an Algerian newspaper during the CMA meeting; when asked if he supported Sayf al-Islam's reforms, he replied that he supported neither Sayf al-Islam nor his father.[32]

Ironically, the incident came at the end of an off-again on-again charm offensive toward the Amazigh community headed by Sayf al-Islam and other government officials, as well as a sporadic dialogue between Qaddafi and Belkacem Lounes, the CMA president at the time.[33] For Qaddafi, his periodic gestures were designed to domesticate the Amazigh community through a government-sponsored organization and to bolster its international image.[34] And even though the threatening demonstration marked an end to these overtures, there were no further consequences, indicating that Qaddafi was still concerned with trying to improve his image in the West.

The Uprising

Perhaps the most difficult political choice that individuals and communities confront is whether or not to take up arms and rebel against their government, as the consequences of failure are likely severe. The decision is itself a charged prospect, creating or exacerbating divisions within the community that could threaten its cohesiveness and adversely affect the outcome. And the more fluid and uncertain the setting, the harder it is to be confident in a particular course of action.

These dynamics were very much in evidence among Libyan Imazighen in early 2011. The reverberations of the Tunisian and Egyptian mass protests were being felt throughout Libya, and Amazigh youth were no exception. While they pushed for action, particularly after the authorities started to arrest potential agitators, community elders tried to hold them back. As they were a vulnerable minority community, the uncertainty about how to react and the possible consequences were especially poignant. In early February, three veteran Amazigh activists, representing three different mountain towns, agreed that, in the event of an uprising in the east, their community should wait to see how neighboring Arab communities reacted before making a decision. The possibility that Qaddafi would use neighboring Arab communities against them was always on their minds.[35]

On February 15, the rebellion was ignited by large-scale protests in Benghazi, which security forces fired on. Unexpectedly, the Nafusa Imazighen's Zintan Arab neighbors, who had a strong presence in the Libyan military, decided to join the rebellion. Their move came after heated internal debate, overtures from the regime, and countervailing pressure from their youth wing. The decision tipped the balance for the Nafusa Amazigh communities, who now joined as well. So did other neighboring Arab towns. Local military councils, supported by deserting officers, were established. Pickup trucks carrying Amazigh fighters often bore Tamazight inscriptions, written in Tifinagh characters, such as *Igrawliyen n Adrarn Infusen* ("Revolutionaries of Adrar n Infusen"), along with Arabic equivalents.[36] Several civilian functionaries did agree to meet with Qaddafi in early March, but they had lost whatever influence they once enjoyed.[37] The National Transition Council, established by anti-Qaddafi forces in Benghazi on February 27, was quickly endorsed by the Amazigh leadership, which sent representatives from different towns, including Yefren, Nalut, Jadu, Ghadames, and Zuwara, to participate. The swift establishment of the NTC and the Amazigh endorsement were partly the outcome of years of periodic discussions, dating to 2005, among several Libyan opposition groups and representatives of the World Amazigh Congress on how to build a post-Qaddafi democratic Libya.[38]

The immediate priority, of course, was the battle: recognizing the NTC enabled Amazigh groups to negotiate external military support for their portion of the insurgency while keeping a distance from the Council. In this, they were not essentially different from other units in the rebellion. While the NTC had formally established a National Liberation Army, it was in practice a loose coalition of independent brigades lacking a unified command structure.

Qaddafi's air force had already begun bombing Yefren on February 20, prompting women and children to take shelter in caves. A more sustained military offensive was launched in early March, and at the beginning of April Yefren found itself besieged; it would remain so for two months. The UN Office for the Coordination of Humanitarian Affairs estimated that nearly 55,000 civilians from Yefren, Nalut, and other towns streamed across the Tunisian border seeking safety, and one knowledgeable scholar cited tens of thousands of families, numbering up to 100,000 persons total. A variety of housing solutions, ranging from UN-run refugee camps to home hospitality and rented rooms, were found, some arrangements lasting four to eight months. The area's own Amazigh population played a key role in mobilizing assistance, and the experience was formative in many ways for both the hosts and the guests.[39] Areas of Tataouine Province adjacent to the Libyan border became a hub for humanitarian supplies to the mountains, supplied by Qatar, the UAE, and Oman, each country directing its aid to specific clients.[40]

During the first months of the rebellion, the hodgepodge of antiregime forces in the western region—Amazigh and Arab, volunteer irregulars, and defectors from the army—were on the defensive and, often, on their own. However, from the beginning of June, the tide shifted, with increasing support from NATO forces. An August offensive seized the strategic western coastal area, including the predominantly Amazigh town of Zuwara and the crucial Zawiya oil refinery 50 kilometers from Tripoli. The city was taken by rebel forces on August 21, and its many Amazigh residents joined the throngs of celebrants, waving Amazigh flags along with the old, pre-Qaddafi Libyan flag that had been adopted by the NTC. Two more months of fighting ensued before the last of Qaddafi's forces were defeated; Qaddafi himself was discovered and quickly put to death on October 20.

Overall, Amazigh fighters had contributed substantially to the rebellion's ultimate success by helping to create an important second front. As Frederick Wehrey observed, "whoever controls the Nafusa commands the western approaches to the capital."[41] Thus, their efforts complemented the main thrust coming from the east. It was a formative collective experience and provided them with a measure of legitimacy for their future actions and demands. Their efforts were also recognized in real time by the Libyan Arab rapper Ibn Thabit, whose songs praised the Nafusa fighters and recognized their deep roots in the country, offering up the possibility that the post-Qaddafi Libyan nation could be inclusive in nature.[42]

Obscure No Longer

Libyan Amazigh communities, emboldened by their struggle and the vacuum left by the withdrawal of regime officials and security forces from the region, asserted their Amazighité in public for the first time. The Tamazight-language song *"Agrawli Itri Enegh"* ("The Rebel Is Our Star"), sung by Dania Ben Sassi and written by her activist father, became one of the anthems of the revolution.[43] The song honors his sister's son, who was killed in the fighting. Ben Sassi performed the song in central Tripoli's renamed Martyr's Square shortly after the eviction of Qaddafi's forces, before large celebratory crowds, Amazigh and Arab alike. It was a moment that seemed pregnant with possibilities for a new Libya, one in which its Amazigh elements might play an integral part.[44]

Ben Sassi's father was from Zuwara and her mother from Belgrade, Serbia (where she grew up). She would appear on numerous occasions before adoring audiences in the years after the revolution. In January 2013, she was joined on stage by the well-known Moroccan Amazigh singer Khalid Izri at a large concert celebrating the Amazigh New Year (Yennayer).[45] Later in 2013, at a festive concert in Paris celebrating Amazigh culture, she sang the unofficial Amazigh anthem, "*A Vava Inouva*," together with its originator, the iconic Idir (Hamid Cheriet, of Kabylia).[46] Izri also performed with them at the concert, making it a truly pan-Amazigh cultural moment.[47] Ben Sassi's presence was an indication of how far her own star had risen as the voice of Libyan Imazighen, how hungry they were for such a star, and how the Libyan Amazigh community was now embedded within the pan-Amazigh cultural and mental map. For her, it must have been a poignant moment, for she had grown up listening to Idir's music thanks to her father. It had been a primary mode through which she began to identify with the Amazigh cause.[48]

From the moment of the uprising, Amazigh flags became ubiquitous, as did symbols in Tifinagh script. A modicum of self-rule was established in Amazigh communities, and Tamazight was introduced into local schools, public spaces, and radio and television broadcasts.[49] The improvised, amateurish nature of the initial efforts mattered less than the fact that they were taking place at all. Teachers were given crash courses on teaching Tamazight, using Tifinagh. They were assisted by hurriedly obtained textbooks and the arrival of educators from Morocco and Algeria; a delegation from the World Amazigh Conference made a five-day visit to the region in August, further deepening pan-Amazigh connections. The first "national" television broadcast in Tamazight took place on May 2, in the midst of the war, on Libya Free People TV, broadcasting from Doha, Qatar. The broadcast and subsequent ones suggested that the incipient new Libya could, and perhaps would, include its Amazigh and other communities within the fabric of a redefined nation.[50]

Anecdotal evidence attested to the transformative effects of the uprising on the Amazigh community, at the communal and national levels. Signs of an emerging modern *ethnie* identity were provided by a resident of Yefren, who noted that previous local divisions had been superseded by a common bond forged in struggle: "The revolution has brought us all together. We all had our tribal allegiances before, and it would be rare for anyone to eat from the same *gasa'a* ('shared plate') as someone from another Amazigh town. Now Nalut, Kabaw, Jadu, Zintan, Yefren, al-Qalaa—we all eat in [from] the same plate."[51] Historical figures from the Nafusa region who had been downplayed or ignored by official accounts of the struggle against Italian colonialism were now publicly iconized. The most important of these was Sulayman al-Baruni (1870–1940), whose father was venerated throughout the Ibadi communities in North Africa, as well as by non-Ibadis in Tripolitania. The well-educated Sulayman was imprisoned several times by Ottoman authorities, elected to the revived Ottoman parliament in 1908 after the Young Turk revolution, and led the early resistance to Italian colonialism while initially aspiring to create an autonomous Ibadi province in the Nafusa region and western coastal plain. Baruni was also one of the leaders of the short-lived Tripolitanian Republic. His later efforts to mediate between Italian authorities and local groups failed, and he ended up in exile, as the Italian authorities suspected his ambitions.[52] Another revived historical figure was Khalifa ben-Askar, executed in 1920 by the Italians, who was especially revered in his native Nalut.[53] By contrast, images of Omar al-Mukhtar, the more widely known lionized leader of the anti-Italian resistance in eastern Libya, were absent.

A broader *imaginaire* seemed to be developing southward as well, to include the Desert Amazigh (Tuareg). Links were forged during the war, as units from Nafusa helped conquer several oasis towns in the Fezzan region and maintained a presence in Sebha, a mixed Tuareg-Tebu town, for several months afterward. Expressions of their common bonds manifested in the first TV broadcast in Tamazight.[54] Years later, hundreds of Tuareg families (if not more) fled intercommunal fighting with their Tebu neighbors and found refuge in Zuwara, where they felt more secure—another sign that bonds had developed between these two very different Amazigh communities.[55] But this was hardly universal. The desert town of Ghadames, whose population included Tuareg and non-Tuareg Amazigh, saw periodic spasms of violent conflict between Tuareg who had benefited from Qaddafi's largesse and revolutionary committees that had taken over after Qaddafi's forces fled at the onset of revolution. Mutual bad blood and several fatalities occurred, for which Ghadames's Tuareg residents paid a heavy price.

Constitutional Battles and the Institutionalization of the Libyan Amazigh Community

From the outset of rebellion, the emergence of militias and sources of authority suggested that assembling a legitimate and stable government with a monopoly on the means of coercion would be a daunting task. Indeed, it proved to be virtually impossible.

As rebel forces closed in on Tripoli, the National Transition Council issued its "Constitutional Declaration," laying out principles to guide the post-Qaddafi era. To the disappointment of Amazigh militants, it stated that Arabic would continue to be the country's sole official language, although the languages of all the elements of Libyan society would be considered "national" languages, with associated cultural rights preserved.[56]

As was true with counterparts in Morocco and Algeria, Libyan Amazigh activists were disappointed that their language would have "national" but not "official" status. If the country was to be a democracy, they said, then it had to be inclusive, representing all of the people equally, and not just one in which the majority could dictate everything. Some activists even saw national status as implying they were not native to the country but were being "nationalized" nonetheless. Others, conversely, thought this status was sufficient for the time being, the priority being establishment of real democracy. Lack of compromise on the language issue, they thought, risked exacerbating tensions and jeopardizing chances for establishing a democratic regime.[57]

On August 12, a body named the Movement for Amazigh Culture issued a document titled "How the Libyan Amazigh Movement Sees the Libya of Tomorrow"; it had actually been sent to the NTC earlier in an effort to influence its thinking regarding a new constitution. One month later, the Libyan T'mazight Congress published an open letter to the National Transitional Council, its executive board, and the public at large. Together, the two documents articulated the Amazigh agenda for the new Libya.

Consistent with long-standing pan-Amazigh discourse, the principles undergirding the new modern and free Libyan state, according to the document, "must emanate from universal human values such as recognition and respect for others, dialogue and tolerance." Therefore, the state should be "secular and democratic," with a decentralized government and a separation of powers among its branches. The Amazigh language was "the heritage of all Libyans without exception" and should be official and equal to Arabic. Concurrently, the Libyan state should promote foreign languages "in order to gain access to science and modernity, to open up to other cultures and civilizations." The symbols of the state should conform to the country's "identity, historical, cultural and intellectual dimensions." No political parties with a religious, regional, ethnic, tribal, "or any other discriminatory basis or in violation of human rights" were to be allowed. Finally, political, civic, economic, social, and cultural rights, including the freedom of expression, were to be guaranteed for all Libyans, men and women alike.[58]

Another open letter issued on September 17, 2011—"Regarding the Justly Deserved Amazigh Rights in Libya"—was sharper in tone. Libyan Amazigh had suffered massive injustices, it declared, the result of systematic, forced

Arabization that bordered on "ethnic cleansing" (*tat-hir al-'unsuri*), in addition to "an inverted and ideological reading of Libyan history, anthropology and extant reality." Having been among the first to rise up against the tyrannical Qaddafi regime and pay in blood and sacrifice along with other Libyans, the Amazigh movement demanded that their rights in all fields—cultural, linguistic, religious, political, legal, administrative, developmental, educational, and media—be enshrined in the new Libyan constitution. This was a matter for all Libyans, it was stressed. The foundational elements of Libyan identity are "Islam, Arabness, and Amazighness, and enriched by Mediterranean and African elements," which are part of the larger fabric of human civilization. (A similar formula, albeit also including the "Hebraic" element, appears in the 2011 Moroccan constitution ratified two months earlier.) There was no such thing as a "majority" or a "minority," "Amazigh Libyans" or "Arab Libyans"— only one Libyan people, who spoke several languages and who together would build a new, democratic, and multicultural state and society. In pursuit of these goals, the Libyan T'mazight Congress had worked with a whole host of Libyan organizations, dating back to the years in opposition, and was continuing to do so.[59]

The sharpened tone of the Congress's statement reflected the militancy of its new head, Fathi Benkhalifa. Born in Zuwara, a chemical engineer by profession, and a longtime activist, Benkhalifa had spent sixteen years in exile in Morocco before moving to Holland in 2010 to avoid possible extradition to Libya. He joined the NTC soon after its formation and was part of a delegation that lobbied European and African governments to recognize it as Libya's legitimate government. The NTC's August 3 "Constitutional Declaration" was unacceptable to him, and he officially left that body on August 20. In the ensuing months, he would sharpen his criticism. At the beginning of October, he was chosen to head the World Amazigh Congress. In selecting Djerba, Tunisia, as the venue for the meeting and Benkhalifa as president, the Congress was seizing an opportunity to expand the pan-Amazigh universe in light of the tumultuous events during the previous months.

Libyan Amazigh activism reached a new peak in the last week of September. On September 26, just nine days after issuing its open letter to the NTC, the first Libyan National Amazigh Congress was held, in Tripoli, under the banner "Constitutionalize the Amazigh Language, Support National Unity." The venue, the heavy media coverage, and huge attendance, including from members of the NTC, reflected the importance of this first-of-its-kind event. In seven months' time, the Libyan Amazigh community had gone from a peripheral, ignored minority to an assertive and relatively cohesive community demanding a share in the post-Qaddafi landscape. To further drive home the point, thousands of flag-waving Imazighen, including fighters in uniform, gathered in Tripoli's Martyr's Square to celebrate freedom and highlight demands for recognition. Wounded veterans of the war against Qaddafi were honored onstage, and the crowd sang the new/old Libyan national anthem in Tamazight.[60]

The post-Qaddafi scene was already becoming contentious. An NTC manifesto had declared that the future constitution could be approved by a two-thirds majority. Amazigh activists rejected that outright, fearing justifiably that they would not be able to mobilize sufficient votes to reject a constitution that did not fully acknowledge their demands, particularly on the language issue. One of the Amazigh Congress organizers, Fathi Salem Abu Zakhar, declared that "language rights are not a matter that is subject to a vote.... We want the government, and the coming government, to grasp that the language is part of the Libyan equation." Thus, the Congress declared its complete rejection of Article 1 of the NTC's "Constitutional Declaration" that had made Arabic the sole official language, characterizing it as "discriminatory and against the linguistic, cultural and social reality of Libya" and "in clear contradiction with the basis for the formation of democratic, civil, plural, modern and just states." Article 1 had also stated that shari`a would be the source of legislation—another red flag for the Amazigh movement, which advocated for a secular state in opposition to Sunni Salafism. Having played a crucial role in the war, and given that their "brave revolutionaries" continued to sacrifice themselves in the ongoing struggle to liberate the rest of the country, Imazighen, the declaration said, must now receive full recognition of their rights. The matter had become even more acute in recent days: the Congress condemned the NTC's announced formation of a provisional transitional government, as its composition was bereft of Amazigh representatives. "The era of the deprivation of Imazighen of their political, economic and social rights is over. The new Libya must be built on the principles of citizenship and just national partnership without any discrimination based on ethnicity, gender, language or religion." Nonetheless, the possibility that the issue would be divisive was worrisome to some, both within and outside the Amazigh community.[61]

On November 22, another post-Qaddafi interim government was unveiled, after a previous attempt failed because it had included people associated with the Qaddafi regime. This one too was controversial and, in retrospect, was only the beginning of the tortuous, unsuccessful efforts to establish a legitimate and functioning regime. While the defense ministry post was given to a Zintani, no posts were assigned to Amazigh representatives, sparking demonstrations in several Amazigh towns. In Tripoli, hundreds gathered outside of government headquarters, chanting "no difference between Amazigh and Arab" and "we are the indigenous people of Libya; give us our rights and we want them now." Following efforts to enter the office of Abdurrahim Abdulhafiz El-Keib, the provisional head of the government, he came out to meet with them wearing a hat with the colors of the Amazigh flag. However, his attempt to placate them failed, and he retreated to his office within minutes.[62]

In reaction, the Libyan Amazigh National Congress announced the next day that it was suspending all contacts with the NTC until a new provisional government was formed that awarded the Amazigh two "sovereign ministries"; that other ministerial portfolios be equitably distributed between the Amazigh and other Libyan regions; and that Article 1 of the constitutional declaration be repealed. It also announced the withdrawal of all Amazigh local council representatives from the NTC, a boycott of the Keib government, and a pledge to continue "peaceful demonstrations and rallies" until their demands were met.[63] The next day, however, the Zuwara representative, after having signed the document withdrawing from the NTC, signed another document pledging cooperation with it.

In a lengthy interview, the new CMA head, Benkhalifa, attacked the NTC, blaming its failed "Arab-Islamist" ideology for Libya's troubles.

> Those people in the NTC are exactly the same as in the previous regime. They're trying to project an image of being liberal and open-minded but the reality is that the majority of them still stick to the same authoritarian old methods.... They want an exclusive Constitution based on Islam.... We cannot accept Libya as an "Islamic and Arab" country.

When asked about NTC chairman Moustapha Abdeljalil's favorable mention of shari`a law, including the permission of polygamy, in an October 24 speech, he responded angrily:

> That was outrageous. Who gave Mustafa Abdul-Jalil the right to say such a thing? He was just the leader of an interim government who had not been democratically elected by the people. This is yet more proof that the current leaders in Libya are unable to adapt to the new times.

As for the language issue,

> some people in the NTC said that our language couldn't be officially recognized because we are a minority. Why didn't you tell us to stop when we were fighting? We didn't fight to achieve nothing at all so we are already starting to mobilize ourselves.[64]

In another interview, he attacked Abdeljalil for stating on a Libyan television channel that Libyan Imazighen were guided by foreign interests. "We thought we were done with the conspiracy theory of the old regime. Abdeljalil's words are dangerous."[65] While not explicitly calling for armed struggle, Benkhalifa did imply on several occasions that taking up arms to defend Amazigh rights was legitimate.[66]

Relations between Nafusa Imazighen and Arab neighbors were now fraught. Fighting broke out in March–April 2012 between Zuwara and the Arabophone towns of Riqdalin and al-Jamil. The latter two had been bases for Qaddafi's forces and joined the revolution only after the fall of Tripoli. Longstanding disputes merged with contemporary issues, primarily over control of lucrative smuggling routes to and from the Tunisian border. Scores on both sides were killed in fighting during March–April 2012. An International Crisis Group report stated that it would be wrong to state the fighting stemmed primarily from ethnic differences.[67] Nonetheless, such differences undoubtedly shaped feelings; the subsequent narrative of the Amazigh movement emphasizes them.

Nationwide elections for the General National Congress (GNC), to replace the NTC, were held in July 2012; a new government would be sworn in that November. The elections and subsequent political maneuvering took place against the background of continuing violence, as armed militias representing a variety of factions and ideologies jockeyed for position. The September 11, 2012, attack on the United States Embassy in Benghazi by the radical Islamist group Ansar al-Shari`a resulted in the death of Ambassador Christopher Stevens and three other American diplomats, highlighting how far the country was from establishing a stable postwar order.[68]

Two-thirds of the seats in the GNC were allocated to party lists, with one-third going to independents. In the run-up to the vote, many parties included Tamazight in their banners, written in Tifinagh script, and expressed support for Amazigh demands to make Tamazight an official language. It was a clear indication of how the Amazigh agenda had taken the national stage. However, as three Libyan Amazigh activists ruefully noted, "once the elections were over, most of those parties forgot about their promises and left many of the Imazighen voters and activists in limbo." Only one party—the small Libyan List for Freedom and Development—stayed true to its promise and advocated for the Amazigh agenda in the GNC, despite pressure against it by other parties.[69]

Not surprisingly, Amazigh activists were disappointed by this marginalization, with only one representative from Yefren, al-Hadi Hinshir, being appointed as minister of water resources. The bigger question was how to push their constitutional demands, as the GNC was scheduled to appoint a body charged with drafting the new constitution.

To that end, a high-profile forum to advance Imazighen constitutional rights was held in Tripoli on January 12, 2013, just one day before Yennayer, which activists across North Africa were demanding be made a national holiday. The gathering was attended by Amazigh GNC members and others from across the Libyan Amazigh spectrum, CMA president Benkhalifa, and Amazigh activists from neighboring countries. Also present were political party representatives, several diplomats from foreign embassies, a representative from the European Union, and the GNC's first president (and Libya's de facto head of state), Dr. Mohamed Magariaf. The well-respected Magariaf had been head of the main opposition group to Qaddafi, the National Front for the Salvation of Libya, and spent most of his previous thirty years in exile in the United States. Unique among the Libyan political elite, Magariaf had already publicly expressed his support for the constitutional recognition of additional languages in remarks at an Amazigh culture festival in the town of Jadu.[70] The extensive media coverage, and the attendance and expressions of support from non-Amazigh Libyan officials, suggested that the Amazigh agenda was gaining traction and that the process of advancing what Eva Pföestl and Will Kymlicka call "transformational minority politics" might not be a pipe dream.[71]

The forum's final statement, issued on behalf of all the Amazigh representatives, announced the establishment of the Supreme Council for the Amazigh of Libya (known commonly as the Amazigh Supreme Council, or ASC). It was the first such countrywide institutional body anywhere in the Amazigh milieu. The forum's recommendations regarding the constitution were clear-cut. It should reflect the "spirit" of the Libyan revolution and thus establish a "state of equality for all citizens"; Libyan identity should be rooted in its Amazigh heritage and be expressed in both symbols and substance by all state institutions; Tamazight should be an official language, backed by fundamental legislation to ensure its presence in public life; and the legislative, ceremonial, and other rights of Ibadi Islam should be relegalized.[72] To bolster the argument, the document included an annex detailing the multiple official languages in South Africa, India, and Switzerland. And the document made sure to quote two passages from the Qur'an that are often referred to by Muslim proponents of religious, cultural, and political pluralism to legitimize their demands: "And among [Allah's] Signs Is the creation of the heavens and the earth and the variations in your languages and colors" [Surah 30: Verse 22]; and "O mankind! We created You from a single (pair) Of a male and a female, And made you into Nations and tribes, that Ye may know each other. . . . Verily the most honoured of you in the sight of Allah is (he who is) the most Righteous among you" [Surah 49: Verse 13].[73]

Unfortunately for the Amazigh movement, Magariaf was soon forced to resign his position as president of the GNC. One month later, Nouri Abusahmen, an independent member of parliament of Amazigh origin from Zuwara, was elected to replace him. This marked the first elevation of a Libyan Amazigh to high office, ostensibly indicating that progress toward recognizing Amazigh identity in a democratizing country was being made. But Abusahmen was more inclined toward the ideology of the Muslim Brotherhood than the Amazigh agenda.

Shortly afterward, the Amazigh leadership's unhappiness with the direction of the constitutional discussions was reinforced by the GNC's approval of a law for the election of a sixty-person committee that would be tasked with drafting the constitution. The law reserved just four spots for Amazigh representatives from their home regions (two from Nafusa and two from among the Tuareg), with two more reserved for Tebu representatives. There was no commitment to the principle of consensus, which was essential for ensuring that the minority communities would not suffer what Edmund Burke, Alexis de Tocqueville, and John Stuart Mill warned against: the tyranny of the majority. For the Amazigh Supreme Council, this was nothing less than a slap in the face, a guarantee that its demand for equality in the new Libya would not be achieved. The committee originally charged by the GNC with drafting the law, they noted, had made explicit that its work should be based on consensus; the GNC's decision to abandon that requirement reflected a "racist and tribal spirit" that betrayed the principles of the Libyan revolution. A constitution that protected the basic rights of all citizens "can only be achieved by embracing the concepts of citizenship, safeguarding human rights principles, protecting freedoms, guaranteeing free expression and the rights of minorities, respecting ideological differences and political pluralism." They announced on July 10 that, if the proposed framework was allowed to stand, the election for the constituent body would be boycotted and that Amazigh representatives would be withdrawn from the GNC.[74]

Seeking to pacify them, the GNC issued on July 30 Law No. 18, which declared that "the language[s] of the Amazigh, the Tuareg and the Tebu are considered part of the linguistic and cultural components of the Libyan society"; and "all linguistic and cultural components have the right to learn their language as an optional subject in the educational curriculum in accordance with the law in the schools located in their indigenous areas and others." The education and culture ministries were charged with implementing the law and promoting festivals and research into the country's Amazigh, Tuareg, and Tebu heritages.⁷⁵ However, the gesture was deemed insufficient. In mid-August, angry demonstrators broke into the parliament building, smashing windows and destroying furniture, in protest against the authorities' continued neglect of Amazigh demands.⁷⁶ And in the following months, Amazigh armed units temporarily shut down oil and gas exports from the port of Mellitah, including the Greenstream gas pipeline to Italy.⁷⁷

Amazigh militancy penetrated the political sphere as well. On February 20, 2014, nationwide elections for the sixty-member Constitutional Assembly were held. As promised, the elections were boycotted in Nafusa and Zuwara and among some of the Tuareg. The two Amazigh seats were not filled. Protesters took to the streets in Zuwara, calling it "mourning day" and "the day of lies" (*n tkerkas*). The previous day, the Amazigh Supreme Council had announced that it was planning to hold elections for its own parliament, without specifying a date.⁷⁸

By this time, parliamentary politics and efforts to forge a new constitution carried an air of unreality. The main story in 2014 was twofold. The country was awash in armed militias, battling for turf and wealth, usually touting some form of Islamism; ironically, many were funded by government largesse and thus aligned with different politicians.⁷⁹ In addition, the jihadist Islamic State was establishing a foothold in the country. The Benghazi-versus-Tripoli fissure that had manifested in February 2011 now reemerged in a new guise. The Tripoli government, dominated by the Islamist-led Fajr Libya ("Libyan Dawn") brigades, was being challenged openly by the Benghazi-based Karameh ("Dignity") forces of the longtime exiled general Khalid Haftar, who created a House of Representatives to rival Tripoli's GNC. For the Nafusa Amazigh, this shattered their wartime alliance with the Zintan. The latter aligned with Haftar's forces, and the Amazigh units lined up with Tripoli. Anecdotal evidence suggested that, among the rank and file, Berber–Arab differences were becoming increasingly salient.⁸⁰

A political dialogue under UN and Moroccan auspices produced a fragile agreement on December 17, 2015, between the warring factions. One month later, Fayez El-Sarraj, head of the Tripoli government, proposed a thirty-two-person unity government, but the process quickly broke down. Noteworthy for our purposes is that Amazigh representatives were not invited to participate in the UN–Morocco talks and that the proposed unity government included no Amazigh, Tuareg, or Tebu representatives.⁸¹

Meanwhile, another institution-building step among the Amazigh took place in August 2015, as elections were held for the Amazigh Supreme Council. A three-week period to register voters and candidates began on August 9, corresponding to the UN-recognized International Day of Indigenous Peoples.

Elections in nearly all the constituencies were held on August 30, Amazigh Flag Day. The number of registered voters was approximately 9,000; of those, approximately 60 percent actually voted.[82] The numbers are modest, but they were not insignificant as a first step. By design, the new body had an equal number of men and women.

The ASC's initial focus was the constitutional question: notwithstanding spreading civil strife, efforts to draft a constitution for the new Libya continued and, with them, Amazigh efforts to improve its wording. A long-awaited draft was published on October 6, 2015. As expected, it provided a fair degree of recognition of the Amazigh and other ethnolinguistic components in Libyan society but fell far short of Amazigh demands. Indeed, a week earlier, the ASC had rebuffed efforts by some Amazigh individuals to mediate between the Council and the state authorities, and it rejected an invitation to discuss the forthcoming draft. Its action stemmed from knowing that Tamazight would not be equalized with Arabic,[83] and it feared that participation would legitimize the existing unequal status. Indeed, Article 30 of the draft did not raise Tamazight to a level equal with Arabic. Instead, it stated: "The languages spoken by a part of the Libyan people shall be considered national languages and a part of their cultural and linguistic heritage; they shall also be a common property to all Libyans. The Arabic language shall be the official language." Further acknowledgment of the non-Arab components of Libyan society was contained in Article 134:

> Every person is entitled to the right to use and learn national languages and to participate in cultural life individually or collectively; the State shall protect them and provide necessary outlets to learn and use them in media outlets. It shall also ensure the protection of national cultures, heritage, customs, literature, and arts, as well as the development thereof and the distribution of cultural services.

Meanwhile, the situation on the ground became increasingly charged. Minority groups, reported the International Commission of Jurists, were again being subjected to xenophobic rhetoric, attacks, internal displacement, arbitrary arrest, and detention. Minorities were being refused the renewal of identification documents, driver's licenses, and passports under the transitional government. Given the history of state-sanctioned discrimination against minorities in Libya, the commission stated they would need much stronger protection than that being proffered in the draft constitution.[84]

Entering 2017, the efforts by outside parties to cobble together an agreement between the warring factions had not produced results, either constitutionally or on the ground. On February 22, 2017—the third anniversary of the election of the Constitution Drafting Assembly that the Amazigh movement had boycotted—the ASC took matters into its own hands, declaring that henceforth Tamazight would be an official language in Amazigh areas and employed throughout the public sphere. In explaining the decision, a Council member took pains to clarify that the decision did not indicate a desire to establish autonomous rule; rather it reflected a determination to protect the Amazigh language and culture, in line with international treaties and conventions that protected the natural rights of indigenous peoples. In addition, the member said, the council would continue to push for Tamazight's constitutional recognition countrywide.[85]

This degree of Amazigh assertiveness was unwelcome in many Libyan quarters, and the level of invective increased accordingly. A fatwa issued by an official under Haftar's jurisdiction condemned Ibadi Muslims as infidels; Haftar himself declared that most Libyans were ethnically Arabs, and he openly referred to his forces as the Libyan "Arab" Army. The ASC declared that these statements were "racist" and tantamount to an encouragement of genocide. "A real national army," it declared, "is an army that includes all the ethnic groups of Libyan society, and refrains from being affiliated with a particular ethnic group."[86] Haftar's declaration, it said, was also a violation of the UN's Declaration on the Rights of Indigenous Peoples.[87] In late December 2017, Rabea Jayasha, an Amazigh human rights activist visiting a friend in Benghazi, was abducted on suspicion of espionage when he was overheard speaking Tamazight on his telephone.[88] He was released a month later, but the incident indicated the contempt that Benghazi authorities expressed toward the Amazigh *idée*.

The "final" draft of the constitution was suddenly confirmed on July 29, 2017, by all but one of the forty-four active members of the Constitution Drafting Assembly (CDA). The Amazigh Supreme Council and Tebu CDA members, who had boycotted the meetings intermittently, jointly rejected the draft and called for a boycott of the planned referendum. Tuareg activists also demonstrated against the draft constitution, stating that Tuareg CDA members, one of whom had voted in favor of the draft, did not represent them.[89]

The confirmation of the draft text came just days after an agreement between Haftar and Sarraj, mediated by French president Emmanuel Macron, to end the conflict and hold a presidential election in March 2018. The agreement quickly fell apart, the election was never held, and the conflict continued unabated. Nonetheless, the text serves as an important indicator regarding the degree to which the political factions were willing to accommodate ethnolinguistic minorities. While maintaining Arabic as the sole official language of the state, it suggests that the Amazigh, Tuareg, and Tebu criticisms of earlier drafts and ideas had not fallen on deaf ears and that the authors desired to placate critics and project a favorable image to the outside world. The word "Arab" was removed from the official name of the country, which would now be the "Libyan Republic" (Article 2). Libya's identity, it declared, was to be based on "inclusive and diverse principles," for Libyans were proud of their "social, cultural and linguistic elements." Libya would be "part of the Arab and Islamic worlds, Africa, and the Mediterranean basin." Similar formulas were used in the Moroccan (2011) and Algerian (2016) constitutions. Libya's languages—Arabic, Amazigh, Tuareg, and Tebu—were declared to be part of a cultural and linguistic heritage and a "common asset" to all Libyans. Moreover, the state was committed to taking all necessary measures for their preservation and development, in teaching and in public life. In addition, parliament was obligated to act to integrate the languages into local and national affairs (Article 2). The rights of all Libyans to learn and use their own languages, and to participate in cultural life with state support, were specifically guaranteed in an additional clause (Article 55); minimum representation was guaranteed in parliament for "cultural-linguistic components" (Article 68).[90]

In the eyes of the Amazigh Supreme Council, the glass was more half-empty than half-full. Not only did Arabic remain the sole official language (Article 2); Islam was the official state religion, and shari`a was to be the sole source of legislation (Article 6). Article 196 of the constitution stated that "the principles on which these two articles were based, as well as those related to guarantees of rights and liberties, political pluralism, the peaceful transfer of power and the country's territorial integrity, could not be compromised." For Fathi Benkhalifa, this meant that Tamazight could never be equalized with Arabic, which had taken on "an aura of sacred inviolability."[91] Still, in the historical context, it marked a major formal acknowledgment by some of the representatives of the country's fractured elites of the rights held by Libya's formerly marginalized and disenfranchised communities. Whether the constitution would actually be adopted, let alone implemented, remained to be seen.

Carving Out Space Between a Rock and a Hard Place

The conflict between Haftar's forces and the Tripoli government reached a new peak in 2019–2020. French and UN mediation efforts went nowhere. Haftar consolidated his control over Benghazi, establishing a strong authoritarian regime that increasingly resembled Qaddafi's. Indeed, several former

Qaddafi loyalists were now placed in positions of influence. So were various Islamist groups—no small irony, as Haftar had earlier billed himself to the international community as an opponent of radical Islam. By the first months of 2020, Haftar's forces, some of whom were mercenaries from Egypt, Chad, Mali, and Niger, and were backed by Russia, Egypt, and the UAE, seemed to be on the verge of conquering Tripoli and unifying the country by force. However, Tripoli's Dawn forces, supported by Turkey and Qatar, inflicted stinging defeats on Haftar in April–May 2020, and a political-military stalemate was reinstated.

For the Nafusa Amazigh, the Tripoli government was the lesser evil. In January 2018, the GNA's commander of the western zone launched a surprise, albeit unsuccessful, attack on the Ras Ajdir border post and the adjacent town of Abu Kammash, which was under the control of Zuwara military units. Tripoli authorities denied authorizing the attack and tried to placate the Zuwaris, but the intent was clear.[92] The decision not to fund a project to train 350 teachers of Tamazight, and the controversy over its place in the school curriculum, were viewed by the ASC as "racist."[93] Nonetheless, the ASC was able to operate openly, in Tripoli and elsewhere, and efforts to advance the Amazigh project continued, due partly to the government's limited ability to dictate the terms of engagement. In January 2019, the mayor of Zuwara decreed the adoption of the Amazigh calendar in all municipal departments. Earlier he had made Tamazight mandatory in all signage and advertising, and the ASC had declared Yennayer an official holiday in Amazigh areas.

There was also space for formal political action. That same year, Fathi Benkhalifa, who had completed his term as head of the World Amazigh Congress, founded a new political party, Libo. Headquartered in Zuwara, with additional offices in Tripoli, the Tuareg-populated town of Ubari in Fezzan, and elsewhere, its aim was national in scope. Its goals dovetailed with those articulated by the Libyan Amazigh current: a redefined nation-state, democracy, multiculturalism, and rejection of the hegemony of Arab nationalism and Islam. They included

> the establishment of a liberal democratic civil regime with a purely liberal Libyan authority stemming from the depth and dimensions of the Libyan cultural identity, without separation, exclusion or differentiation. [The party] provides a Libyan political identity to the world, which is based on the living reality, not the imported slogans, ideas and doctrines. . . . In addition to the provisions of the Libyan Constitution, which are conditional on national consensus and participation, our party also references the universal system of human rights adopted in international covenants, as common human values

that are binding on those who ratify them. [Our goal is to] build a state of truth, law and democracy while respecting the beliefs and beliefs of all Libyan citizens and citizens without exception.[94]

The crystallization of Libyan Amazigh agency, from the moment of the February rebellion and continuing throughout the decade, was seen not only in the military and political-constitutional spheres but also in civil society. A detailed study of the numerous organizations that sprouted up in the Nafusa towns and Zuwara during 2011–2012 emphasized the "vital role in mobilizing local society by providing stability" during the country's initial transition period. In essence, these were created "from nothing." Naturally, many were devoted to the promotion of language, culture, and heritage. The new atmosphere of freedom witnessed the establishment of at least ten local independent media groups that provided young Amazigh activists opportunities to pursue numerous projects in news, information, film, and culture. Other associations focused on women's and children's issues, human rights, general human development, and charity.[95]

To be sure, their effectiveness was often limited by a lack of experience and organizational skills. Thus, the authors of the study—themselves activists who had been imprisoned by Qaddafi—emphasized the need for administrative reorganization and maintenance, as well as increased collaboration among associations, local authorities, and supportive international organizations. The latter were essential for providing skills to civil society activists and funding of sustained projects, "particularly in the field of women's empowerment and indigenous rights."[96]

One such group was the Tamazight Women's Movement (TWM). Founded by a small group of committed activists in 2016, it aimed to "research, report and advocate on the intersectional gender issues amongst indigenous groups, particularly Tamazight women in Libya." Its cofounders emphasized a commitment to bringing the stories of indigenous women—not only Amazigh but also Tuareg and Tebu—to the national discourse. As an example of their thinking regarding intersectionality, they point to the relationship between the language issue and gender-based violence, with non–Arabic speaking women unable to receive help, owing to the cultural stigma of being raped and the basic language issue.[97] "Hundreds of indigenous women are targets of sexual and gender-based violence simply because they belong to communities such as the Tebu, the Tuareg and my own people," TWM's Inas Miloud stated to a UN Security Council panel on sexual violence.[98]

TWM's work was anchored in UN Security Council Resolution 1325, which addressed the issues of women, peace, and security, particularly the special needs of women and girls in conflict zones and postconflict reconstruction. As elsewhere, women in Libya have been severely impacted by violence.[99] Support from a Canadian government fund in 2016 enabled the TWM to undertake capacity-building training to female municipal government members and civil society actors; funding from the Dutch foreign ministry enabled the TWM to partner with two Dutch organizations and an additional Libyan one in 2017–2019 to strengthen the resilience of civil society organizations working with women and youth regarding issues of peace and security.[100]

The obstacles, of course, were formidable. One of TWM's founders, Fatma al-Omrani, had expected "much more" from the 2011 uprising, believing that women would play a bigger role in post-Qaddafi Libya, with full rights. "Unfortunately," she told a journalist, "it's not the case as religion is always used against us in courts and all aspects of life."[101] The escalation of fighting during 2019–2020, the authorities' suspicion of civil society actors, and deeply ingrained cultural norms that militated against discussions of violence against women were exacerbated in 2020 by the COVID-19 crisis. TWM cofounder Asma Khalifa noted that women were paying a heavy price from the fighting. For example, on April 7, 2020, shelling by Haftar's forces damaged the maternity ward of Tripoli's Al Khadra Hospital, and another hospital was destroyed entirely. With women making up the majority of the hospital staff, the war damage and the already existing shortage of supplies made them especially vulnerable to COVID-19 infections.[102] As for the Tripoli government—committed to submitting a report to the United Nations on how it was advancing policies to promote long-term sustainable development—there was a deep disconnect between the picture it was presenting and realities on the ground. Risking repercussions from the government, TWM set up a coalition of civil society organizations across Libya in order to produce a report to inform their government of their on-the-ground insights. "As our national institutions and government are weak themselves, we are forced to take on this risk," said TWM's Zorgh Madi. "We need to ensure that the peacebuilding and statebuilding process of Libya, and the road towards the achievement of the [UN's] 2030 Agenda [for Sustainable Development], continues. It is the only way forward."[103]

A different sort of civil society organization was TIRA Research & Studies (TIRA: Tasuggurt d Tizrawin). TIRA (lit., "writing") focused primarily on the language issue—the development and dissemination of Tamazight in schools and local governments—as well as a variety of projects centering on women, youth, conflict resolution, and cultural preservation.[104] It received modest funding from international NGOs and foreign governments, as well as from Libyan bodies.

The National Democratic Institute, funded by the US Agency for International Development (USAID), supported grassroots efforts to promote citizen engagement, particularly among women, young people, and ethnic minorities. Among the steps taken were training Amazigh and Tuareg groups in getting out the vote in municipal elections,[105] lobbying government officials to support education in native languages, and convening a meeting of twenty-five Amazigh, Tuareg, and Tebu representatives "to identify common advocacy issues and areas of mutual support between the communities." The result was the printing and distribution of 6,000 Tebu-language (Tudaga) textbooks and workbooks across the Tebu region for school-age children in 2019. Amazigh educators shared their recently acquired expertise on the subject, another small indication of the common interests and ideology among Amazigh and Tebu communities as they sought to refashion the nature of the Libyan state.[106]

On the whole, these were modest beginnings. Libyan civil society had been completely gutted during Qaddafi's long rule, contributing to a mind-set that the government should "do everything," as opposed to citizens empowering themselves. The extreme dependence of local authorities on the central government for funding reinforced this passive mind-set, impinging on the capacity to undertake local initiatives.[107] Hovering over everything was the continuing civil war and uncertainty for the future.

The threat posed by Haftar to the Amazigh movement was driven home in 2019. On March 31, one of the spokesmen in the Libyan Salafist *madhkhali* current,[108] which supported Haftar, declared that the "liberation" of western Libya should begin with Nafusa. Hostile to the prevalent Ibadi doctrine there, he compared it to Da'esh (ISIS).[109] Within days, Haftar's forces launched a major offensive to force a military solution that would make him ruler of the whole country. Zuwara forces participated in efforts to repel them. In August 2019, the Supreme Fatwa Committee in Benghazi labeled Ibadi Islam as an "aberrant and misguided sect" and "infidels without dignities."[110] In December, Haftar's forces bombed a civilian airstrip in Kabaw, in the Nalut District, 70 kilometers west of Jadu.

However, as noted above, the tide turned in April–May 2020. What was intended by Haftar to be a climactic offensive resulted in a stinging defeat. Just as Nafusa fighters had contributed to the success of the 2011 rebellion, so too did they in 2020. The Amazigh Supreme Council welcomed the outcome, "bowed to the memory of our Amazigh martyrs ... as well as all the heroic martyrs from all the cities and regions of Libya," wished a speedy recovery to the wounded, and called for Libyans to unify their ranks and establish "a civil state based on democracy, a state of justice and law." Only thus could equality between all Libyans be guaranteed.[111]

The Amazigh contribution to the victory did not go unnoticed by the authorities in Tripoli. In mid-April, as the tide of the battle turned, the minister of the interior issued a tweet written in Tifinagh characters ridiculing a Haftar-backed video that allegedly showed Turkish mercenaries fighting for the Tripoli government when in fact the soldiers were speaking Tamazight (i.e., they were "true Libyans"). His tweet brought a sharp rejoinder from Benkhalifa, who emphasized to his followers that the GNA was no friend of the Amazigh and that the minister had praised Haftar in the past.[112] However, a shift was now afoot. On May 28, the Tripoli House of Representatives head office published a declaration saying that the Amazigh language—*as an official language of the country along with Arabic*—would be added to all official documents issued by the House. With the country still divided into two parts, and without a constitution and zero plans for its implementation, the statement raised more questions than it answered; it could be revoked just as easily as it was issued.[113] But the statement indicated how far the Libyan Amazigh current had advanced during the decade, established a baseline for future efforts in the legal-constitutional sphere, and brought Libyan Amazigh a step closer to the legal status of counterparts in Morocco and Algeria. For what it was worth, US ambassador Richard Norland held a virtual meeting on June 12, 2020, with ASC representatives, expressed support for its activities, including those in partnership with USAID, and emphasized that UN-led efforts to encourage a political dialogue in Libya could succeed if there was "meaningful participation of Libya's indigenous and ethnic groups, including Amazigh, Tebu, and Tuareg Libyans."[114]

Conclusion

For Libyan Amazigh, the 2011 rebellion that toppled Qaddafi's regime had far-reaching consequences. In taking up arms in support of the rebellion, Nafusa Imazighen became, almost overnight, a meaningful part of the larger fabric of the country's contested space. Their military contribution to the opposition's ultimate victory could not be denied and provided them a new degree of legitimacy for advancing demands in the post-Qaddafi era. Indeed, most young urban Libyans barely even knew of their existence prior to the war.[115]

War has always been a formative experience in the life of nations; the death of hundreds of Amazigh fighters in the 2011 war, and the continuing, though intermittent, violence since then, resharpened self-awareness among Nafusa Imazighen as an ethnocultural collective. The sudden withdrawal of Qaddafi's "fierce state"[116] provided them with an unprecedented opportunity, which they seized, to renew and practice their language in the public sphere. The post-Qaddafi generation of schoolchildren in Amazigh areas has developed literacy in Tamazight (written in Tifinagh characters) to a degree that was previously unimaginable. In higher education, a Department of Amazigh Studies was opened for the first time in Libya, in the Faculty of Arts at Zawiya University, in 2015.[117] Tamazight language expression in broadcast, print, and social media flourished, cultural icons emerged, and preservation and development of historical sites and new historical narratives proceeded apace.

The messages contained in Tamazight-language instructional materials closely followed the Amazigh movement's promotion of a multicultural and tolerant society. This was strikingly apparent in a textbook for sixth-graders: a lesson on tolerance emphasized the need to respect the religions of all peoples, and reported that some Amazigh used to be Jewish. It was accompanied by pictures of an imam, a priest, and a rabbi![118] The last remnant of Libya's historic Jewish community, some of which was Judeo-Berber in origin, had departed the country under duress following Qaddafi's seizure of power, and native Christianity had disappeared in the centuries after the Islamic conquest. Including Christians and Jews within the definition of the Libyan nation constituted nothing less than a conceptual revolution.

Politically, Libyan Amazigh quickly organized to weigh in on the efforts establishing a governing system for the new Libya and to develop agency in their own areas. The efforts to institutionalize their activities reached a peak in 2015 with the elections for the Amazigh Supreme Council. No such parallel body existed in either Morocco or Algeria. Amazigh input into the extremely contentious process of drafting a (still-unratified) constitution resulted in formal acknowledgment of the Amazigh component of Libya's national identity and the legitimacy of its language. Similarly, the earlier acknowledgments in Morocco and Algeria were unsatisfactory to Amazigh currents, which continued to demand recognition of Tamazight as an official state language. This goal was ultimately achieved in both Morocco (2011) and Algeria (2016). Libyan Amazigh activists responded the same way. Moreover, the issue merged with larger questions over the nature of the gestating Libyan state and how it would be governed. Was Libya to be a democratic country of all its citizens? With safeguards for linguistic and cultural rights and religious freedom? Or were its Arab and Islamic elements to be privileged? For most Amazigh activists, the 2017 draft constitution emphasized the latter, notwithstanding some conciliatory language. Moreover, the proposed system privileged a numerical majority over consensus, a vital component to safeguarding their rights. Thus, they declared that any ratification vote would be boycotted.

Khalid al-Haftar's consolidation of power in the eastern half of Libya, and his fourteen-month offensive in 2019–2020, brought Libya no closer to resolving the stalemate and fashioning a consensus-based post-Qaddafi state. Indeed, Libya had become an arena for foreign intervention, which only complicated its prospects. Most of the international and regional actors operating there were hostile to the ideas of linguistic and cultural pluralism, the bedrocks of the Amazigh platform.[119] For the Amazigh movement, the stalemate, however problematic, was the best possible outcome for the time being. Throughout years of uncertainty, the Amazigh discourse had been resharpened and a degree of agency achieved, at least in its own regions. As they sought international legitimacy and protection, statements from the Amazigh Supreme Council made increasing reference to the UN-endorsed rights of indigenous peoples.[120] Terms such as "autonomy" and "self-determination" were now being used by Amazigh activists, even if their meanings remained vague. One notion put forth by an ASC member was a decentralized Libyan state in which the Amazigh would have an autonomous region of their own.[121] Given the proximity of Amazigh and Arab populations in the Nafusa and Zuwara regions, such a scenario was likely to prove controversial, to say the least.

The 2011 rebellion and subsequent fractured status of the country had provided Libyan Amazigh with sudden and unprecedented opportunities, notwithstanding their limited capacity to influence events on the broader national canvas. But when Haftar's yearlong offensive reached a decisive phase, Amazigh armed units joined in the fight and, as in 2011 against Qaddafi, contributed to the victory against him. They were rewarded with the Tripoli parliament's statement that Tamazight was an official language and would be added to all official documents. Preserving, and even expanding, on their gains was now the top priority. With that in mind, the Amazigh Supreme Council expressed anger over international diplomatic efforts to mediate a solution between the GNA and Haftar because they failed to include it.[122] Still, barring a grand deal between the GNA and Haftar that would result in a strong and hostile centralized state, the prospects for strengthening Amazigh agency—including a degree of de facto autonomy in the Nafusa and Zuwara regions, as well as some input into the larger Libyan fabric—seemed reasonably achievable.

CHAPTER 3

Azawad: The Abortive Republic

On April 6, 2012, the Tuareg-led Mouvement National de Libération de l'Azawad (MNLA) proclaimed the establishment of a new breakaway state, which it called "Azawad,"[1] carved out of Mali's northeastern, mostly desert region encompassing no less than 900,000 square kilometers—65 percent of Mali's total territory.

According to the MNLA, Azawad's population was approximately three million, half of whom were in exile. Sixty percent were either Tuareg or labeled "Moor."[2] The move came after a swift string of victories over the disintegrating Malian army, leaving the region's main cities—Kidal, Timbuktu, and Gao—under MNLA control. The proclamation of the new republic was the culmination of a chain of events triggered by the rebellion in Libya that broke out in February 2011. In the larger context, it was the latest iteration of Tuareg resistance to French colonial rule and then to the central governments of Mali and Niger that had been imposed on them at the moment of French decolonization.

For Amazigh partisans in North Africa and the diaspora, Azawad's proclamation of independence seemed to be nothing less than a great leap forward. The hard-won constitutional recognition of Tamazight as an official language of Morocco in 2011, the deepening of Kabyle militancy in Algeria, and the sudden combative self-assertion of Libya's Amazigh community were important interim steps that ideally would lead to some form of self-determination. In a single act, this seemed to have been achieved in Azawad by the Tuareg—the most socially, economically, and historically differentiated from all other Amazigh communities and, ironically, the least affected by the modern Amazigh identity movement. For a moment, this background did not seem to matter: the declaration of independence's emphasis on the new state's commitment to democracy, ethnic pluralism, and secularism seemed to fit hand-in-glove with

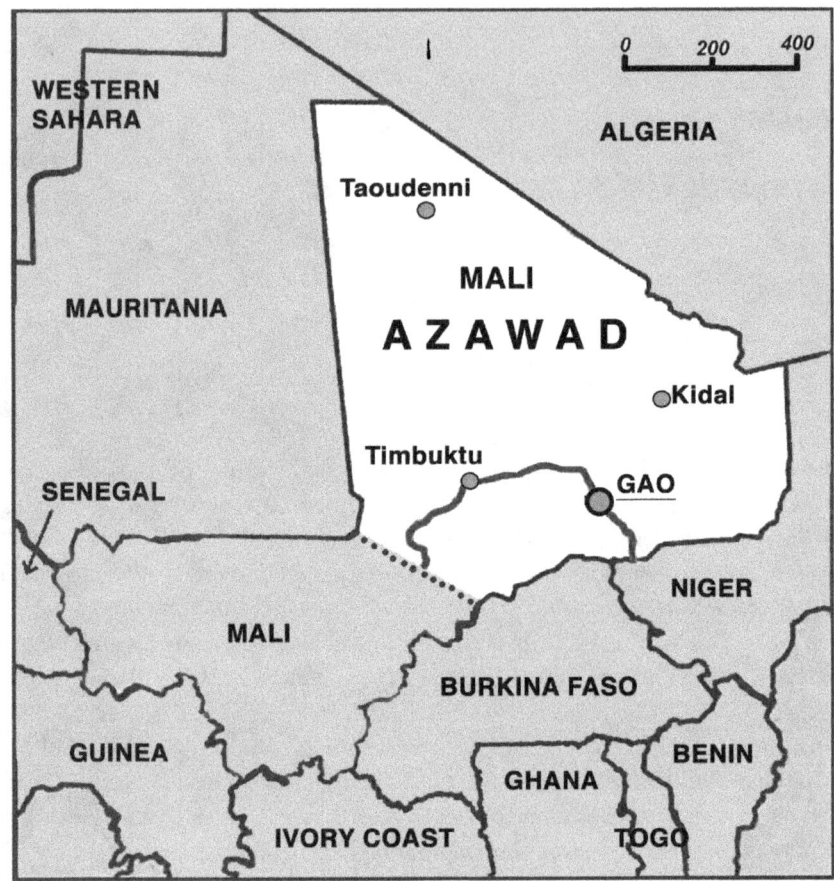

Map 3.1 Azawad, https://commons.wikimedia.org/w/index.php?search=Azawad &title=Special:Search&ns0=1&ns6=1&ns12=1&ns14=1&ns100=1&ns106=1#/media/File :Azawad_map-english.jpg

the overall Amazigh agenda. The Movement for Kabyle Self-Determination (on the MAK, see chapter 1), the World Amazigh Congress (on the CMA, see chapters 2 and 4), and Tamazgha-France all expressed enthusiastic support for the new state and provided logistical assistance in Paris for the MNLA's media efforts.[3] The CMA would subsequently name a representative of Azawad as one of the organization's vice presidents.[4]

However, the optimism was short-lived. Azawad lacked the capacity to establish a functioning regime on the ground. Unlike South Sudan and Eritrea—two African states that had successfully challenged heretofore sacrosanct colonial-imposed borders—Azawad's establishment was recognized by no other state and was rejected forcefully by the Economic Community of West African States, the African Union, and the United Nations. Worst of all, the MNLA's ethno-secular elements were thrust aside by a mix of local and international jihadi Islamist groups, which in turn caused a French-led military intervention aimed at beating back the jihadists and stabilizing the region. In 2015, the MNLA formally abandoned its demand for independence as part of an Algeria-brokered agreement with Malian authorities that promised to address their grievances in a reformed Malian state. Five years on, however, the same underlying conditions that had led to the creation of the Azawad "parastate"[5] were still very much present. Going forward, the successful reconstitution of Mali along lines desired by civilian democrats and Western backers will depend on the degree to which Tuareg grievances, both material and symbolic, can be addressed. In that regard, the Mali–Tuareg story is now a variation on the theme of Amazigh–state relations throughout North Africa.

Azawad's abortive moment of independence sheds light not only on the Tuareg predicament but also on the position the Tuareg hold in the collective Amazigh universe. As such, it is an integral part of the Amazigh story.

Background and Context

The traditionally pastoral-nomad Tuareg have been romanticized in Western travel literature as the "blue men of the Sahara" (owing to men's blue veils and the resulting bluish tint on their faces from the dye). Their lands are spread across the vast reaches of the Sahara-Sahel region—"the Central Saharan mountain ranges—the Ajjer, Hoggar, Aïr, and Adagh n Ifoghas—as well as the adjacent Sahel-Saharan plains on the southern edge of the desert and the interior bend of the Niger River."[6] There are various theories about the meaning of "Tuareg." The most widely accepted is that it stems from "inhabitant of *Targa*" (lit., "drainage channel"), the Tuareg name for the Fezzan region of Libya.[7] Their more common self-designation is Kel Tamasheq/Tamajaq, or "those who speak Tamasheq/Tamajaq," the generic names for Tuareg dialects (there are eight main ones), which in turn belong to the Tamazight language family. Another common self-designation is Kel Tagelmust, or "veiled people." Estimates of their numbers vary: The largest single concentration is in Niger (2.6 million, according to the CIA's *World Factbook*, where they constitute 11 percent of the population);[8] estimates of their numbers in Mali range from 500,000–800,000,[9] with approximately 400,000 in Burkina Faso, 100,000 in Algeria, 20,000 who are native to Libya, and smaller numbers in

Tunisia and Mauritania (as well as in Europe and North America). Their social organization has always been tribal, with a high degree of stratification. These numbers now generally include former slaves who were assimilated into the Tuareg milieu. In addition to pastoral nomadism, Tuareg tribes traditionally controlled the long-distance trans-Saharan caravan routes. In modern times, they have played important, although not exclusive, roles in cross-border contraband operations involving cigarettes, drugs, arms, and people.[10]

France's conquest of the Tuareg lands and their incorporation into French West Africa at the end of the nineteenth century inaugurated a century of profound change that shaped every aspect of Tuareg society—social, economic, political, and conceptual. As Hélène Claudot-Hawad notes, Tuareg resistance to French conquerors and their subsequent numerous rebellions—first against their colonial overlords and then against the postcolonial states that had been established according to the French-designed territorialization of the region—shared many features. At the same time, the contexts were different, owing to the ever-evolving dynamics between Tuareg communities and the new administrative authorities, in addition to accompanying social and economic transformations. Thus, the "semantic register" of the Tuareg struggles changed over the course of a century: the idea of liberating "Tuareg country" (*akal n Imajaghen*) from foreign rule eventually was transformed, at least for some, into a focus on liberating "Azawad,"[11] indicating the acceptance, and even embrace, of the Westphalian system that ran completely counter to the precolonial Tuareg experience.

To be sure, they were not alone in their resistance, often establishing multiethnic coalitions and mobilizing preexisting alliances. Neither was resistance the unanimous and unambiguous choice among Saharan communities. Depending on the circumstances, and the particular calculations of their interests, cohabitation, submission, and even collaboration were preferred at times.[12] This has continued to be the case to the present day.

Even as French colonial authorities idealized and romanticized the Tuaregs' alleged "essence,"[13] their insistence on including the Tuareg in administrative frameworks imposed from the outside guaranteed Tuareg "otherness," minority status, and alienation. This was shared to varying degrees by other populations in the Azawad region (Arab and Fulani nomadic pastoralists; Songhay, Arma, and Fulani agriculturalists; and Bozo and Sorko fishermen).[14] Some scholars point to a never-realized project put forth by French colonial officials in the early 1950s—the Organisation Commune des Régions Sahariennes—as a stimulus for rethinking the meaning of sovereignty among the Tuareg and other peoples in the northeast region of French Soudan, soon to be the independent state of Mali. Until that point, sovereignty had been conceived by the region's people in personal and communal, not territorial, terms. Now, as decolonization approached, a prominent Arab leader from Timbuktu gathered signatures from Tuareg chieftains, joined by notables, merchants, and community leaders among the Tuareg and other nomadic and sedentary minority communities, to petition French president Charles De Gaulle, at the very moment of his return to power on May 30, 1958, to include them in the "French Sahara" (which by definition included the Saharan portion of Algérie Francaise and its own Tuareg tribes). One excerpt laid out the first claim to self-determination, however vaguely defined, by the people of Azawad:

> If there exists a right to self-determination for a people, we would like to believe that we are allowed to make our aspirations known.... We manifest our formal opposition to being integrated in an autonomous or federalist Black Africa or North Africa.... We demand the incorporation of our country ["notre pays et sa Boucle du Niger"] in the French Sahara of which we are part, historically, emotionally and ethnically.[15]

The letter was referred to explicitly in the MNLA's "Political Platform" in September 2012 in order to highlight the continuity between past and current struggles.

By 1960, it was clear that France was leaving. Tuareg chieftains in Niger made clear their demands for self-determination, beseeching French officials on behalf of the Kel Aïr and all the other Tuaregs to restore the freedom that had been taken from them by French forces.

> Since you are leaving the Tuareg country ["le pays Tuareg"], return our country to us as you snatched it from us.... We want to lead ourselves and bring our whole society together, wherever it is.... We want our country to be one country.[16]

Baldero and Raineri periodize Mali's state-building efforts and the Azawad-Tuareg responses to them between 1960–2012 according to three distinct stages: (1) independence and modernization (1960–1968), during which time Tuareg opponents to the centralizing policies of President Modibo Keita's government engaged in their first revolt (between 1962–1964); (2) authoritarian upgrading under a military regime (1968–1992) during periods of severe drought, resulting in social, economic, and demographic upheavals throughout Tuareg lands; and (3) the shift toward being a neoliberal state (1992–2012), which generated large-scale revolts during the first half of the 1990s, unresolved agreements, and smaller revolts that set the stage for secession in 2012.

The pattern in Niger was broadly similar up through the first decade of the 2000s, but so far Niger has not witnessed any comparable challenge to its legitimacy and territorial integrity.

The first rebellion, in the early 1960s, was limited to the one area dominated by the Kel Adagh. Moreover, in addition to the opposition generated by the government's efforts to centralize, sedentarize, and implement Mandefication (the adoption of Mande languages for teaching in schools), the rebellion was also motivated by revenge, as it was led by the son of a rebel leader who had been executed by the French a decade earlier.[17] The resulting suppression of the revolt was harsh, and thousands fled the country. But the social order in Azawad was not fundamentally altered by the government's policies. At the same time, it reinforced the tendency in Malian society to view the Tuareg with suspicion.

The real change came as a result of the severe droughts throughout the Sahel in 1972–1974 and 1984–1985. The devastation was far-reaching. Hundreds of thousands of people died. The preexisting rural society, in which pastoralists and agriculturalists coexisted through a complex set of negotiated alliances allowing access to land and water, could not be sustained. Many pastoralists lost access to the Niger River for watering their herds as agriculturalists were forced to extend the areas of their cultivation. In some locations, Tuareg established farming villages of their own; many more were compelled to migrate to urban centers within Mali or to seek refuge in other countries in West Africa, Libya, and Algeria or even Europe.[18] For most, livelihoods became based on wage labor, and new consumer goods were introduced. The resulting geographic and economic changes "brought about shifts in gender relations; cultural forms of expression; education; and politics."[19]

Baz Lecocq elaborates on the new way of life among the uprooted Tuareg, embodied by the term "*teshumura*," which according to the iconic Tuareg poet Mahmudan Hawad is a Tamasheq derivative of the French *chômage* ("unemployment"). Over time, *teshumura* became a cultural marker, as the experiences of the *ishumar* generation gave new meaning to their existence and raised them to positions of leadership in the community, challenging the old notables and religious leaders. Ines Kohl stresses the *ishumar* generation's agency, its "creative strategies for dealing with and participating in the outside world ... and ... impressive capability to adapt and cope with transformation processes." *Ishumar*, she says, "stands for 'borderliners,' characterized by transnational movements in the borderlands between Libya, Algeria, Mali, and Niger and by ruptured, modified, and newly invented traditions, norms, and values."[20]

The *ishumar* played a central role in the Tanekra, the large-scale rebellion of the 1990s. Although there were multiple factors and vectors leading to the rebellion, much of its leadership came from Kel Adegh members born during the late 1950s and early 1960s, the traumatized "orphans" of the rebellion a generation earlier.[21] The *ishumar* were complemented in their efforts, somewhat uneasily, by those who had managed to attain a modern education and employment with the government and international NGOs. As Tuareg identity began to acquire more modern ethnonational features, Tuareg *evolués*,[22] some of whom were located in Europe, contributed their own organizing and media skills to the cause.

Preparations for the rebellion had begun in the late 1980s, and a low-intensity conflict between a group called the Popular Movement for the Liberation of Azawad (MPLA) and the Malian government of Moussa Traroé broke out in 1990. An Algeria-mediated cease-fire agreement in 1991, and a follow-up National Pact in 1992, conferred an undefined "special status" on the northern region, but it was never implemented. Traroé was overthrown in a coup, and the next few years were marked by escalating violence on several fronts: between the regime and rebel groups; between the Tuareg and other communities; and among rival Tuareg groups. It was only in 1996 that a fragile peace was negotiated among all of the factions and communities, which lasted for a decade.[23]

Mali's democratization and decentralization policies seemed to provide an opening for a new deal with Azawad. A 1996 law recognized Tamasheq as a national language, along with twelve other indigenous languages. More important still was the plan to integrate former rebel combatants into the state's security forces. Implementation was controlled largely by faction heads and other leaders who used the integration project as a resource to attain greater mobility and influence to the detriment (and dissatisfaction) of their rivals.[24] The influx of foreign assistance begat widespread corruption and greater dissatisfaction with the regime. Matters were further complicated when the region became a center for smuggling of drugs and arms and a haven for radical Islamist armed groups, notably al-Qaeda of the Islamic Maghreb (AQIM).

Beginning in 2005, the Malian and Niger governments again found themselves in confrontation with armed opposition groups. Its reactivation was generated by those groups who had not benefited from the policies of the previous decade (or who faced discrimination even if they had). Libya and Algeria engaged in mediation efforts as each sought to advance their own interests. Yet another Algeria-brokered agreement in 2006 echoed earlier agreements to provide greater autonomy to the Kidal region; economic development; the integration of former opposition fighters into the national army and the creation of "Special Units for security" in which insurgent officers would take pride of place; and a larger presence of the Tamasheq language and culture in the national media and within education.[25]

For the Algerian state, these interests were twofold: (1) defeating AQIM, the latest iteration of a radical Islamist terrorist organization that had fought against it during the 1990s; and (2) maintaining the sanctity of its international borders, thereby walling off its own Tuareg population from the unrest to the south. Of course, the latter was no easy task, as Tuareg refugees and migrants had been crossing into Algeria since the first drought back in the 1970s. The regime was also concerned about possible deleterious influences from the opposite direction. In the wake of the large-scale unrest in Kabylie in 2001, Algerian president Abdelaziz Bouteflika visited the towns of Tamanrasset, Djanet, and Illizi in what was traditionally the Tuareg-populated region of Algeria's deep south to show his commitment to the area's well-being. But he was greeted by street demonstrators whose essential message was: "If he [the North] didn't want the South to be part of Algeria, he was just to let them know!" In other words, their eyes were not on Kabylie but on their brethren south of the border.[26]

Throughout his four decades of rule, Libya's Muammar Qaddafi had sought to play an outsized role in African affairs, particularly in the Sahara–Sahel region. Extending patronage to rebel groups was part of his modus operandi as a self-styled revolutionary; in that regard, dissatisfied and uprooted Tuaregs, reeling from the catastrophic droughts of the 1970s and 1980s, found a haven in Libya. Thousands answered Qaddafi's invitation in 1980 to receive military training and were incorporated into Libyan security forces; some even managed to attain papers enabling them to legally live and work in the country. They brought their training to bear during the Tanekra in the 1990s and would do so again with far greater impact in 2011–2012.[27]

Tinariwen

Aficionados of the amorphous "world music" genre were thrilled by the decision to have the iconic Tuareg band Tinariwen ("Deserts"; plural of the Tamashek word *ténéré*) perform at the opening ceremonies of the 2010 World Cup finals tournament in South Africa. Two years later, it received a Grammy Award for Best World Music Album and was nominated for another in 2021. It would be fair to say that the vast majority of those who have attended a Tinariwen concert, or listened to any of their eight albums, are barely aware of the context in which the band's music was crafted or the backgrounds of its star members.

The band's first manager, Andy Morgan, stated that the band's origin story is "a complex drama of exile, wandering and the *clandestino* life, in which fact, memory and nostalgia are entwined like spaghetti in a bowl." For example, a key founding member, Ibrahim Ag Alhabib, witnessed as a small boy his father's execution in 1963 for providing succor to antigovernment rebels. Following his father's death and the accompanying destruction of the family herd, his grandmother took him to Algeria, together with a single cow that died on the journey. From a young age, he became a quintessential wanderer, where "survival was by any means necessary, or not at all." Along the way, he taught himself how to play guitar, using whatever improvised parts he could cobble together. Together with two other founding members of the band, *ishumar* all, along with two female singers, they began playing together in the southern Algerian oasis town of Tamanrasett in 1979. During the 1980s they migrated to Libya and took up Qaddafi's offer to receive military training while continuing to develop their music. The charismatic Tuareg leader Iyad Ag Ghali recognized the value of their music and provided equipment and rehearsal space, and they began gaining a reputation, as their electrified music circulated on poor-quality cassettes through the so-called ghetto-blaster grapevine. Older members of the band took part in the rebellion that broke out in Niger in 1990, as well as in Mali the following year.[28]

The link between Tinariwen's music and its politics is organic. The lyrics of their songs are a repository of their generation's experience, in turn expressing anger, determination, despair about their plight and internal divisions, and nostalgia. One song, written by a band member in 1983, included the following verse:

> The fire has been burning for far too long
> In our lost slumbers
> For the burnt animals and the aged dead
> At the gates of Kidal we must assemble
> And fight
> As strong as you might be
> You will burn in your fire

A sometime-member of the group, the poet known as Japonais, referred to the difficulties of his Libyan experience:

> Dear Mother, since the time I left for Libya with patient steps
> I arrived but I have been feeling aimless
> I search for the money I need by any means necessary
> But it refuses to accumulate

Another song, written by Ibrahim Ag Alhabib, defiantly reflects his own traumatic childhood experience:

'63 has gone, but will return
Those days have left their traces
They murdered the old folk and a child just born
They swooped down to the pastures and wiped out the cattle ...
'63 has gone, but will return.[29]

Many of his songs center on *assouf* ("loss"), which Morgan says is

the most important word in Tuareg poetry. Assouf is the pain that is not physical, the pain in the heart. It's nostalgia. It's loss. It's grief. It's the coldness of a camp that used to be inhabited but there's no one there anymore.

Assouf is the central theme of the music of other important Tuareg bands as well.[30] As the anthropologist Susan Rasmussen shows, the term also possesses older meanings:

In ritual healing and cosmology, this denotes approximately "the wild" or "solitude"; it is at once a mental state, a place where the soul of a possessed person travels, and also a literal remote space, far from the nomadic tent and camp.... Paradoxically, it is a place to which some are tempted to travel, but also an abyss of suffering.

Its redeployment in various contexts provides evidence of the depth of Tuareg cultural practices and notions and their revitalization and adaptation to new circumstances.[31]

Once the rebellion ended in 1996, the band, which Morgan characterizes as "an extended musical family," kicked into a higher gear. Tinariwen's international career took off at the beginning of the 2000s. But their message of protest, defiance, and commitment never wavered. As another of the band's members told a journalist in 2012:

We are military artists! Today, if we see that our brothers need fighters rather than musicians, we will go to the front, because we are always ready to answer the call of the preservation of our land, our values, and our culture. This is what we do through music, and we will do it again with arms![32]

The Amazigh Movement and the Tuareg

The veneration of Tinariwen is part of a larger picture. Music, poetry, and art have been integral elements in the fashioning of a modern ethnocultural Amazigh identity. In recent years, social media and other internet platforms have become essential tools for their dissemination, blurring the boundaries between "virtual" and "actual" communities. Thanks to this technology, Tinariwen has achieved iconic status throughout the Amazigh milieu. One indication is provided by dozens of articles on the band found at Tamazgha.fr, the primary Paris-based website for Amazigh activities. The lead article in the section "Tinariwen: un combat pour l'existence" confirms the band's mission and the band's self-definition as "military artists."[33] Fans' veneration points to the evolution of the Amazigh-Tuareg relationship.

Within the Amazigh milieu, the Tuareg have always stood apart from the rest—geographically, historically, and in their ways of life. The emergence of the modern Amazigh identity movement in Algeria's Kabylia and portions of Morocco during the 1960s and 1970s was remote from extant Tuareg realities. Still, from the movement's perspective, the Tuareg were very much worthy of attention and inclusion. After all, their language was unquestionably part of the Amazigh language family. The perception of them as "pure" and "uncorrupted" Imazighen who had maintained endogamous practices over the *longue durée*, and their preservation of the ancient Tifinagh script—a crucial modern marker of Amazigh uniqueness and indigeneity—gave them special cachet.[34] So did the widespread belief that the status of Tuareg women within their society was superior to that of Arab women, owing to the practice of matrilineal descent and women's considerable power in domestic affairs. Mouloud Mammeri, the Kabyle intellectual luminary who stood at the center of the emerging movement during the 1960s and 1970s, included the Tuareg within the purview of his research, as did the Paris-based Académie Berbère.[35]

As shown by Cynthia Becker, Amazigh artists have taken up Tuareg motifs with gusto. Nomadic life is depicted as idyllic and pristine; designs inspired by the Tifinagh script are ever-present; pre-Islamic symbols, including those related to ancient Egypt and Phoenicia, are sometimes used as well, which serve to emphasize Amazigh indigeneity; and women are valorized as both the guardians of their culture and symbols of women's essential agency. For example, statues of Tuareg women created by the France-based Kabyle sculptor Dalila Aoudia resemble classical statues of Greek and Roman women. The effect is twofold and contradictory. On the one hand, it reinforces the colonial myth of Imazighen as being biologically related to Europeans; on the other, "for an Algerian immigrant in France, the Tuareg represent both ethnic and gender empowerment" in the face of an alien and alienating society.[36] These themes are ubiquitous on Instagram and Facebook pages devoted to Tuareg and Amazigh subjects.[37]

Pan-Amazigh Institutions and the Tuareg

Initial steps to institutionalize pan-Amazigh action in 1994–1995 included the Tuareg, giving further tangible expression to the "imagining" of Tamazgha. A 1994 film festival in Douarnenez, Brittany, was devoted to the *"peuples Amazighs."* Among the twenty-five Amazigh associations who organized the festival was a Lyon-based Tuareg body named Temoust ("Identity"). Its very existence indicated that an emerging Tuareg diaspora experience was shaping Tuareg collective identity in new ways. The festival's conclusion included a declaration of support for the Tuareg against Malian and Nigerian government repression, whose "massacres" and "genocide" were being carried out, the declaration said, with help of the French military and French economic aid that should be halted. It also called for the United Nations to stop ignoring the matter. Pan-Amazigh, diaspora-based organizations have engaged in lobbying governments and international bodies on behalf of the Tuareg ever since.

A follow-up conference a year later, which would be a prelude to the 1997 official establishment of the World Amazigh Congress, readdressed the Tuareg plights in Mali and Niger. Representatives of two Tuareg associations based in France, and one in Mauritania, attended, as did the poet Hawad. Emphasizing the right granted by international law to the Tuareg and every other people to decide their own fate, and "considering that the fight of the Tuareg people is an integral part of the Amazigh people's fight for its dignity and its inalienable right to live in freedom and equality in a land undeniably theirs," the Congress "affirm[ed] its engagement to make the Tuareg people's fight its own, until its rights are effectively recognized." It appealed to the United Nations, the Organization of African Unity, and the European Union to do everything in their power to stop the "massive massacres," and it called "for the creation of an international tribunal to try the persons responsible for this genocide."[38]

The instantiation of the Tuareg within Amazigh movement institutions was finalized in 1997 with the official establishment of the World Amazigh Congress at its meeting in Las Palmas, Canary Islands. Tuaregs were included in the Congress's governing bodies, and the Congress issued a resolution calling for Tuareg self-determination.[39] Similar resolutions were issued at subsequent conferences. On the very eve of the 2011 uprisings, the Congress's Federal Council, meeting in Marrakech, issued strong statements condemning the treatment of Tuareg in Libya, Niger, and Mali. In Libya, the Federal Council contended, thousands of Tuareg who had migrated there suffered from rank discrimination and marginalization and were being manipulated to renounce their own identity in favor of an Arab one. In Mali and Niger, "Tuareg people are surviving between the anvil of drought and the hammers of states and multinational corporations which occupy their territories and ruthlessly exploit their natural resources."[40]

The Rise and Fall of the Republic of Azawad

In November 2010, a meeting in Timbuktu of mostly Tuaregs resulted in the founding of the Mouvement National de l'Azawad (MNA). It did not call for an armed rebellion, but its establishment indicated a rising militancy and frustration with the central government's failure to address the region's grievances. Malian president Amadou Toumani Touré launched several initiatives during the first half of 2011 to ameliorate the situation, but his efforts were overtaken by events.

The rebellion in Libya was the immediate trigger for the upheaval that would follow. However, the planning for it had been several years in the making, spearheaded by Ibrahim Ag Bahanga, "Mali's public enemy number one and the recalcitrant hero of hawkish Tuareg everywhere."[41] Bahanga had rejected the 2006 agreement, engaged in armed operations as part of a short-lived alliance with Tuareg rebels in Niger, and ended up in Libya under Qaddafi's patronage. There he linked up with Tuareg veterans of the 1990s rebellion who had assumed senior positions within elite Libyan army units, particularly that of Colonel Mohammed Ag Najm. As Qaddafi's regime began to crumble in early 2011, he put his plan into action, persuading Ag Najm and other Tuareg officers to desert and return to Mali with their weapons and followers. By midsummer, they were on their way, along with considerable amounts of weaponry, including ground-to-air and ground-to-ground missiles. Bahanga would soon die in a car crash—whether by accident or design is not clear.[42] But the basis for the rebellion had been set. Intense discussions on the best course of action resulted in the establishment of the MNLA, whose main objective was "to free the people of Azawad from illegal occupation of Azawadian territory by Mali." A conscious decision was made to frame the MNLA's demand in nonsectarian, territorial terms, a vision that was subsequently spelled out in its "Political Platform" (see below). To emphasize the point, an ethnic Songhai was named as MNLA's vice president.[43] However, the MNLA leadership was overwhelmingly Tuareg in composition and perceived as representing Tuareg interests.

There was a general consensus among the armed elements and the younger generation of media-savvy, educated Tuareg who had formed the basis of the MNA: the time was ripe for action. Thus, efforts by the Malian government and the region's representatives in the Malian parliament to delegitimize the

MNLA leadership and forestall the outbreak of rebellion were rebuffed.[44] Nonetheless, the veneer of Tuareg unity was thin. Tribal, clan, caste, generational, and ideological divisions were endemic and shaped the unfolding of the 2012 rebellion. The charismatic Iyad Ag Ghali, of the *ishumar* generation, who had led the rebellion during the 1990s and again in 2005, made repeated efforts to assume the leadership position again, but he was rebuffed for a variety of reasons. Ghali belonged to the "wrong" clan among the Ifogha Tuareg (the warrior/nobility caste) and had long sought to become its first nonhereditary leader. To that end, he had been bolstering his religious credentials by linking up with the proselytizing Tablighi Jama'at stream of Salafi Islam.[45] These ties may have been one reason for his failed bid for leadership. He then proceeded to form his own organization, the radical Islamist Ansar al-Din. In turn, Ansar al-Din forged links with AQIM, which had infiltrated Mali over the previous decade, thanks in no small measure to the tolerance of the Malian authorities,[46] and an offshoot, the Movement for Unity and Jihad in West Africa. Although Ansar al-Din received military and financial assistance from AQIM, Ghali made sure to assign the top political positions to longtime allies from the Tuareg nobility and even to some of his erstwhile rivals.[47]

The early months of 2012 were decisive and nearly shattered the Malian state. The rebellion was launched on January 17, 2012, with an attack on Malian government forces in the town of Menaka. At first, MNLA and Ansar al-Din units worked in coordination, gaining the upper hand against government forces and progressively taking control of the region's major towns, even up to Tessalit, near the Algerian border. Looting, war crimes, interethnic tensions and violence, and civilian flight became features of the expanding conflict. On March 22, Touré was removed from power by army officers who blamed him for the government's failure to quell the rebellion. And on April 6, MNLA Secretary-General Billal Ag Achérif, a relative of the late Ag Bahanga, issued the declaration of independence for Azawad. The declaration touched all the relevant bases in claiming legitimacy for Azawad: international law; the principles of the UN Charter and the UN's Declaration on the Rights of Indigenous Peoples; the request for independence in 1958 to France and France's failure to consult with the population of Azawad before attaching them to Mali; and the ensuing fifty years of "humiliations, spoilation, massacres and genocide." Boundaries with neighboring states would be respected, and the declaration called on the international community to recognize the new state and thereby contribute to the peace and stability of the region.[48]

On paper, the new state appeared to have an institutional shell. The declaration was issued after consulting the movement's "Executive Committee, Revolutionary Council, Consultative Council, State-Major of the Army of

Liberation, and regional bureaus." Two months later, a ceremony installing the members of the Transitional Council of the Azawad State, headed by Ag Achérif, took place in Gao. And in September, the MNLA issued its detailed "Political Platform" that expounded on the historical justification for Azawad's establishment and its vision for the future.

Although the leadership was 80 percent Tuareg, the official platform declared that Azawad would be a multiethnic democratic state within defined boundaries. Its four ethnic groups—Tuaregs, Moors, Songhays, and Fulas—"have historically lived in harmony," and their "shared cultural, historical, economic and social links ... cemented the sense of their belonging to the Azawad territory. Their shared attachment to the land and water had reinforced their will to live together well before the arrival of the first colonists." The fundamental problem, the platform stated, was that Azawad had been illegitimately included within the Malian state, which had immediately proceeded to sow division among its components and subjected the Tuareg and Moors, in particular, to "humiliation, harassment, massacres and genocides." After a half-century of this, with repeated rebellions and broken promises, the only choice was to pursue a divorce—a right anchored in international law. The MNLA, "a political and military organization without tribal, ethnic, cultural or religious affiliation," was committed to building "a democratic and modern society and guarantee[ing] the fundamental and individual freedoms for the common good of our people." Multiparty democracy, a free media, and the dynamism of civil society would underpin the country's health. All the communities of the Azawad people would be guaranteed cultural, social, and economic freedom to develop in conformity with the principle of human rights, particularly the Declaration of the Rights of Indigenous Peoples:

> Respect and promotion of cultural and language specificities of the various components of society ... [are] absolutely essential in order to rehabilitate every historical element of the Azawad body, which has been disintegrated by decades of feelings of contempt for our culture and of political uniformity imposed by the Bamako-based political elite.

In addition, Azawad would institute "the separation of religion and state in order to guarantee religious freedom," an important point given the opposition to traditional religious practices by increasingly intrusive Salafi-jihadi currents. Along those same lines, the platform declared that

> meticulous attention will be paid to the issue of equality between men and women. One of the main characteristics of the specificities of our society, of

which we are proud, is the place, role and status which our society has given to women. Our project of society does not only aim to safeguard this tradition and practice but also to fight against all alien and retrograde political and religious elements which stand in the face of progress and the march toward modernity.

To that end,

schooling of girls and boys and providing opportunities for both men and women to have access to highly rewarding jobs on the basis of meritocracy and not on the basis of their sex or ethnic origins, will be guaranteed.

The platform was short on details regarding the projected state institutions but emphasized the "great resonance" in Azawadi collective memory of "our traditional social and political systems." Decentralized economic development, according to the specific needs of the local population and the fragile ecosystem in which they lived, was an absolute must. Such policies would combine respect for the traditional pastoral economy with emphasis on clean energy and proper exploitation of natural resources.[49]

For supporters of a modern, liberal multicultural society, the platform's vision was inspiring. But it was divorced from the existing circumstances. The proclamation of Gao as Azawad's capital had alienated the Songhay population, who viewed themselves as the heir to the Songhay Empire of the fifteenth and sixteenth centuries. Moreover, there were multiple instances of MNLA fighters targeting Songhay and Bella populations for rape, abduction, and theft.[50]

More important still was the fact that Ansar al-Din and its allied jihadist groups had in the meantime pushed aside the MNLA, taking control of the main towns in the region and instituting a strict regime of Salafi-jihadi rule. An agreement had been signed between the MNLA and Ansar al-Din on May 26 to coordinate their activities, but its implementation stalled. In an interview published on June 13, Ag Cherif still expressed confidence that the two groups would be able to work together in consolidating the new state and that Ansar al-Din would remove AQIM from the equation. When asked what the new constitution would be based on, he replied "on the Qur'an, as well as on other principles arising from international treaties that do not go against Islam."[51] Within days, however, the MNLA had been pushed aside. Its September platform reflected this new reality, referring to the "dark forces which are threatening the Azawad, the sub-Saharan region and the rest of the world," and the MNLA's support for the separation of religion and state.[52]

The international community's response was fairly swift. Following a UN Security Council resolution, a Franco-African military operation, launched in January 2013, rolled back the jihadis' control of the territory and restored it, at least ostensibly, to the Malian central government. The MNLA regained its footing and took control of the northern city of Kidal, defeating Malian government forces that had previously pushed out the jihadists. Along with two other groups, it formed the Coordination des Mouvements de l'Azawad (CMA). Other armed groups emerged as well, as dissidents from the MNLA, Ansar al-Din, and elsewhere sought to advance their respective interests. A series of agreements between 2013–2015 culminated in one between the Malian government, the CMA, and a rival coalition of mostly non-Tuareg pro-government armed groups (known collectively as the "Platform"). Sponsored by Algeria, the centerpiece was the MNLA's withdrawal of its demand for independence in return for a real change in the relationship between the central government and the long-neglected northern region.

The broad outlines of the agreement were essentially reiterations of the previous failed ones. This one would also flounder, and several years on, the situation in Mali was more precarious than ever. A cogent analysis published by the Washington-based Center for Strategic and International Studies laid out the shortcomings of the accord (its limited focus on Mali's northern region only, as well as the exclusion of important actors) and the absence of any true commitment by the signatories. Armed groups had proliferated, and corruption and the smuggling of drugs and weapons among all of Mali's actors were as rife as ever. Islamist and ethnic militias killed more civilians in 2019 than in any year since 2012, displacing tens of thousands of people and engendering widespread hunger.[53]

Still, it is worth noting the Algiers agreement's main themes. Azawad, stated the agreement, was "a socio-cultural reality, both commemorative and symbolic, shared by the different populations of Northern Mali." An institutional structure "based on territorial collectivities ... with extended powers" was to be established; along with "effective management of their own affairs" through regional bodies with financial and judicial powers, the populations in the north were to be represented in greater numbers in national institutions, including in the areas of defense and security.[54] This emphasis on decentralization, local management by territorial collectives, and power-sharing was an approach that had become increasingly attractive in Amazigh circles, from the Moroccan Rif, to Kabylia and the Mzab, to the Libyan Amazigh community. As such, it provided further evidence underscoring the central theme of this study: the rising salience of the political, territorial, and socioeconomic dimensions of the Amazigh movement and of Amazigh-state relations.

Conclusion

Only time will tell whether a Tuareg-dominated territorial entity will reemerge and prove to have more staying power than the Azawad parastate of 2012. In looking back at the chain of events, it is clear that the circumstances may have been propitious to launch a rebellion, but the ability to sustain it and establish a functioning independent state was beyond the MNLA's capacity. A host of factors militated against them: the absence of a real consensus among Azawad's ethnic groups for whom the MNLA claimed to speak; the determination of the Salafi-jihadi groups to impose their own program; the complete rejection of Azawad's independence by the international community; and, perhaps most important, the deep-rooted internal divisions and rivalries within Tuareg society. Interestingly, the Azawad episode did not have a parallel set of developments in Niger, where the relationship between the formerly rebellious Tuareg and the central government has become less charged and more cooperative.[55]

Notwithstanding the deep-rooted tribal and ethnocultural underpinnings of Tuareg society, one must also acknowledge the newer aspects of Tuareg collective identity that have emerged against the backdrop of profound upheavals: a degree of wider collective consciousness; new cultural markers; the growing impact of the Tuareg diaspora; the employment of social media as a mobilizing tool; a desire for self-determination within a defined territory; and a degree of solidarity with Tuareg beyond the borders drawn up by French colonial rulers. Of course, the degree to which these ostensibly modern aspects are salient varies widely depending on the circumstances.[56]

The Tuareg have a special place in the Amazigh *imaginaire*. Thus, Amazigh militants in neighboring North African states and the diaspora strongly support Tuareg ethnonationalism, both as a matter of principle and because it confirms and reinforces their own activities. This position is not fully reciprocated by Tuareg militants or the rank and file, as their own life experiences and requirements are different from those of northern Amazigh communities. Nonetheless, the lobbying of pan-Amazigh associations on behalf of the Tuareg, the connections forged between Tuareg and other Imazighen in the diaspora, and the expansion of social media as a mobilization tool all point to the strengthening of Tuareg links with the broader Amazigh universe. Even as the context varies from place to place and events unfold in diverse ways, the Azawad episode belongs not only to Mali and the Tuareg but also to the increasingly politicized agenda of the Amazigh communities throughout North Africa and beyond.

CHAPTER 4

Tunisia: The Amazigh Factor Enters the Realm

Tunisia, where the spark for regionwide upheavals was lit (literally) by a despairing young man in December 2010, is the singular success story of the Arab Spring uprisings. It is the only country that transitioned from a strong authoritarian regime to a pluralist, democratic one, anchored in a new constitution.

Its success to this day can be ascribed to several underlying factors, all of which point to social cohesion and stateness, sharply contrasting with neighboring Libya. These include: (1) its long history as a distinct political entity within a defined territorial space, dating back to at least the seventeenth century; (2) center-periphery relations that tilted decisively to the center, not to the tribal periphery; (3) a substantial level of ethnic and religious homogeneity, although the whole issue of ethnicity and the existence of minorities in Tunisia is now under reexamination; (4) a degree of openness and tolerance stemming from its history of being a Mediterranean trading country; (5) a less traumatic experience with European colonialism compared to Algeria and Libya; (6) the emergence of a substantial, educated middle class, accompanied by the highest rate of female literacy and lowest rate of population growth in the Middle East–North Africa region, owing to systematic policies designed to raise the status of women; (7) a tradition of active civil society organizations, particularly labor and lawyer unions; and (8) a smaller, nonpoliticized military. Taken together, these factors contributed to a willingness among the country's political and social forces to fashion a functioning consensus on core issues, contain centrifugal tendencies, and avoid dangerous ruptures.

To be sure, Tunisia's democratic experiment remains fragile: the performance of successive coalition governments since 2011 has left much to be desired in addressing the country's underlying socioeconomic maladies, particularly in peripheral regions that helped fuel the original uprising; alienation and cynicism toward the political class are widespread; rival views regarding the role of Islam in society and related sociocultural orientations remain ever-present; and jihadist terrorism has not been entirely eradicated.

Tunisia's Amazigh community has generally been ignored by scholars and policy makers, owing to its extremely small size, commonly estimated at no more than 1–2 percent of the country's approximate twelve million people. Active speakers of the language are concentrated in several villages on the southeast periphery and the island of Djerba.

As has happened elsewhere in North Africa, Tunisian Imazighen have also migrated to major cities. In Tunis's *medina* (old city), for example, they have established pockets of communities engaged in daily commerce and crafts.

Amazigh groups strongly contest these estimates. They are also problematic for other reasons, raising the larger question Who is an Amazigh? (for a fuller discussion, see below). Regardless, the community's existence has long been barely acknowledged, and its long-term survival as an ethnolinguistic community is at risk. Tunisia's much-heralded 2014 constitution makes no reference to it, in contrast to the new constitutions of Morocco and Algeria and Libya's draft text.

Nonetheless, the Amazigh dimension is part of Tunisia's post–Revolution of Freedom and Dignity (*thawrat al-hurra wal-karameh*) story. The toppling of the long-serving autocratic president Zine El Abidine Ben Ali had an immediate salutary effect. Amazigh activists seized on the sudden and massive expansion of freedom in the public sphere to assert their collective existence, promote their culture and language, and demand official recognition from authorities. In doing so, they were following in the footsteps of compatriots in Libya, Morocco, and Algeria. International Amazigh organizations were quick to embrace them, expand advocacy on their behalf, and deepen connections with local activists. The World Amazigh Congress even held an extraordinary meeting in Djerba in October 2011—something that would have been unthinkable during the Ben Ali era—and appointed a Tunisian representative to its Federal Council for the first time. An additional session of the Congress was held in Tunis in 2018. For some of Tunisia's liberal intellectuals, reference to the country's previously ignored Amazigh heritage and culture now became an additional element in their toolbox, as they sought to promote a multicultural and liberal vision for the country. These discussions also extended to the need to acknowledge and valorize the country's historic Jewish community (numbering 120,000 at the moment of independence, approximately 1,000 nowadays), as well as its black African population (10-15 percent of the country's total population).[1] At the same time, Amazigh identity activism in Tunisia was viewed suspiciously, or worse, by many sectors of society and some of the state apparatus. Ten years into Tunisia's new era of pluralist democracy, state

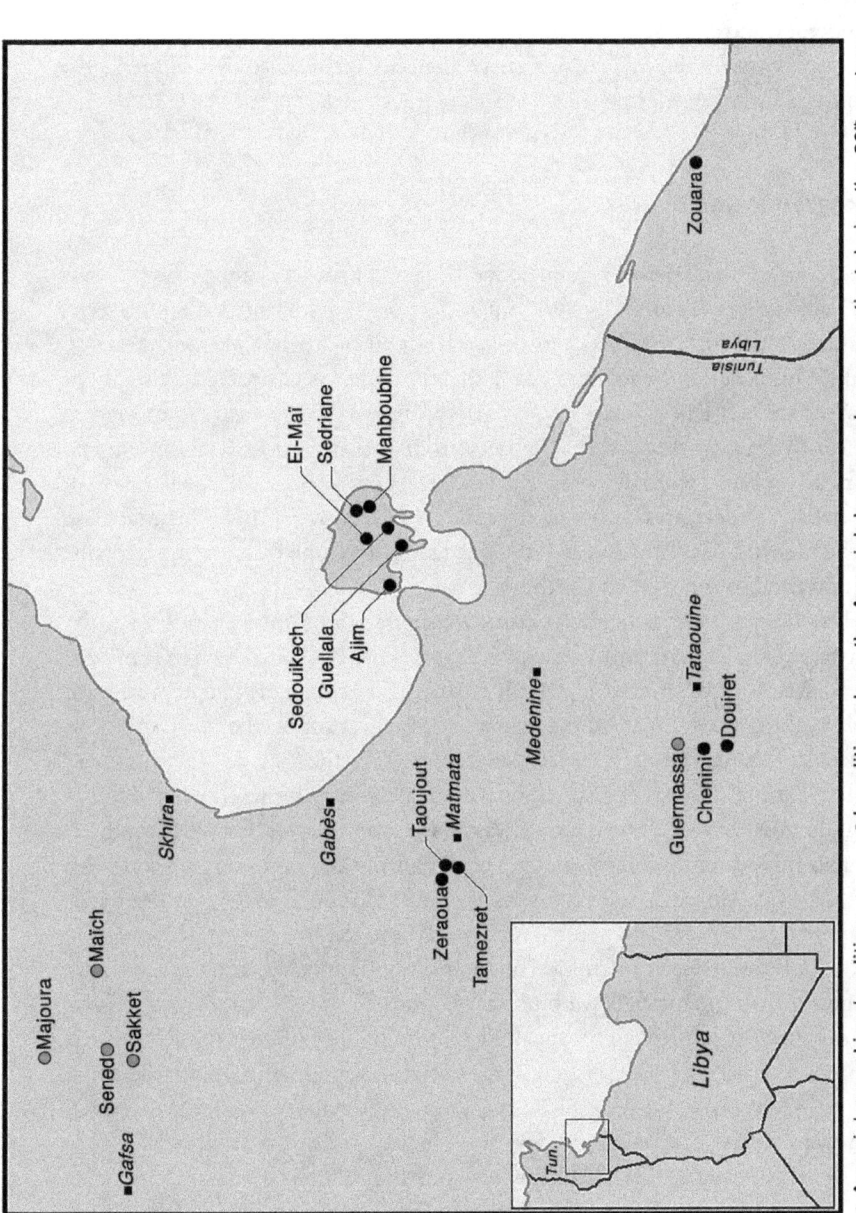

● Amazigh-speaking localities   ○ Localities where the Amazigh language became extinct during the 20th century

Map 4.1 Amazigh-speaking concentrations in Tunisia, https://upload.wikimedia.org/wikipedia/commons/550//Tunisia-Zuwara_Berber_Map.png

institutions are only barely becoming attentive to Amazigh demands. Yet, overall, the subject is now part of a larger debate over the parameters of Tunisian democracy and the meaning of Tunisian identity. The contested place of the Amazigh community in Tunisia's evolving polity is thus also part of the larger Amazigh story.

Background and Context

Tunisia's very small percentage of active Tamazight speakers belies the fact that the country was historically very much part of the Amazigh tribal universe. The name "Tunis" is believed to derive from an old Amazigh root meaning "halt," "bivouac," or "encampment"; ancient Tunes was probably already in existence when Phoenician traders arrived to establish nearby Carthage in the ninth century BC.[2] In that same vein, it is now generally accepted that "Africa"—a Latin word denoting the lands west of the Nile Valley and north of the Sahara Desert, and subsequently rendered as "Ifriqiya" in Arabic, referring to the Central Maghreb lands—derives from the name of an Amazigh tribe that dwelled to the west of Carthage.[3]

The story of the indigenous Amazigh populations' interactions with the Carthaginian, Roman, and Byzantine Empires has been analyzed in some detail by Michael Brett and Elizabeth Fentress.[4] Subsequent chapters in their pathbreaking book focus on the transformative impact on the Amazigh populations of the centuries-long Islamization and Arabization of North Africa.[5]

For Tunisia's Amazigh population, the process was ultimately destructive in ethnolinguistic terms. The country was an early destination for Arab conquerors and subsequent tribal migrations coming from the east: the garrison town of Qayrawan, 115 miles south of Tunis, was established in 670 AD as the headquarters for the expansion westward; it would eventually become an important center of Sunni Islamic learning. Topographically, Tunisia lacked the mountain ranges, and attendant well-watered valleys and remote oases, that were crucial for the survival of Tamazight-speaking communities in Algeria and Morocco. Moreover, it became a major hub in the global Islamic trading network. Thus, unlike in Morocco and Algeria, Islamization and Arabization occurred earlier and were far more extensive in Tunisia—linguistically, culturally, and demographically. A key aspect of this process was the progressive abandonment of the Ibadi-Kharijite creed of Islam between the fourteenth and eighteenth centuries by most of Tunisia's Amazigh tribes, owing to heavy pressure from zealous orthodox Sunni Maliki missionaries and marabouts. The abandonment of Ibadism, explain Brett and Fentress, prepared the way for the abandonment of the Berber language itself.⁶ Ernest Gellner confirmed this process, stating that folk legends in southern Tunisia connect the region's linguistic Arabization to "the religious reconversion or expulsion of Kharijite dissidents." Moreover, he stipulated, southern Tunisian Berbers make the link between Berber speech and the Ibadi creed and thus have a self-consciously "Berberist" grasp of the world. Conversely, the same link is viewed by non-Berbers with opprobrium: for example, those who venerate a southern Tunisian saint credit him with having displaced the local heretics (Ibadis) and Berbers.⁷

Belgacem Hamza's doctoral dissertation elaborates on the dynamics by which Sunni maraboutic tribes established their dominance and how their *zawouiyat* (Sufi lodges, often built around the tombs of marabouts) became Arabic-language religious and educational centers at the expense of Tunisian Berber, which retreated into exclusively private use and would eventually disappear in many instances. Nomadic Berber tribes, numbering approximately 250,000 persons, had been fully Arabized by the end of the eighteenth century. At the same time, according to Hamza's study, nearly all of the south continued to be known as "Wouerghemma," the name of the large tribal confederation that included eleven groups of Berber-speaking tribes, each with a unique dialect, as well as Arabized Berber tribes. Indeed, the term "Wouerghemmi" has continued to be used by Tunisian Arabic speakers to denote most inhabitants of the south and anyone who speaks Berber.⁸

France conquered the Ottoman Regency of Tunis in 1881 and established a protectorate regime that lasted seventy-five years. As was the case elsewhere in North Africa, France's primary investments were in *utile* areas. In that regard and others, French policies marked a broad continuity with the previous local/Ottoman order. The declining use of the Tamazight language continued apace as well. A French linguistic census taken in 1923 reportedly counted only 20,601 Tamazight speakers out of a population of two million.⁹ That being said, French policies toward the region are remembered by some in a positive light. According to Ahmed Gwirah, president of the Taoujout Association for the Preservation of Amazigh Villages: "The situation for us in Taoujout was better under the French. They built a lot for us, including two wells. They also built the roads connecting us [to the outside]." The real problems, he said, followed independence.¹⁰

Tunisia's first president, Habib Bourguiba, was an autocratic ruler who towered over public life for more than three decades before being deposed in a bloodless coup in 1987 by Ben Ali. Styling himself after Turkey's Kemal Attatürk, his nation-building and state-building projects emphasized the primacy of a uniform national identity that had emerged over time from the successive imprints of a mosaic of cultures; economic modernization and centralization;

improving the status of women; and a reduction of the role of Islam in public life. The latter was reflected, albeit opaquely, in the wording of Article 1 of the 1959 constitution: "Tunisia is a free, independent and sovereign state. Its religion is Islam, its language is Arabic and its type of government is the Republic." One analyst noted that this was more like a sociological statement than a declaration that Islam was the religion of the state.[11] The deliberate ambiguity legitimized Bourguiba's quasi-secularizing policies. For example, Tunisia is the only member of the League of Arab States to have officially banned polygamy; Bourguiba nationalized the *habous* institution (Islamic charitable endowments) and put the higher Islamic educational institute (Zaytouna College) under state control; and he famously drank a glass of orange juice in public during Ramadan to promote greater productivity during the religiously prescribed month of daytime fasting. Bourguiba was a fervent opponent of Egyptian president Gamal Abdel Nasser's brand of radical pan-Arabism yet maintained a pro-Western orientation in foreign policy. His good relations with Tunisia's Jewish community (numbering approximately 120,000 at the moment of independence) enabled it to emigrate almost entirely in an orderly fashion over the ensuing decades, reflecting a pragmatic view of the Arab-Israeli conflict. Although Arabic was the sole official language of the country, French remained the language of the economic and cultural elites and much of the political elite as well.

None of Bourguiba's autocratic liberalism carried over to the Amazigh community, however. The country's "ancestral diversity," wrote the anthropologist Stéphanie Pouessel, "was presented as something of the past, that is now over, and that is not politically threatening."[12] Bourguiba was hardly an Arab nationalist. Nevertheless, Tunisia's constitution clearly emphasized the Arabness of the country not only linguistically but also by defining it as part of the Greater Arab Maghreb (*al-maghrib al-`arabi al-kabir*), with which it aspired to unify, and as belonging to the "Arab family" (*al-'usra al-`arabiyya*). The Amazigh language, if acknowledged at all, was defined as an archaic local dialect of Arabic. As a component of Tunisian society, Amazighness was useful for its exotic folklore aspects that could be marketed to foreign tourists, and also as part of the country's pre-Islamic history that enabled Tunisia to promote itself as a country with a unique Mediterranean heritage. But in terms of Bourguiba's requirements for the country—national unity, integration, and modernization—there was no place for Amazigh-speaking elements, which needed to be absorbed into the larger body politic.[13] Consequently, their children would be educated in Arabic, like the rest of the country, and they were strongly encouraged to move out of their hilltop towns into new lowland settlements that made them more accessible, legible, and thus malleable to state authorities.¹⁴ The fact that many Amazigh in the south had supported Bourguiba's rival Salah Ben Youssef during the internal struggles leading up to independence, and had participated in armed attacks against French outposts, reinforced his instincts.¹⁵ Cumulatively, these policies accelerated the existing long-term processes of Arabization of Amazigh communities in the south, as well as emigration from them in search of a better livelihood. Of course, the socioeconomic distress in Tunisia's southern peripheral region was not unique to its Amazigh population.

Two important measures taken early in the Ben Ali years repeated the exclusion of Amazighité in determining the parameters of Tunisian national identity: The 1988 National Pact between the government and the country's main political forces emphasized the country's Arab and Islamic nature, including the "civilizational requirement" of Arabization; and in 1995, the code of child protection proclaimed the need "to raise the child with pride in his national identity . . . and the sense of civilization at the national, Maghreb, Arab and Islamic levels."[16]

Hamza's detailed 2006 study of the state of Tunisian Berber highlights the extent to which the language had become endangered. Among the eleven Berber groups in the historic Wouerghemma confederation, only four had maintained their language up through the nineteenth century. By the middle of the twentieth century, they had adopted Arabic as a daily language, and by the end of that century Berber had completely disappeared from some villages. The transmission of the language to the younger generation ceased during the 1980s, especially in urban areas such as Tunis. According to Hamza, Tunisian Berber "is hardly used except by [those] over [fifty], and then only in certain circumstances such as social gatherings and intimacy."[17] The fact that Arabic had higher social capital, and that Berbers had often been shamed by Arab speakers when they did speak Arabic, redoubled families' determination to give priority to Arabic for their children. A similar phenomenon was noted by Mohamed Errihani while researching the attitudes of Moroccan Amazigh parents toward their children learning Tamazight in schools.[18]

What Are the Numbers? Who Is an Amazigh?

Hamza's field work was carried out in 2000; his dissertation was submitted in 2006. His conclusion was not quite unequivocal: the Tunisian Berber dialect is endangered and may be dying, he said, but predictions of other scholars of its imminent death were exaggerated. To be sure, he noted, the language itself was not only falling into disuse; even when it was being employed, it had become increasingly Arabized. And where there once had been a continuum of Tunisian Berber speakers covering most of the south of the country, there were now only "four localised dialects separated from each other like islands in a sea of Arabic." Hamza put the total number of Berber speakers at 60,000.[19] Similar, concurrent estimates of the number of Berber speakers put it at less than 0.5 percent of the population.[20] In 2012, UNESCO classified Tunisian Tamazight as a "severely endangered language" and gave credence to local estimates of 40,000–50,000 speakers.[21] Others cite even lower figures.

However, this is not the whole story. Hamza provides anecdotal evidence that Tamazight is still spoken in certain social situations, even if the speakers are no longer fluent in it, and that the loss of language has not erased many people's continued self-identification as being ethnically distinct from their Arab neighbors. This also appears to be the case among much of the population that originated in the south and now live in Tunis and other major cities, going back generations. Thus, determining the actual number of Amazigh in Tunisia depends on how one defines it: language, culture, place of origin, history, and self-identification. The World Amazigh Congress states that 10 percent of the Tunisian population is Amazigh (approximately one million), obviously using a more expansive ethnocultural definition of "Amazigh" than common estimates, which focus on active Tamazight speakers.[22] Hamza argues that Tunisian Imazighen should be seen as a "speech community," defined as "speakers who share the same culture, history, values and the communicative know-how with the rules of speaking, without the necessary use of the same language."[23] Numerically, he states, 90 percent of those who originate in southern Tunisia (25 percent of the country's total population) are of Berber origin, as are 80 percent(!) of the country's total population, based on his survey of family names and patterns of migration northward.[24]

Such a huge gap may seem like a historical curiosity without relevance to contemporary affairs. However, the whole subject of Amazigh existence—whether defined narrowly (an endangered ethnolinguistic community) or broadly (constituting the historical, cultural, and sociolinguistic underpinnings of Tunisian society)—began creeping into the Tunisian public sphere starting in the mid-1990s. Left-wing activist historians at Manouba University took the lead in this regard, employing a discourse emphasizing "minority heritages," which included Tunisia's black and Jewish populations.[25] Prior to the 2011 revolution, Tunisian Imazighen were themselves extremely reticent about speaking Tamazight in public settings, let alone discussing the issue. But with the emergency of the Amazigh identity movement in Morocco, Algeria, and the diaspora, their precarious state entered into the pan-Amazigh discourse and, through them, reached the attention of international forums, which periodically challenged Tunisian authorities on the subject. In 2003, the UN Committee on the Elimination of Racial Discrimination (CERD) pressed Tunisian representatives to provide concrete information regarding the situation of its Amazigh population. One committee expert suggested that it recognize them as an indigenous minority, and another asked what was being done to protect and promote Amazigh language and culture. Tunisian officials pushed back, denying there was any problem and even rejecting use of the term "Amazigh," as "there were only Berbers, whose traditions had prevailed over many years, as the first inhabitants of the territory."[26]

CERD revisited the subject in 2009. Tunisia's official submission to the committee and replies to questions were detailed but did not differ in substance from previous denials. "Tunisian-ness," Tunisia's permanent representative to the UN in Geneva told the committee, did not mean assimilation or a denial of the diversity of Tunisian society. "Tunisians were Berber, Phoenicians, Jews, Vandals, Byzantines, Arabs, and so forth.... Homogeneity did not mean a monolithic structure, nor the negation of differences.... That the Berbers were an ethnic minority did not mean that their specificities were denied. They freely practiced their religion, with a clergy of their own" (a reference to the Ibadi community in Djerba). In any case, the representative said, Berbers were fully integrated into the life of the country and had no complaints.[27] On this occasion, though, the leading Amazigh association in France, Tamazgha, submitted a fifteen-page alternative report that attacked the Tunisian government's submission and called for concerted international action. The report laid out a detailed critique and coherent historical narrative that would be articulated repeatedly by both international and Tunisian Amazigh associations; it was viewed with sympathy by UN bodies and international NGOs alike.

As in all of North Africa, the report declared, Tunisia was experiencing a serious cultural and identity denial (*un très grave déni culturel et identitaire*) as it sought to Arabize its Berber speakers in violation of the Universal Declaration of Human Rights and other international texts. Since ancient times, North Africa had been populated by Berbers who professed multiple religions, as attested to by Ibn Khaldun and other respected historians. From the outset of independence, however, the Tunisian state authorities had sought the de jure erasure of the country's Berber language and culture: this was exemplified by the 1959 constitution, official Arabization policies, and the disappearance of Berbers from Tunisian official history. As a result, the Berber language was now in serious danger of a "slow death." Such policies, the report declared, constituted "one of the most horrific crimes, for they deprived Tunisia of an essential component of its history, identity and culture" (*l'un des crimes les plus horribles à savoir priver la Tunisie d'une composante essentielle de son histoire, identité et culture*), which was also the heritage of all humanity.

One of the tools of this policy of denial, the report emphasized, was the economic marginalization of Berber-speaking regions, which drove Berber speakers to emigrate to Arabic-speaking regions, where they were inevitably subjected to deculturation, assimilation, and Arabization processes. Another tool was Berbers' exclusion from official cultural and educational fields: Their language wasn't taught, and their heritage was denied. Although there was no official prohibition against them, Berber cultural associations were not allowed to operate in any manner. Neither were Berbers allowed to give their children Berber names, a prohibition the Tunisian government refused to acknowledge. At bottom, the report said, the state's claims that the Berber language was oral (not written) and only spoken by 1 percent of the population (a figure disputed by Tamazgha) were specious. If there was no written production of the language, it stated, this was because the state didn't allow it or promote it, unlike in other North African countries and in France. And if the language was spoken only by a small number of people, that was all the more reason for it to have official protection under international conventions.

The Tamazgha report concluded with the standard demand of the Amazigh movement throughout North Africa: constitutional recognition of Tamazight as a "national and official language." In addition, it demanded the right to establish associations for the protection and promotion of the Berber language and culture; media programming on the subject; compulsory teaching of Berber in Berber regions; integrating its teaching into all educational and training programs; allowing Berbers to use their language when engaging with the justice system and in official matters dealing with personal status; state support for Berber cultural activities; and an economic development plan for Berber regions.[28]

These demands were clearly not going to be met. However, they did resonate with CERD. The committee's final report again expressed dissatisfaction with the incongruity between the Tunisian state's insistence on the country's homogeneity and its reference to particular ethnic groups such as Berbers and sub-Saharan Africans, while simultaneously failing to provide reliable statistics on the ethnic composition of Tunisian society. This needed to be remedied in future reports, in line with previous UN recommendations "concerning the self-identification of members of racial and ethnic groups.... [The Tunisian State needed] to take account of the way in which the Amazigh perceive and define themselves ... [and] guarantee ... the enjoyment of the rights they claim, notably the right to their own culture and the use of their mother tongue and the preservation and development of their identity." The state should also provide information proving how Amazigh (and migrants from sub-Saharan Africa) were being guaranteed their "enjoyment of civil, political, economic, social and cultural rights and fundamental freedoms without racial distinction." Apart from the demand for constitutional recognition of the Tamazight language, the CERD report included all the "Tamazgha" demands, giving them an important measure of international legitimacy that had been lacking.[29]

The New Tunisia and the Amazigh Issue

The dramatic toppling of the Ben Ali regime in January 2011 opened a new era for the Tunisian body politic. Even as the country's political factions agreed on establishing a democratic regime, its exact content—and particularly the relationship between religion and the state—would be a subject of enormous contention fraught with tension. Almost three years passed before polarization between the Islamist and secularist camps was moderated and a laboriously negotiated constitution completed and ratified. The National Dialogue Quartet (its members being the country's leading labor union, employers' association, bar association, and oldest human rights association) was awarded the Nobel Peace Prize in 2015 for shepherding the process to a successful conclusion.[30]

Tunisia's Amazigh activists moved into the open during the weeks and months following the fall of the old regime. Taking advantage of the country's new atmosphere of freedom, they began establishing cultural associations and sought official recognition of their language and culture, even while rejecting the label "minority" (*aqaliya*), which they viewed as calling into question their identity as Tunisians. The first such organization—Association Tunisienne de la Culture Amazighe (ATCA)—was established in June (after the Ministry of Interior nixed the original name, Association des Amazighs de Tunisie).[31] Promoting culture was one thing, but promoting group rights was viewed as an affront to Tunisia's proclaimed homogeneity and unity.[32]

The Amazigh idea received initial support among non-Amazigh secular intellectuals and politicians. Some of this was instrumental, as they sought to brand the electorally strong Islamist Ennahda Party as intolerant and to ensure that the new Tunisian constitution would protect the secular values that had underpinned the national discourse since independence.[33] Ironically, the Ennahda Party received 70 percent of the vote in predominantly Amazigh areas in the initial postrevolution elections for the Constituent Assembly, pointing out the gap between secular activists and the more traditional and pious base.

Tunisian officials also spoke the new language of cultural diversity, pluralism (*ta'adudiya*), and democracy. However, they rejected applying the label "minority" to the Amazigh population for the same reason that the Interior Ministry had forced a name-change for the first Amazigh association. Admitting the existence of a distinct ethnolinguistic group within the Tunisian Arab-Muslim *umma* ("nation") somehow threatened integrity and cohesion. This approach was part of a larger opposition to acknowledging the presence of non-Muslims and Africans as well as Imazighen.[34] Throughout the decade, Tunisian state authorities refused repeated requests from UN committees to provide disaggregated data on the numbers of different ethnic, religious, and racial groups.

One of the recurrent accusations against members of the Tunisian Amazigh current is that they were "separatists."[35] It was a specious notion given their limited numbers and the absence of a homogenous territorial core. But the accusers could point to encouragement by international Amazigh organizations, as well as links forged with Tunisian activists. Language teaching materials were provided by Morocco's Royal Institute of Amazigh Culture (Institut Royal de la Culture Amazighe, or IRCAM). A preparatory meeting of the World Amazigh Congress was held in the southern town of Tataouine in April 2011. Convening at that location just as tens of thousands of Libyan Amazigh families fleeing the war between the Qaddafi regime and rebel forces had found refuge in the area, particularly among Tunisian Imazighen, highlighted the "pan-Amazigh" aspects of the movement that cut across existing state borders.

The sudden influx of Libyan Amazigh fleeing violence was, according to the anthropologist Katherine Hoffman, "a key moment in Amazigh minority history." Hoffman's real-time, on-site research highlights how Amazigh activists played a central role in organizing housing and basic needs, as well as how the four- to eight-month experience resulted in the forging of new links and renewed self-awareness of a common ethnicity that transcended borders. At the same time, there were many differences between them, differences that emerged based on divergent colonial and postindependence experiences.[36]

In October, the Congress convened in Djerba, where an Ibadi Amazigh community has existed for many centuries. Holding the meeting there during Ben Ali's time would have been impossible. Now, thanks to the revolution, Tunisian Amazigh were officially part of the pan-Amazigh milieu. The head of ATCA was elected to the Congress's Federal Council, and the Congress accordingly assumed the role of promoter and defender of Tunisian Amazigh rights. However, according to Tunisian activists in Djerba, the gathering highlighted clashing approaches regarding Amazigh identity and integration into the respective nation-states. For example, they were deeply offended by the antistate militancy expressed by Kabyle and some Moroccan participants, which included criticism of Djerba residents for speaking Arabic in shops and cafés.[37]

Official permission to hold the conference in Djerba did not make the Congress any less militant in addressing Tunisian Amazigh issues. One month later, it drew up a report for the UN Human Rights Commission detailing the Tunisian state's failure to uphold Amazigh rights, pre- and postrevolution regimes alike. Particularly grating, it declared, was that an Amazigh child was subject to an "education system that falsifies his story, offends his personal convictions, represses his freedom of conscience and despises his culture." The report concluded with demands for a fundamental shift in state policies on everything touching on Amazigh social, cultural, and linguistic rights so that their place in Tunisian history and society would be guaranteed.[38]

In the constitutional sphere, however, Amazigh activists came up empty. There were no Amazigh representatives in Tunisia's 217-member Constituent Assembly, charged with drafting the new constitution. None were willing to meet with ATCA representatives, and only two supported the call for cultural and linguistic rights to be officially recognized.[39] Thus, Article 1 of the 2014 constitution repeated the text of Article 1 of the 1959 constitution word for word: "Tunisia is a free, independent, sovereign state; its religion is Islam, its language Arabic, and its system is republican." Moreover, the article could not be amended. The country's Arabness was reiterated in several other places as well. The Preamble emphasized Tunisia's "cultural and civilizational affiliation to the Arab and Muslim nation"; Article 5 affirmed anew that Tunisia "is part of the Arab Maghreb and works towards achieving its unity and takes all measures to ensure its realization"; the Preamble also declared that "strengthening Maghreb unity [was] a step towards achieving Arab unity"; Article 39 emphasized that the educational system "shall also work to consolidate the Arab-Muslim identity and national belonging in the young generations, and to strengthen, promote and generalize the use of the Arabic language and to openness to foreign languages, human civilizations and diffusion of the culture of human rights."[40] This last article especially raised the ire of Amazigh activists: Why, they asked, should there be an openness to foreign languages but not to Tamazight?

To be sure, the constitution also included language that proponents of Amazigh and other minority rights could point to in the ongoing battles for recognition and justice. Article 42, for example, declared that "the state encourages cultural creativity and supports the strengthening of national culture, its diversity and renewal, in promoting the values of tolerance, rejection of violence, openness to different cultures and dialogue between civilizations"; it shall also "protect cultural heritage and guarantees it for future generations." The troubling Article 39 emphasized the "principle of positive discrimination" in seeking social justice and sustainable development for different regions.

However, translating these general principles into concrete improvements was difficult. Amazigh culture and heritage associations were now able to operate freely, and several sprouted up in southern villages, but they were unable to obtain state funding for their activities and thus were extremely limited in scope. ATCA's president summed up the situation to a journalist: "The state no longer represses us as it once did, but it doesn't give us any financial support. They seem bothered by us." As a result, the organization could not even afford to maintain an office in Tunis, forcing it to close down its Amazigh language classes and to conduct meetings with interested journalists in cafés.[41] The World Amazigh Congress used harsh language in a 2016 report on the situation to the UN Committee on Economic, Social, and Cultural Rights: Funding for Amazigh organizations was lacking, the country's political and religious discourse demonstrated anti-Amazigh prejudice, and the 1962 ordinance that in effect prevented parents from giving Amazigh names to their children remained in force. Unfortunately, the report declared, the "Tunisian pseudo-revolution" had produced nothing for the country.[42] The Tunisian authorities could not have been pleased. One indication was the complete lack of press coverage for the Congress's 2018 gathering in Tunis.

To the Congress's great satisfaction, the UN committee was sympathetic to its message. It repeatedly challenged the Tunisian government's representative during their discussions and produced a final report that endorsed many of the Congress's demands. Expanding and sharpening the demands contained in the earlier CERD reports, the committee called on the Tunisian state "to recognize the language and culture of indigenous Amazigh people and to ensure their protection and promotion"; "take legislative and administrative measures to ensure the teaching of the Amazigh language at all school levels and encourage the knowledge of Amazigh history and culture"; "facilitate the development of cultural activities organized by Amazigh cultural associations"; and repeal the decree preventing the registration of Amazigh first names to newborn children.[43]

The internationalization of the Tunisian Amazigh issue continued apace during the remainder of the decade and slowly began to affect official attitudes and behavior. An NGO, the Minority Rights Group International, put the issue on its agenda, linking it to the plight of other minorities (broadly defined) in Tunisia: its black population, estimated to be 10 percent of the population; the LGBTQ+ community; and women. The UN Office of Human Rights was particularly engaged on the subject.

An important achievement came in October 2018, when the Tunisian authorities, following the CERD and 2016 UN committee recommendations, passed a law barring all forms of racial discrimination, defined as "any distinction, exclusion, restriction or preference operated on the basis of race, color, ancestry, national origin or ethnic or any other form of racial discrimination within the meaning of international conventions."[44] And official doors were no longer entirely closed to Amazigh representatives: on July 15, 2019, Amazigh associations met with Minister for Relations with Constitutional Bodies, Civil Society, and Human Rights Organizations Mohamed Fadhel Ben Mahfoudh to push for implementation of the 2016 UN recommendations. The minister reportedly took action to place this issue on the agenda of forthcoming government meetings.[45]

Clearly, though, implementation would not be a simple matter. In May 2019, for example, a pharmacist in the southern town of Matmata was threatened with legal action by authorities if he did not take down a sign written in Tifinagh script over his shop. Similar incidents had occurred in Morocco in the early 1980s, indicating just how far behind Tunisian Amazigh still were compared to compatriots in neighboring states. A March 2020 report to the UN's Human Rights Committee by Minority Rights Group International and several Tunisian civil society organizations called on the government to ensure the implementation of the 2018 law. Moreover, it also called for comprehensive legislation prohibiting all forms of discrimination including "gender, ethnicity, religion, language, indigenous status, sexual orientation or gender identity, in line with international standards." It also reiterated the specific demands of Tunisia's Amazigh groups, including Amazigh names for children. A separate report by eight other Tunisian civil society groups did the same.[46] The inclusion of Amazigh issues on the agenda of Tunisian civil society groups indicated that the Amazigh question was no longer absent from the public discourse—an achievement in and of itself.

The problem of registering Amazigh names to newborns continued to rankle. Notwithstanding a 2013 Ministry of Interior directive to municipalities to register only Arab first names,[47] authorities claimed at times that there was no such prohibition; on the ground, however, requests were handled arbitrarily depending on the whims of local officials. In 2018, one parent managed to achieve a favorable court judgment in Sfax after his request had been turned down by a local official. The judge was immediately moved to another region, apparently as discipline for his ruling.[48] But in July 2020, the Ministry of Municipal Affairs issued a directive officially lifting restrictions on parents' rights to name their children. For Amazigh rights proponents, it was an important symbolic step; it also demonstrated that authorities were no longer entirely tone-deaf to the efforts of international and local organizations.

Akal—A Turn Toward the Political Arena

In May 2019, a group of Amazigh activists announced the establishment of the Akal ("Land") political party to field candidates in the parliamentary and presidential elections scheduled later that year. According to its head, Samir Nefzi, the party's founders had concluded that efforts by Amazigh NGOs to promote Amazigh causes were not sufficient and that it was necessary to enter the political arena. They were inspired by the efforts of the Kurds, as well as the RCD party in Algeria, which had a national orientation but also a clear Amazigh foundation.[49]

Akal's founding statement emphasized political and socioeconomic goals. Changing Article 1 of the constitution to confer full recognition of the Amazigh identity in public institutions was a top priority. The teaching of Tamazight in schools and its use in the media should also be guaranteed. Ameliorating the dire situation of Amazigh villages in the south was considered to be another must.[50] More vaguely, the party advocated a political, social, and economic program that was claimed to be "neither East nor West." Nefzi criticized "the mentality of hatred cultivated by the nationalist Arabs and Islamic currents," in addition to "ideas coming from the North, such as the socialist or capitalist thought, which did not fit into the nature of the Tunisian people." The alternative would be building a national economy in partnership with North Africa and the Mediterranean region—"an absolute priority." To that end, Nefzi said, Akal was in contact with groups throughout the Amazigh milieu for the purpose of establishing an overarching representative body.[51]

Neither the Tunisian state nor other Amazigh organizations were enthused about thrusting the Amazigh issue directly into the political sphere. State officials tried to obstruct Akal's efforts: initially, authorities denied that the party had submitted the requisite documents, as required by law, which wasn't the case. Then, authorities demanded a change in the party's name because it was not an Arabic name and the law forbade parties that appealed to only one ethnic group. On the latter point, Nefzi rejected the accusations of ethnic particularism, insisting that the party was open to all Tunisians, who, by definition, were Berbers, as Tunisia was a Berber land.[52] From one angle, the response might appear to be sleight of hand. From another, though, it confirms anew that ethnicity is a fluid and malleable construct.

Akal's establishment was a controversial step among Tunisian Amazigh activists as well. Most groups preferred to focus on projects promoting the linguistic and cultural dimensions of their identity, and many feared that entering the political arena would be counterproductive. ATCA's president was blunt: "The situation is not ripe enough to launch a political party, which could be illegal, given that the law forbids ethnically based parties. A lot of prior awareness-raising work needs to be done. It is a project doomed to failure that will rather harm our cause." The question of how politically active and confrontational one should be had been debated by Amazigh groups throughout North Africa for decades. Tunisian civil society groups were also concerned over the prospects of igniting civil strife. Nefzi, for his part, was withering in his criticism of such groups, accusing them of being "linked to the circles of power in Algeria or Morocco" that sought to confine the Amazigh issue to cultural matters.[53]

The party did not make a dent in the 2019 elections. Nefzi's candidacy for the presidency was rejected, owing to his inability to provide onerous financial and logistical guarantees. It did manage to field candidates for parliament in three districts but did not win any seats. According to Nefzi, this was "due to the abundant money that competitors were using to buy votes." In any case, as far as he was concerned, this was only the beginning.[54]

Nora Gharyéni—Promoting Amazigh Culture Through Music

Music has played an important role in the fashioning and dissemination of a modern Amazigh consciousness over the previous half-century: examples of iconic artists who promoted Amazigh culture through their songs include Idir, Lounes Matoub, and Louis Aït Menguillet, all Kabyles; the Moroccan band Saghru and singer Khalid Izri; and the many Tuareg bands, headlined by Tinariwen. In 2011, Libya's Dania Ben Sassi joined the list of celebrated singers, and in 2016–2017 Silya Ziani emerged as the "Voice of the Rif." Today, Amazigh music and culture festivals are an integral feature of societies throughout North Africa and in the diaspora.

Nora Gharyéni is a young Tunisian singer committed to the preservation and development of Amazigh culture. Her song "Takrust" ("The Knot," or "The Problem"), released in a video clip produced in the ruins of the Byzantine fortress of Younga south of Sfax, is a strong pushback against the Arabization and resulting effacement of Amazigh culture. "The Knot," she explained, was

> the complex of the poet, who lived a childhood of linguistic and identity marginalization, in a historical context that did not allow him to express himself with his own language ... at a time when speaking Tamazigh was a crime and the Amazigh question was a taboo:

> Yemma imet oughini aselmadh n tsarghint?
> Nitch ekhsa idlisin n Tamazight.
> Asalmadh yennay tasarghint dh awel n tamsount
> Nighass Tmazight d awel n tililli d tafsouth
> Nitch ekhsa atharya isekkilin n Tamazight
> Tikkaz n nanna d amezriw n tamagit
> Ekhsa ssalmedha tadelsa d tagharma n idherfan
> Akkal d awal d afkan n igharsen
> Imaddukal n tamourt oufin agherbez tsallast
> Tefout n Tmazight taqqas ljaj g uammess.
> Yemma nitchin neggour d effer n thbabenna
> Anarraz ur neknou fi fadnenna.

Translation:

> Mom, why did they bring me an Arabic teacher?
> I need Tamazight books
> My teacher told me Arabic is the language of paradise
> I answered him Tamazight is the language of freedom and spring
> I want to write with the Tifinagh letters
> The tattoo of my grandmother is the history of my identity
> I want to study the culture and the civilization of free people
> Motherland, language and human roots
> My peers in the village found the school in darkness
> The light of Amazigh will shine in it everywhere
> Mom, we are walking on the path of our ancestors
> We may break, but not bow ... that's the title of our grandchildren.[55]

Her background and motivations shed light on the sparks of modern Amazigh identity in Tunisia, as well as the difficulties facing its advocates—both of which are reflected in the song's lyrics. She was born in the city of Sfax (derived from the Berber name "Sfaqes," or "the one that is surrounded by ramparts") on the country's southeastern coast; both her parents were of Amazigh origin. The family's last name indicates that it originated in the city of Gharyan, in the predominantly Amazigh Jebel Nafusa in Libya. She herself did not grow up in an Amazigh-speaking environment. However, her parents were proud of their origins, and she took an interest at an early age in learning about her roots; she ascribes much influence to her artist-mother, who spent eight years in the town of Métlaoui (Gafsa Governorate), where she was inspired by the material culture, traditions, and habits of Amazigh women, all of which are reflected in her paintings.

She related an early incident from her days in secondary school during which she clashed with a teacher who insisted that Berbers were nothing but "savages" who had contributed nothing to Tunisian civilization. In 2016, while still in high school, she founded the Club de la Culture Amazigh à Sfax, whose objective was "raising awareness and spreading Amazigh culture to discover its historical, cultural, civilizational aspects." It was an uphill battle to find space and persuade people to participate; even hanging an Amazigh flag at meetings was frowned on by the owners of the meeting place. But she remained committed.

Singing in Tamazight, despite her lack of proficiency in the language, was a conscious choice. She has already performed at cultural festivals in Algeria, Tunisia, and France and is currently collaborating with other artists across North Africa. She has just received a BA in psychology from Sfax University and intends to combine her music career with civil society activism, including raising awareness about the stigmas associated with mental illness.[56] Her future career trajectory bears watching not only musically but also with regard to her place in the Amazigh cultural sphere.

Conclusion

Tunisia's Amazigh dimension slowly made its way onto the public stage in the decade following the toppling of the Ben Ali regime. The 2011 revolution made it possible for Amazigh activists to openly establish associations to promote their language and culture for the first time since the country achieved independence in 1956. As an endangered and historically marginalized ethnolinguistic community, its battle for recognition and support from state authorities and civil society was arduous. Mobilizing the large number of Arabized Amazigh to identify with, and participate in, such efforts was even harder. The first modest initiative to enter the electoral political sphere in 2019 was controversial within the community and beyond, and it made no tangible impact.

Nonetheless, while the proverbial glass was not close to being even half-full, neither was it entirely empty. United Nations bodies, international NGOs, and Tunisian civil society groups followed the lead of pan-Amazigh associations and kept up a steady stream of missives and remonstrations to authorities, who now realized that the previous strategy of wholesale denial was no longer viable. Although the parliament was distinctly unresponsive, other areas of the state administration and civil society were showing signs of being more sympathetic. In writing about Tunisia's "democratic turn," Stéphanie Pouessel pointed to signs of a "neo-diversity" discourse in Tunisia's evolving body politic, replacing an outmoded, monolithic insistence on linguistic, ethnic, and cultural homogeneity with one that acknowledged and celebrated the country's diverse elements. Its proponents argued that such an approach would not only *not* damage the national fabric, as opponents had charged, but instead reinforce it at a time when Tunisia's fragile democracy very much needed help. Promoting Tunisia's Amazigh heritage, language, and culture was a natural part of this conversation. In that regard, the ongoing efforts to promote Tunisia's Amazighité and the responses of both state and larger society promised to be a bellwether for the health of Tunisian democracy in the years ahead.[57]

The small number of Tunisian Amazigh who were actually proficient in Tamazight raises questions about the nature of Amazigh ethnicity. Belgacem Hamza's study and Nora Gharyéni's artistry highlight the continued existence and potential vitality of Amazigh ethnic identification even after having been linguistically Arabized. The unattractiveness of Arab nationalist ideas for Tunisians not affiliated with the Islamist current made "being Amazigh" a potential alternative pole of identification that at the very least could be blended with other elements. While the particular context was Tunisian, the questions raised, and the possible courses of action to be adopted, were applicable throughout the Amazigh universe—in North Africa, the Sahel, and the diaspora.

CHAPTER 5

Moroccan Imazighen and the *Makhzen*: From Recognition to Malaise

Morocco's Democracy Spring protests in 2011 were different from those held in neighboring states. The guiding mantra was *al-`sha`b yurid islah al-nizam* ("the people want to reform the regime"), in contrast to Tunisia, Libya, and Egypt, where the protesters demanded *isqat al-nizam* ("toppling the regime"). Unlike in Algeria, demonstrations were coordinated, had a clear message, and showed a degree of staying power. As was the case in Jordan, where protesters also called for *islah al-nizam*, Morocco's monarchical regime was headed by a young king who possessed a degree of legitimacy and authority that provided a cushion against the protests. Moreover, King Mohamed VI was proactive in his response, seizing the initiative by promulgating a ballyhooed set of constitutional and political reforms. These proved to be cosmetic, but they were effective politically. They produced a coalition government led by an Islamist political party, and took the wind out of the sails of the protests, while leaving real power in the hands of the Palace and affiliated elites. Throughout the ensuing decade, it was business as usual in the political sphere, as authorities continued proven methods of manipulation, co-optation, and selective repression to prevent the emergence of any serious challenges to the status quo, thereby maintaining the essential hollowness of the official multiparty political system.

To be sure, many of the underlying social, economic, and political grievances that sparked the 2011 uprisings elsewhere were present in Morocco as well and remained throughout the decade. Although Morocco showed improvement according to United Nations Human Development Index parameters, including life expectancy, per capita income in terms of purchasing power, and level of education, it remained in the third tier ("medium development") of countries, ranked number 121, which is lower than most other Arab League member states, including Libya and Iraq. In 2019, about 43 percent of the country's 35.6 million citizens were under the age of 24, the share of the population aged

15–24 was almost 17 percent, and the unemployment rate at the end of 2018 stood at 27.4 percent. Not surprisingly, 60 percent of 15- to 24-year-olds expressed a desire to emigrate from the country,[1] and many would imperil their own lives attempting to do so.[2]

Signs of alienation and a desire to challenge the status quo were widespread, from peripheral towns to football stadiums, where teams' die-hard supporters ("ultras") raged against the country's ruling elites.[3] There was a widespread (and justifiable) perception of official corruption,[4] as it reached the highest levels. A 2009 Wikileaks document reported that three people were responsible for all decisions related to major investments in commercial real estate: the king and his two top advisers, Fouad Ali El Himma and Mounir Majidi. In the same document, a former US ambassador expressed displeasure with the "shocking greed" of the king's associates.[5] The king himself had accumulated extraordinary wealth—$5.7 billion, according to one report.[6] The economic activity of the king, his family, and associates reached into the banking and insurance sectors, mining, communications, the cement industry, energy, food, agricultural production, and more. Many of the details appear in the book *Le Roi prédateur* ("The Predator King"), published in France in 2012. Its sale was completely banned in Morocco, but in practice it is within the reach of anyone with internet access.[7]

It was against this background that a 2018 study by a Moroccan think tank predicted a new wave of protests in the coming years due to high expectations of citizens whose horizons were blocked—among both the university educated and poorer sectors, in both urban and rural areas—and the inability of authorities to meet them.[8] The acclaimed French Moroccan author Taher Ben Jelloun captured the mood:

> Il y a trop d'injustice, trop d'inégalités, trop d'égoïsme, trop d'autosatisfaction. Pendant ce temps-là, les jeunes issus de milieux modestes ou carrément pauvres se débrouillent. La violence qui leur est faite, ils la retourneront un jour contre les autres.[9] ["There is too much injustice, too much inequality, too much selfishness, too much complacency. During this time, young people from modest or downright poor backgrounds manage. The violence that is done to them, they will one day turn against others."]

It remained to be seen whether the authorities would re-contract with their increasingly alienated populations and adapt fast enough to successfully meet the challenges from below.

Morocco's large and diverse Amazigh communities were integral actors in the country's increasingly contested public space, in a multitude of ways: from the initial 2011 demonstrations and the constitutional reform process, to diverse, uncoordinated protests over socioeconomic issues in peripheral regions, to the large-scale and sustained protests in 2016–2017 under the banner of the Rifian *Hirak al-Sh`abi* ("Popular Movement"). In the legal-constitutional sphere, the Amazigh movement achieved its central goals. However, translating them into a fundamental shift in the country's sociolinguistic landscape, addressing concrete and symbolic grievances, and fundamentally revamping the long-dominant national narrative remained distant goals. Thus, entering the 2020s, the mainstream Amazigh current found itself at a crossroads. As for the Rif, the alienation that had powered the 2016–2017 protests remained, with new wounds and bitterness piled on top of older grievances. The unfolding of the Amazigh question in Morocco, in all of its varieties, over the decade since 2011 forms the heart of this chapter.

The Twentieth Century—Colonialism and Independence

The bulk of Morocco's Imazighen belong to one of three main ethnolinguistic groups: the Tashelhit-speaking tribes and communities of the High Atlas Mountains and southern valleys (the Souss region); the Tamazight[10]-speaking tribes of the Middle Atlas region; and the northern Rifians. Taken together, they constitute the largest Amazigh population, by total number and percentage of population, among all the North African states. In fact, entering the twentieth century, they constituted a majority of the country's overall population.

France's protectorate regime in Morocco lasted forty-four years (1912–1956). Resistance by recalcitrant Berber tribes was not subdued until the early 1930s.[11] French policies toward the Imazighen varied, in line with the different realities of each community. After having been subdued, fragmented Middle Atlas tribes were targeted as potential assets, with children of notables receiving schooling in French to help train future junior administrators. The near-mythical Mohamed bin Abdelkrim al-Khattabi led a five-year rebellion in the Rif against Spanish authorities that was eventually defeated in 1926 by combined French and Spanish forces. In the south, France made common cause with Thami el-Glaoui and other "Lords of the Atlas"—the all-powerful heads of large tribal confederations that controlled vast swaths of territory and main trade arteries.[12] In 1930, France propagated the infamous Berber *dahir* (royal decree), which sought to elevate the status of Berber customary law and thus, at least implicitly, push Berbers away from shari`a and the urban-based, Arabic-speaking Muslim establishment. However, even as France pursued a

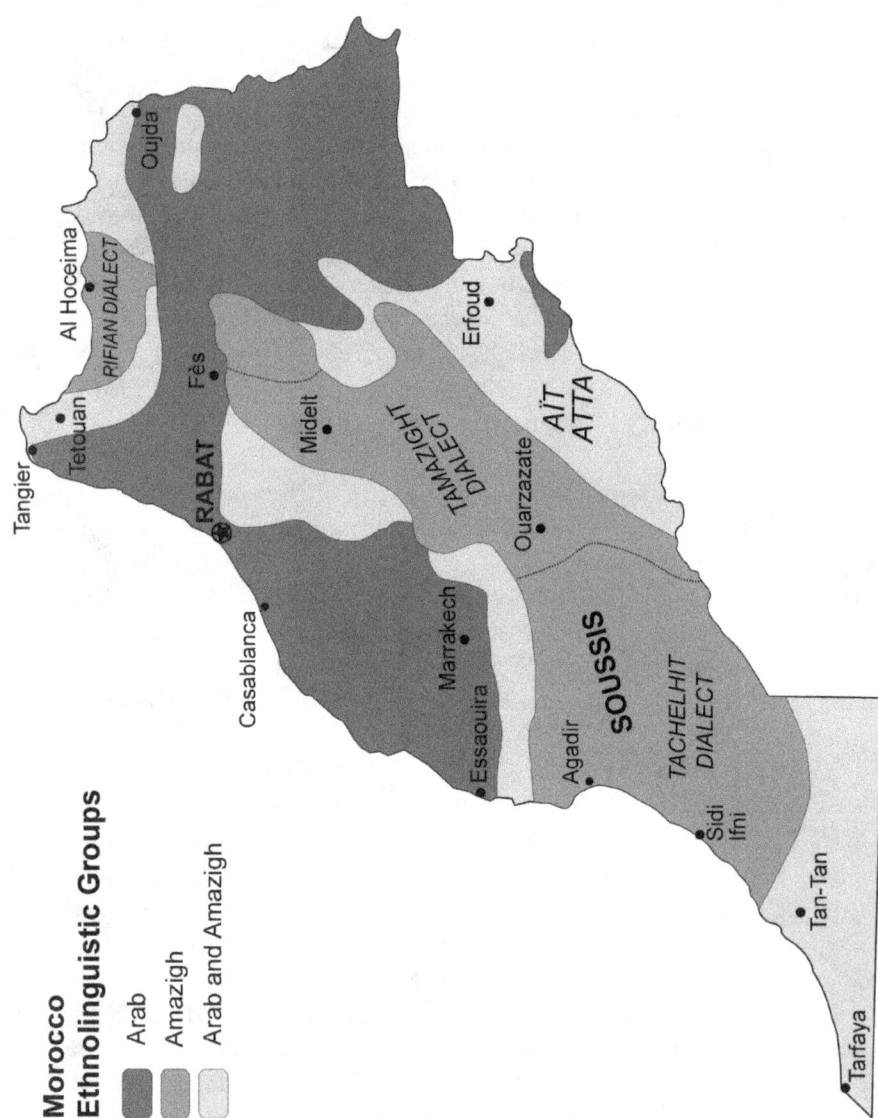

Map 5.1 Amazigh-speaking regions in Morocco, https://www.cs.mcgill.ca/~rwest/wikispeedia/wpcd/wp/d/Demographics_of_Morocco.htm

divide-and-rule policy, its economic and security policies also led to greater integration of the territory, and many young Berbers were recruited to the French military.

In the early 1950s, France mobilized Glaoui and his supporters to depose Sultan Mohamed, who was now openly supportive of the Moroccan nationalist movement. The move boomeranged badly, reinforcing Mohamed's status and pushing Middle Atlas Berber tribes to armed revolt, leading to France's decision to grant Morocco independence. As for Glaoui, his territorial and economic empire collapsed.[13]

Morocco's postindependence state-building and nation-building projects had important, albeit contrarian, Berber aspects. A 1958–1959 rebellion in the Rif was brutally crushed by forces led by Crown Prince Hasan (soon to become king) and his strongman, General Mohamed Oufkir, himself a proud Berber from the southeastern Tafilelt region. The monarchy's alliance with rural Berber Middle Atlas notables was crucial in ensuring its hard-won hegemony over all other political forces.[14] But in the early 1970s, two nearly successful military coups, both led by Berber officers (the second one by Oufkir himself), severely stigmatized the Berber community for many years to come in the eyes of Arabophone urban elites.

Meanwhile, urban-based Berber intellectuals began pushing back gingerly against the state's official national narrative that foregrounded its Arab-Islamic heritage, in line with the evolving trends in Algeria's Kabylia region and the diaspora. During the 1980s, state authorities forcibly blocked manifestations of modern Berberism, fearing a spillover from Algeria's Berber Spring. By the early 1990s, however, King Hasan II's initial steps to liberalize political life enabled the renewal of Berber activism. The first noticeable manifestation was the 1991 Agadir Charter for Linguistic and Cultural Rights, which called for an end to the systematic marginalization of the Amazigh language and culture "in the context of building the national democratic culture."[15] Three years later, Hasan partially legitimized the Amazigh agenda on a nationwide television broadcast with a notion of promoting national unity.[16]

Mohamed VI—A New Era

Mohamed VI's ascent to the throne in July 1999 following his father's death inaugurated a new liberalizing era in Moroccan politics, with important consequences for the Amazigh issue. The next few years were marked by several significant actions by the king, and increasing public assertiveness by Amazigh intellectuals. Mohamed VI began his rule by making a high-profile reconciliation visit to the alienated and long-neglected Rif region. Six months later, approximately 250 Amazigh intellectuals signed the Berber Manifesto, a 9,000-word document that articulated a sharp counternarrative to the country's official one and fleshed out demands first laid out ten years earlier in the Agadir Charter. The document concluded with a clear answer to accusations that the Amazigh agenda was one that endangered national unity and ultimately separatist in nature:

> We the Amazigh . . . who are proud of our Amazighity . . . are brothers to the Arabs. . . . We jointly form one body . . . [with] our fellow citizens who are proud of their "Arabity." We believe that diversity is an enrichment . . . and a sharpener of human designs. . . . What causes separatism and group splitting is [not] multilingualism . . . but a lack of civilizational maturity.[17]

A year later, the king spoke on national television favorably about the Amazigh dimension of Moroccan history and society. He then gave the force of law to this endorsement: the Amazigh *dahir* authorized the establishment of a royal institute to promote Amazigh culture (IRCAM) for the benefit of Morocco's democratization and development. Symbolically, he issued the *dahir* from the Middle Atlas region of his mother's Berber tribe while wearing traditional Amazigh headgear.[18] The edict and accompanying speeches by the king constituted an official acknowledgment that Morocco's history and culture were bound up with its Tamazight-speaking populations, as well as a commitment to ameliorating their socioeconomic plight and ending their long-standing marginalization.

On May 16, 2003, a series of five coordinated suicide bombings by homegrown Islamist extremists killed forty-three people in Casablanca. It came as a shock, as many Moroccans considered the country immune from jihadi terrorism. The king's response was slow, but multipronged: harsh and sweeping antiterrorist legislation that could be wielded to curtail political opposition,[19] followed some months later by (1) a long-delayed reform of the family code that greatly enhanced women's rights;[20] and (2) the inauguration of Tamazight-language classes in Moroccan primary schools, a prime demand of the Amazigh movement, nine years after his father had first endorsed the idea.

The king's partial embrace of the Amazigh movement's ideas marked a sea change in official attitudes toward the issue. It fit hand-in-glove with the monarchy's time-honored strategy of balancing competing interests within the kingdom while maintaining royal dominance.[21] In this case, the promotion of women's rights and the Amazigh current served as a counterweight to Islamist parties and movements. While being understandably suspicious of the king's embrace, most Amazigh activists saw the benefits of royal patronage as outweighing the liabilities.

To be sure, a gap remained between symbol and substance. Tamazight-language classes were inaugurated without preparation, attaining poor results, and rural Amazigh regions continued to suffer from neglect. Nonetheless, Amazigh activism gradually expanded to campuses and even rural areas. The Amazigh presence also gradually spread in the audio-visual media, which eventually included the establishment of an Amazigh television channel.

The 2011 Protests and Royal Response

Inspired by the success of counterparts in Tunis and Cairo in early 2011, Morocco's internet-savvy Generation Y created Facebook groups protesting endemic corruption, including individuals close to the king, and calling for a genuine change of the nature of the regime in favor of a parliamentary monarchy. In addition, several individuals immolated themselves, following Tunisia's Mohamed Bouazizi, whose desperate act had sparked the initial protests there. By mid-February, they had congealed into the heterogeneous February 20 movement (F20), mobilizing 200,000 demonstrators on February 20 in fifty-three cities and towns, with weekly protests continuing for months afterward.[22] F20 served as an umbrella "for all those left outside the public space who wished to re-claim that space, democratize it, and transform it into a genuine avenue for debate."[23] These included a cross-section of activists ranging from leftist groups to members of the officially banned but reluctantly tolerated Islamist movement al-'Adl wal-Ihsan ("Justice and Beneficence"). It was more of a "transgressive" political movement than a "contained" one,[24] and it constituted the most significant challenge to the existing civil order since the mid-1960s.

The question of whether or not to be part of the F20 protests caused some division within Amazigh activist circles. The central bureau of the Reseau National Amazigh pour la Citoyennete´, an umbrella organization for hundreds of local Amazigh associations, left the decision to participate in F20 protests to its constituent members, and approximately one-third of them did take part,[25] alongside people acting individually. Amazigh activists displayed their movement's flag at the protests and demanded full cultural and linguistic recognition as part of the overall reform of political life. Among the Rifian Amazigh, the protests had more pronounced regional aspects. The initial one, on February 20, was attended by 30,000 in Al Hoceima and ended in the death of five, the result of a fire inside a bank. While the authorities blamed the protesters for looting and vandalism, there was some evidence to show that the violence had been incited by proregime thugs and that the five dead activists had been "disappeared" the previous night, tortured, and killed, with the fire being staged as a cover-up. Al Hoceima's F20 chapter condemned "this tragic event that took Moroccans back to the years of repression and to the historic tension between the state and the Rif that resulted from those years."[26]

On March 9, just over two weeks since the first large protests, King Mohamed sought to take back the initiative. In a nationwide television address, he announced plans for fundamental constitutional reform that would consolidate the rule of law, including enhanced powers for an elected parliament and prime minister, and "elevat[e] the judiciary to the status of an independent power." Notably, he emphasized that the new constitution would "enshrine ... the Amazigh component as a core element and common asset belonging to all Moroccans."[27]

Keen on winning broad legitimacy for his efforts and thus derailing the energy released by the F20 protests, the king appointed a blue-ribbon commission to study and formulate the new text. Headed by a senior constitutional jurist, it included representatives from across the political and social spectrums, although not from groups associated with F20. Significantly, the subcommittee charged with drafting the language relevant to the Amazigh question included Professor Lahcen Oulhaj, dean of the Faculty of Juridical, Economic, and Social Sciences at Mohammed V University–Agdal and a militant proponent of Amazigh identity. Oulhaj's input was crucial, and he even threatened at one point to resign if his proposals were rejected. As a result, the subcommittee produced a draft text that fully equalized the status of Tamazight to Arabic, stating that both would be official languages of the state. However, to Oulhaj's dismay, the king's counselor, Mohammed Moatassim, watered it down before issuing the final version.[28] Article 5 of the new constitution now stated that "Arabic remains ... the official language of the State.... Likewise, al-Amazighiyya [Tamazight] constitutes an official language of the State, being common patrimony of all Moroccans without exception." The process of implementing Tamazight's official status was to be defined by an Organic Law. A National Council of Languages and of Moroccan Culture, charged with protecting both Arabic and Tamazight, was also to be established, governed by another Organic Law. Most of the decade would go by before the laws were finally approved by parliament.

The Amazigh issue was addressed more broadly in the constitution's preamble. The final version emphasized the theme of diversity within unity, declaring that Morocco's national identity had been "forged by the convergence of its Arab-Islamic, Amazigh and Saharo-hassanian components, nourished and enriched by its African, Andalusian, Hebraic and Mediterranean tributaries" (*rawafid*). The original draft had spoken only of "Amazighité and Arabité," without reference in this clause to Islam. Neither had the original draft defined Morocco as a "Muslim state," whereas the final version did. The draft text had also placed the Saharo-Hassanian element in the secondary ("tributary") category, but it was upgraded in the final version. The motivation for this was clearly political: to reinforce Morocco's claim to the disputed Western Sahara territory.

Although Arabic retained pride of place in the new constitution, Morocco's identity was no longer defined as exclusively Arab. The new constitution also deemphasized the Arab orientation in at least one additional way. While committing to strengthening fraternal ties with the "fraternal peoples" (*shu`ub al-shakika*) of the Arab and Islamic *umma* ("nation"),[29] Morocco's number-one foreign policy priority was the building of the "Maghrib Union." The official name of the five-country regional organization, established in 1989, was the Arab Maghrib Union: the removal of "Arab" was a nod to the Amazigh movement's insistence that North Africa was not exclusively Arab. Some months later, Foreign Minister Saad Eddine El Othmani, himself an Amazigh originating from the Souss region in the country's south, caught his fellow AMU foreign ministers by surprise when he proposed to drop the word "Arab" from the name of the organization.[30]

On June 17, the king returned to the airwaves, presenting the draft constitution to the public and calling for everyone to confirm it with a "yes" vote in the upcoming July 1 nationwide referendum. To make sure of the results, the Moroccan media limited any mention of criticism of the new constitution, and security forces clamped down harder on protests.

As expected, the new constitution was overwhelmingly ratified in the referendum (officially by 98 percent of the voters, with a 70 percent turnout rate). The February 20 movement, including its Amazigh components, had called for a boycott, owing to its lack of input into the process, the state's prevention of any real debate on the subject, and the repressive measures being taken by security forces.[31] The boycott call had no discernible effect, however. Over the summer, F20's energy dissipated, as internal divisions over tactics and strategy came to the fore. In particular, al-`Adl wal-Ihsan withdrew from the movement. Another structural problem was the difficulty of mobilizing rural populations, which were generally skeptical about the potential benefits that might accrue from joining up with the urban-based F20.[32] The king's proactive measures to reassert control over the political field were completed with the November parliamentary elections, which brought the Islamist Justice and Development Party (Parti de la Justice et du Développement, or PJD) to power at the head of a coalition government.

The election results were sobering for the Amazigh current. Contemporary Islamist movements have always been hostile to the Amazigh *idée*. The PJD's achievement (winning 23 percent of the vote and earning 27 percent of the seats in parliament) and the participation of the venerable Islamic modernist Istiqlal Party (12 percent of the vote and 15 percent of the seats) in the new PJD-led governing coalition confirmed to Amazigh militants that PJD and Istiqlal were two sides of the same coin—both dedicated to subordinating the Amazigh language and culture to the country's dominant Arab–Islamic paradigm. Conversely, Foreign Minister (and later prime minister) Othmani was also a member of PJD, and Istiqlal supported the Amazigh demand to make the Amazigh New Year (Yennayer) a national holiday, indicating that Islamists were hardly of one stripe in their approach to the Amazigh issue. (As of May 2021, Yennayer had still not been declared a national holiday, in contrast to Algeria, where the authorities had done so in late 2017.)

As for the constitution itself, Oulhaj and other militants were disappointed with the watered-down final version and skeptical about its likely implementation. Nonetheless, its adoption was a symbolic achievement regarding a core demand of the Amazigh identity movement. Morocco now became the only North African state—and only the second core Arab League member state (after post-2003 Iraq)—in which Arabic was not the sole official language. The achievement would be a bellwether for Amazigh activists across North Africa.

One of the most salient questions regarding the Amazigh movement is whether it would be capable of forging alliances with other social and political groups and thereby generate what Eva Pföstl and Will Kymlicka call "transformative minority politics" (i.e., achieving genuine recognition of Amazigh ethnocultural demands as part of a broader democratic transformation of North African states and societies).[33] Daniele Rossi-Doria's interviews with F20 activists, Amazigh as well as non-Amazigh, provide valuable evidence of the difficulties and possibilities faced in achieving such a goal. For example, there was friction over the fact that many non-Amazigh members of leftist-democratic groups did not view Amazigh demands as a vital part of the protests. Opinions about the substance of the demands varied: Some saw them as worthy; some viewed them as populist and unrealistic; others thought they were appropriate for Amazigh-dominated regions exclusively within the larger context of a desired decentralization of authority; and still others, including some Imazighen themselves, feared that the whole issue would be divisive and cause interethnic divisions. Amazigh associations were also divided about whether to participate in the F20 protests and, in some cases, left it up to individual members. In any case, there was a general consensus that this represented one more episode in the long-term struggle to achieve Amazigh rights.[34]

The Rural Dimension—Human Insecurity and the Amazigh Factor

Human insecurity has long been a fact of life in Morocco's peripheral regions. This is reflected in many of the indicators determining Morocco's ranking on the UN Human Development Index: adult illiteracy—25 percent for males and roughly 40 percent for females, with the rate among rural adult women being close to 90 percent; maternal mortality (69th highest in world rankings as of 2015); infant mortality (76th highest, as of 2017); and GDP (PPP) per capita (116th). Although poverty rates in the country have steadily declined since the turn of the century, perhaps 75 percent of those at or under the poverty line live in rural areas.[35]

To be sure, the Moroccan state's penetration into rural regions has increased exponentially. This includes expanded electrification of villages (96.5 percent in 2009, compared to just 18 percent in 1996—i.e., more than 35,000 villages and 11.5 million people); construction of schools and roads; and increased access to potable water (from 20 percent in 1990 to 87 percent in 2009 and presumably well over 90 percent today, with a 15 percent jump over five years to full access in the northern Al Hoceima region).[36] In addition, migrant workers from rural areas, who spend parts of the year in big cities or extended periods in Europe, provide crucial injections of cash into village families' economies. Nonetheless, the deprivation in remote Middle and High Atlas mountain villages and valleys, which are populated primarily by Amazigh communities, remained high.

One shocking episode occurred in the winter of 2007, when approximately thirty infants died within just a few days from an illness exacerbated by severe temperatures and the absence of basic medical services in the village of Anfgou in the eastern High Atlas Mountains. Thanks to the efforts of Amazigh activists, the event went viral on social media, highlighting the village's isolation and extreme poverty. The nearest hospital was seventy miles away, the village was accessible only via a rocky path alongside a riverbed that often flooded in winter, and it had no electricity, telephone network, or potable water. The shock reached the royal palace, generating a series of actions to ameliorate the situation, beginning with two visits by the king himself, and resulting in infrastructure projects that substantially improved the life of the 1,700 villagers, although they remain deeply impoverished and dependent on others for their existence.[37] For Amazigh militants such as Mouha Moukhlis, Anfgou and surrounding villages remain symbols of what they view as the willful neglect of Arab-Islamic–oriented authorities, including members of parliament who "read the Fatiha after the death of Saddam Husayn, but failed to do so after the Anfgou tragedies," as well as the neglect of "city-dwelling" Amazigh who prefer to sit home and watch Al Jazeera and ARTE.[38]

Devastating floods in late November 2014 highlighted the poor infrastructure that still prevailed in much of the interior. More than fifty people were killed, hundreds of houses were destroyed or heavily damaged, and cattle and many roads were washed away. Official aid and rescue operations undertaken were considered to be insufficient. The population was furious at the use of garbage trucks to transport the numerous corpses. A month later, 200 Amazigh activists—men and women—from across the country demonstrated in downtown Casablanca in solidarity with the victims of the floods and to denounce the treatment they had received from authorities. Among the slogans chanted by the demonstrators and written on signs: "We are not Arabs," "Men and women are equal," "Billions go to Palestine and we are looking for crumbs for us to feed," and "We were born in this country; we want our rights."[39]

Another set of protests that grabbed authorities' attention took place in summer 2017 in the town of Zagora, in the southeast. Angered over the lack of drinking water for hours or even days at a time, residents organized regular peaceful protests, which they dubbed *Hirak al-'Atash*. Commonly translated as the "thirst protests," the use of the term "*Hirak*" was clearly designed to emulate the large-scale *Hirak* protests in the Rif. It certainly caught authorities' attention. An eventual police crackdown sent several people to prison, a government minister visited the town and promised help, the prime minister promised to take emergency measures, and the king appointed a commission to address the problem of water shortages nationwide.[40]

Given the neglected state of the largely Amazigh peripheral regions in Morocco, one would expect them to be a natural and fertile base for political recruitment and mobilization. However, the Moroccan *makhzen*[41] has always pursued a sophisticated and generally successful strategy that combines cooptation and repression that makes it difficult for would-be challengers to build a sustained base of support. Indeed, one of the country's oldest and most durable political parties has been the staunchly promonarchy Mouvement Populaire, whose ties to the Palace enabled it to benefit from the king's largesse and dispense patronage services among its Amazigh electoral base, primarily in the Middle Atlas region.

In addition, one of the persistent shortcomings of Morocco's Amazigh movement has been the disconnect between urban-based intellectual leadership focusing on the cultural, linguistic, and historical dimensions of Amazigh identity, versus the very different and difficult socioeconomic realities in the Amazigh hinterlands. Just as the F20 movement struggled to mobilize support in rural regions, the converse was also true. Local protests in peripheral regions failed to win the requisite sustained backing of wider sectors within Moroccan society, whereas urban Amazigh associations—even when sympathizing with rural causes—lacked the mass mobilizational capacity to make a major impact on specific issues. The authorities, for their part, were keen to maintain this disconnect and used a variety of means to that end.

That being said, there was some movement in bridging the urban-rural divide thanks primarily to a new generation of politicized Amazigh youth from peripheral areas who studied in universities in Agadir, Marrakech, and elsewhere. F20 did succeed in establishing a presence in outlying areas, organizing protests in numerous provincial towns. Rossi-Doria's research in Al Houz Province showed that leaders of local Amazigh associations and urban-based F20 militants, particularly those affiliated with the Tamaynut ("New") association, registered some success in coping with what Paul Silverstein calls the "scalar dilemma," which requires different strategies and discourses depending on the arena (tribe, village, national stage, religious sphere, transnational networks, and so on). The result was some ability to mobilize local residents on behalf of concrete grievances (e.g., a lack of infrastructural investment, as well as the expropriation of tribal lands by state and private interests).[42] Students' militancy also included insistence on fair compensation for the remaining elderly combatants of battles against the French conquerors, plus separate demands for the rehabilitation and restoration of local *qasbahs* ("fortresses") and *qsours* ("fortified villages"), concrete symbols of Amazigh culture and history, most of which are in advanced states of decay.

Amazigh student activism has a history that stretches back to the 1990s, when the Amazigh Culture Movement first appeared on the scene. Beginning in the early 2000s, Amazigh student groups clashed violently with Marxist and pro–Polisario Sahrawi groups on numerous occasions.[43] The latest iteration came in January 2016, when Omar Khaleq (known as "Izem," or "Lion"), a student at the University of Al Cadi Ayyad in Marrakesh, died of injuries inflicted by Sahrawi students. The funeral in his home village of Boumalen Dades was attended by thousands, as was a commemorative march on the first anniversary of his death. His gravestone, which included the inscription *shahid* ("martyr"), was later defaced by unknown persons. Seventeen persons were convicted of involvement in Khaleq's death and sentenced to prison terms.[44] Conversely, in 2016, two Amazigh students in Meknes were released from prison eight years after being convicted of killing another student. Throughout their years of incarceration, during which they were subjected to torture, they were held up by Amazigh associations as political prisoners.[45]

The pan-Amazigh movement has placed increasing emphasis in recent years on the threats posed to the rural Amazigh world—its land, natural resources, and way of life—by modern postcolonial states, which were building on prior actions taken by colonial rulers. The discourse of indigeneity was central to these efforts: The longtime Moroccan Amazigh activist Hassan Idbalkassm served for many years as senior member of the UN Permanent Forum on Indigenous Issues; and with the UN's adoption in 2007 of the Declaration on the Rights of Indigenous Peoples, indigeneity was embraced as a useful part of the movement's toolbox. As a result, Amazigh activists were able to promote their agenda in sympathetic UN and other international forums and establish links with activists from kindred movements. The increasing international legitimacy of Amazigh indigeneity, and the accompanying recognition of their grievances, now represented something that authoritarian regimes could no longer dismiss out of hand.

A 2017 international conference on "The Rights to Land and Natural Resources in the Countries of Tamazgha (North Africa)," held in the city of El-Hajeb in the Fez-Meknes region, brought the issues facing Morocco's rural Amazigh into sharper focus. The conference highlighted the engagement of the World Amazigh Congress and other pan-Amazigh groups in addition to sympathetic international actors, including the chairwoman of the UN Permanent Forum on Indigenous Issues and her counterpart in the African Union, international human rights officials, and NGO activists. The 200 participants heard numerous testimonies regarding land theft, evictions, illegal exploitation of resources, prohibitions of access to pasture lands, forests, and water sources, exclusion from development projects, and repression of activists. The overriding theme common to these cases was that the state's neoliberal policies of development—themselves a variation on French colonial policies—were being carried out at the local populations' expense, with severe consequences for livelihoods and well-being.

The conference concluded with a series of recommendations. Among other things, states were asked to "constitutionally recognize the inalienable rights of Amazighs to their land, territories and natural resources, including the right to natural resources of the soil and the subsoil"; abolish all French colonial and Moroccan laws that had enabled the expropriation of Amazigh lands and resources; ensure local representation in all relevant decision-making processes and policy making; bring domestic law into line with relevant international law, particularly regarding indigenous peoples; suspend all projects exploiting

Amazigh lands and resources until new agreements regarding their parameters could be reached; make an independent assessment of all damages done; return all confiscated lands and, where such would be impossible, provide equivalent compensation in land or with agreed-upon indemnities; and rehabilitate, compensate, and defend activists who had been repressed by authorities. UN and African Union organs were asked to organize further meetings and fact-finding missions on the subject of defending Amazigh and other indigenous people's rights and to conduct training sessions for local Amazigh representatives regarding their rights to land and natural resources.[46]

One high-profile development project was the massive solar energy power plant being built on land previously owned by an Amazigh tribe just outside the city of Ouarazazate. Although framed as a win-win situation in which allegedly "unusable" land would be transformed into being "usable," thereby generating investment that would create new opportunities for the local population, the actual outcome was quite different. In the words of the anthropologist Sarah Ryser, in this and other cases, "reality shows that access to new opportunities is not usually for local people but rather for (elite) capital accumulation." Although the project, championed by King Mohamed VI, generated little opposition when it was first announced, the lack of genuine consultation with the people most affected by the so-called green grab of land and water resources generated several protests.[47]

To be sure, the often nefarious effects of neoliberal policies on the rural world were not limited to Amazigh areas. And in the case of the *soulaliyate* women's movement, the responses were part of a larger developing culture of protest and a challenge to traditional social practices. Present in both Arabophone and Amazighphone communities from diverse geographical areas, *soulaliyate* tribal women demanded equal rights and shares when the communal lands on which they lived were being privatized or divided up. Overall, their efforts registered several successes, placed the issue on the public agenda, and overlapped with the increasing visibility of issues related to the status of women.[48]

Imider

One of the most noteworthy episodes in this regard centered on Imider ("Imiter"), a collection of seven villages, with a total population 7,000, of the Aït Bouknifen, the largest clan of the Aït Atta tribe, in southeastern Morocco, 130 kilometers northeast of Ouarzazate. From ancient times, the area was known for its rich deposits of silver.[49] In 1969, an extremely profitable mine was established on what had been tribal land. Extraction began in 1978, and the mine was privatized in 1994. La Société Métallurgique d'Imiter is a subsidiary of Managem, the mining branch of the Société Nationale d'Investissement, a massive holding company whose largest shareholder is the royal family. The mine produces 240 tons annually, making it the largest silver mine in Africa and the seventh-largest in the world.[50]

For villagers, the mine was an ongoing symbol of how state authorities and affiliated elites extract enormous wealth from their traditional lands, literally the ground underneath them, while leaving them struggling to eke out an increasingly impoverished existence. Moreover, the mine's operations required an enormous amount of water; according to an Amazigh source, 1,555 cubic meters of water were needed per day, twelve times the village's daily consumption.[51] In 2006, an association devoted to protecting agricultural water rights, including an endangered system of subterranean irrigation canals (*khettaras*), was founded. In essence, the association constituted a counterelite in opposition to co-opted local leaders.[52] Periodic protests, crackdowns, and meetings with authorities repeatedly failed to produce equitable arrangements that would safeguard the villagers' ability to sustain themselves.

Matters came to a head in the summer of 2011. University students returning home following the end of the academic year found that their traditional seasonal jobs working for the mine were no longer available, adding a concrete dimension to the general sense of embitterment and discrimination. Paradoxically, the villagers wanted both the jobs the mine provided and a change in its operation in order to protect them from its harmful effects. As Ramadan approached, the faucets bringing drinking water to the village began running dry, and the water they received had an increasingly foul smell. According to villagers, the damage to people's health, crops, and livestock was great. The young people of the villages decided to act: hiking up 1,400-meter Mount Alban to a water tower serving the mine. There they shut down one of the water pumps to redirect water to the village. Mobilizing sufficient numbers of local inhabitants to protect their achievement, they established a permanent encampment. Organized under the banner "Movement on Road 96 Imider,"[53] they periodically conducted marches along roads in the area. Stone structures decorated gaily with graffiti replaced tents, and some bore inspirational inscriptions from civil and human rights leaders such as Martin Luther King Jr. and Mother Teresa.[54] They also linked their struggle to global environmental concerns, pointing to the ecological degradation caused by widespread use of poisonous substances such as mercury, zinc, and cyanide in the mining operation. Among the global-oriented activities was a special march by hundreds of women organized to mark International Women's Day. Their impressive staying power, and the levels of organizational sophistication and communal solidarity, were documented by the activist Moroccan filmmaker Nadir Bouhmouch. His film *Amussu*, made in collaboration with Imider villagers, won the Grand Prize at a documentary film festival in Agadir in 2019.[55]

The authorities had crushed a smaller protest against the mine in 1996, with one person being killed. This time, their methods were less brutal and more sophisticated, combining both carrot and stick. The mine's operators conducted yearlong negotiations in 2011–2012 with members of the local communal council, supported by a Ministry of Interior representative. An agreement was reached, but according to Moha Tawja, one of the chief activists, it did not live up to the community's expectations and was rejected by a collective petition. The standoff continued.

Village leaders and local representatives of several political parties continued to be offered incentives to cooperate, and the resulting internal divisions gradually weakened the protest, as intended. Thirty protesters were imprisoned for a few months, and three activists, who had been arrested in March 2014, were convicted of disturbing public order and sentenced to three years in prison and fined 60,000 dirhams each. Their crimes included "establishment of a criminal gang," "embezzlement," "assembly without permit," "disorderly conduct," and "premeditated aggression."[56] The protest finally lost steam and ended in September 2019—eight years after it started. Moroccan authorities quickly destroyed the empty encampment. For the time being, though, the water pump that had been shut down in 2011 remained closed.

Social movement studies generally focus on three fields: grievance theories, political opportunity theories, and resource mobilization theories. In the case of Imider, one can locate the grievances that were the trigger and focus of the protest; one can also point to increased opportunities for political expression that evolved during the reign of Mohamed VI, particularly the ferment that characterized Morocco's public sphere during the first half of 2011, when the Imider protests began. They were also part of a larger pattern of protest on socioeconomic issues in small Moroccan towns over the previous decade. The political scientist Koenraad Bogaert has cogently written about this phenomenon, emphasizing the contemporary form of global capitalism, class politics, and the relations of power and exploitation that produce food insecurity, poverty, and inequality.[57] With regard to resource mobilization, however, the picture is more clouded, which perhaps helps us understand why the Amazigh movement has not become a mass movement in the conventional sense. By way of comparison, it may be useful to look at the successful Movement of Rural Landless Workers in Brazil, which has acquired land for more than 300,000 families since it began organizing in 1984. One of its central pillars was official support from the Catholic Church, which provided crucial means of organization of movement activities throughout rural Brazil.[58] No such comparable support from the state-controlled Moroccan religious establishment could possibly exist in the Imider case (or regarding Amazigh grievances in general), as imams in rural areas are controlled by Interior Ministry agents. Indeed, authorities were keen to prevent any linkage between religion and Imider activists. One year, the local imam was banned from conducting a prayer service at the protest mountain encampment during the Muslim Eid al-Adha holiday celebrations; the activists did manage, however, to clandestinely bring in an imam from a remote area to do the job before an audience of 3,000.[59]

Other research on social movements seeks to understand the motivations of the participants, the ways in which they are personally affected and even transformed, and the attendant social dynamics of the protest groups. Why do people join? Are the social ties strong enough to persuade people to join and make it stick? How is it sustained? With what means? What are the internal dynamics within a group of protesters? How much opposition is there? Is there a strategy other than sitting around and waiting for grievances to be addressed?[60]

The personal accounts of three male Imider protesters add depth to the story and partially answer questions posed by social movement theorists. To be sure, their answers to my written questions are themselves part of their struggle to get their story out and thus cannot be accepted uncritically. However, neither can they be dismissed. In general, they displayed a high degree of commitment and determination and described a degree of solidarity among the local population that cut across place of residence, age, and gender. They placed high value on the weekly consultation and decision-making process—a general assembly (*Agraw*) in which anyone could participate and vote, as well as specialized committees.[61] Their families were supportive and participated in the ongoing protest actions and marches. When asked about the "fear factor," one of them expressed defiance. Having reached a stage in the decades-old struggle over the mine in which there was nothing more to lose, he declared: "There's a time to live and a time to die, and it's better to die in a fight for truth than to live lies." Another interviewee, however, acknowledged an awareness of the long arm of the authorities, "which never forgets," and could even reach all the way to the university in Agadir where he studied, creating a climate of fear that inhibited behavior. One of them also emphasized that the initial actions were taken in the context of Morocco's Democracy Spring protests, as well as a similar protest against the national phosphate company in Khouribja, 120 kilometers southeast of Casablanca.[62]

The interviewees displayed an intimate knowledge of local history yet framed their grievances within the larger struggle of the Aït Atta tribal confederation against French colonial conquest and the subsequent expropriation of collective lands, a policy that was continued by the Moroccan state. This is, of course, part of the larger Amazigh narrative. They also reported on a specific ethnic grievance: the decision by authorities to import Arab workers from another region to replace local labor. While one of them emphasized that theirs was a social protest, and not a political movement per se, he acknowledged that, for him, the movement was inseparable from the larger themes of promoting both Amazigh identity and democracy. Another emphasized more directly the ethnic underpinning of his actions, linking the struggle to remain on the land and prosper to the efforts of his forebears across generations.

Discussing the achievements and failures of the protests, Moha Tawja, one of the chief activists, reported on several concrete measures taken by Managem to improve the local road and water infrastructure, in addition to providing an ambulance and some vehicles for school transportation. All of the interviewees were proud of having raised the consciousness and determination of the population, their self-reliance in collecting donations of funds and supplies, and the partial improvement to the state of their water, thanks to the estimated three million tons of water that had been saved. However, they feared that their main achievement—shutting down part of the water supply to the mine in 2011—was not permanent and that Managem would resume pumping in violation of the 2012 agreement. Their lack of trust in the system and lack of faith in the future were palpable. Morocco, one related, was not a state of citizens whose rights were respected. No less disappointing was the sporadic nature of support given by urban-based Amazigh associations, Moroccan human rights associations, and the political classes. Even the various Amazigh associations that existed in neighboring towns and villages kept their distance from the Imider protests due to a combination of fear of authorities' heavy hand and the entrenched localism that inhibited efforts to establish a broader-based movement.[63] Following the end of the protests, a group of activists made their way to the north, seeking a way to Europe, like so many other Moroccan youth.

The Rif—From Abdelkrim to the *Hirak*

In contrast to the numerous but mostly unconnected social protests in the country's central and southern peripheral regions, the northern, predominantly Amazigh, Rif offered a more coherent narrative. Three rounds of large-scale, angry confrontations with state security forces took place between 2011–2017: the third, beginning in late 2016, crystallized the *Hirak al-Shaʿbi*, which the regime tried and failed to contain with its usual tactics before ultimately crushing it in summer 2017. The reasons behind the repeated, interconnected episodes had everything to do with the Rif's historic alienation and marginality from the centers of state power, going back to precolonial times. This was especially acute during the twentieth century, and despite the unprecedented symbolic and material efforts of Mohamed VI to ameliorate the situation, the degree of alienation remained high during the decade leading up to 2011.

For many Rifians, the key figure and reference point in the story, dating back to the 1920s, is Mohamed bin Abdelkrim al-Khattabi. A gifted and charismatic leader of the Aït Waryaghar, the largest of the notoriously fractious and quarrelsome Rifan Berber tribes, he managed, together with his brother M'hamed, to unite them and establish an embryonic state, the Republic of the Rif. Its most celebrated moment was inflicting a catastrophic defeat on advancing Spanish forces at the Battle of Anoual in the summer of 1921, in which more than 10,000 Spanish soldiers died and thousands more were captured. It was the worst defeat inflicted upon any colonial army in the twentieth century up to that point, and news of the battle reverberated throughout the Middle East and beyond. The subsequent guerrilla tactics of both Ho Chi Minh, who was studying in Paris at the time, and Mao Tse-tung are said to have been influenced by Abdelkrim's methods. It would be five years before the combined power of Spain and France would crush the republic and send Abdelkrim into exile, never to return.[64]

Moroccan official history systematically downplayed Abdelkrim's resistance to colonialism, concentrating instead on the subsequent efforts by the younger generation of urban Arabophone elites to establish a national movement. In so doing, it reflected and replicated the distance between Fez (the seat of the sultan and the urban Arabophone religious-minded Fassis who provided much of the backbone for the *makhzen*'s administrative apparatus) and Ajdir (Abdelkrim's headquarters, near the northern coastal town of Al Hoceima). Although the *makhzen* was under the thumb of the French colonial power, fear of Abdelkrim's "uncouth" Rifan Berber tribal warriors helps to explain why the Fassis did not rise up in support of Abdelkrim's rebellion.

Rif–*makhzen* relations following independence were similarly fraught. Tribal unrest in 1958–1959 was crushed by Morocco's newly constituted armed forces, commanded by Crown Prince Hasan,[65] who subsequently refrained from visiting the Rif throughout his thirty-eight-year reign as king. Purposefully kept economically marginalized, the region became Europe's primary source of hashish, as well as a center for smuggling goods and people. In 1984, riots sparked by sharp increases in the price of bread and other staples were dealt with mercilessly, accompanied by harsh rhetoric from Hasan reminding

Rifians that what he had done to them as crown prince could easily be replicated as king.

Well aware of this legacy, Mohamed VI sought to turn the page, beginning with a high-profile motorcade visit through the region just weeks after ascending to the throne. It included a symbolic acknowledgment of Abdelkrim's historic role—including a meeting with his son, who flew in from Cairo for the occasion—and the investment of large sums to promote economic development in the region, centering on the Tanger-Med port complex, the largest in Africa and third-largest in the Mediterranean.[66] By acknowledging the legacy of Abdelkrim, albeit in a supporting role only to his grandfather Sultan Mohamed V, Mohamed VI sought to send a message that Rifian Berbers—and thus Moroccan Imazighen as a whole—were an integral part of the Moroccan fabric. It was a clear strategy: expand the boundaries of collective Moroccan identity while ensuring that the monarchy remained the central axis of the Moroccan polity and society.

The first decade of Mohamed VI's reign was one of significant but controlled political liberalization. One prominent theme of his annual addresses to the nation was his commitment to "advanced regionalization" to enable local and regional governments to better address the needs of their populations. It would be enshrined in the 2011 constitution. For the disputed Western Sahara, the king went even further, proposing in 2007 "broad autonomy" for the region as an alternative to the long-stalled UN plan for a referendum on the territory's future. As it happened, "advanced regionalization" was mostly a slogan, as power remained in the hands of the Ministry of Interior and other central governmental bodies. Moreover, the regions themselves were purposely demarcated so as not to be too closely congruent with Amazigh population concentrations. Similarly, the broad autonomy plan for the Western Sahara also remained merely a slogan, but its political purpose—winning the support of key international actors—was achieved.

Nonetheless, the newly liberalized atmosphere, the king's reconciliation gestures, and his rhetoric of regionalization and autonomy had an effect. During the first decade of the new century, Rifian civil society and local elites became actors within the larger political game, but they also shaped it from the outside. One result was to foster a new regionalist debate. Discussions on possible governance models for the Rif ranged from enhanced regionalization to territorial autonomy. According to Angela Suárez Collado, the illegal Movement for the Autonomy of the Rif (Mouvement pour l'Autonomie du Rif, or MAR), which drew inspiration from Algeria's Kabyle autonomists and support from diaspora groups, was especially popular among Rifian youth. MAR even developed a comprehensive institutional roadmap for Rif regional autonomy, with Tarifit as an official language.[67] To be sure, these discussions and plans remained just that. But their very existence indicated a deep unhappiness with the status quo.

The 2011 and subsequent mass protests demonstrated that the Rif's historically alienated "otherness" remained. As mentioned above, five of the six fatalities registered in Morocco during the 2011 protests occurred in Al Hoceima. Over the course of the next year, Rifian activism was progressively divorced from the national February 20 movement, as well as expanding beyond Al Hoceima to include surrounding regions. What Suárez Collado calls the "localization of contestation" reached a new peak in spring 2012. Protest marches that included prominent displays of Abdelkrim's Rifian Republic flag expanded in tandem with harsh crackdowns by security forces.[68] As was the case in the 2001 Black Spring confrontations in Kabylie, the gendarmerie stationed in the area were viewed as a foreign occupier.

Shared memory, said Anthony Smith, is as essential to the survival of a collective cultural identity as is a sense of a common destiny.[69] For Rifian Amazigh, the emphasis and elaboration on the history and legacy of Abdelkrim has become especially important in the increasingly contested and highly charged environment that characterizes Morocco in the twenty-first century. Of necessity, this emphasis ignores certain aspects of his legacy (e.g., his rejection of popular religious practices in favor of Islamic reform). A colorful graphic novel for children titled *The Amir, Ibn Abdelkrim*, published in Arabic, French, and Dutch (with an eye to the large Moroccan Amazigh, mainly Rifian, diaspora in the Netherlands),[70] was especially instructive, owing to the background of its author. Mohammed Nadrani spent eight and a half years in prison for his militant Marxist opposition to the regime during the dark "Years of Lead,"[71] a period during the 1970s and 1980s when political dissidents and associated family members were tortured and imprisoned. Nadrani learned to draw during his years of isolation, using a piece of charcoal to sketch on the floor of his cell. His decision to write the book, he explained, came from a desire to recover a history that had been erased and denied by authorities. "We have to revive this history," he said, "in order to safeguard the memory of our people."[72]

On October 28, 2016, Mohcen Fikri, a thirty-one-year-old fishmonger in Al Hoceima, was crushed to death in a garbage truck compactor. Desperate to retrieve his wares (100 kilograms of swordfish) that had been confiscated and thrown into the back by policemen,[73] he jumped into the truck to retrieve them and died after someone ordered the driver to "grind him" (*t'hanmu*).[74] The incident was captured in the gathering darkness by a cell-phone camera and went viral, touching off widespread protests in the Rif and beyond. Demands to bring the perpetrators to justice were combined with condemnations of the regime's *hogra* ("contempt") toward the region. In the city of Nador, the demonstrators chanted "No reconciliation with the *Makhzen* as injustice and *hogra* continue!" while in Tangier one protest sign read "From the Years of Lead to the Years of Grinding . . . What has changed???"⁷⁵

The collective anger and alienation were encapsulated in an angry declaration that very first night by Nasser Zafzafi, who would become the acknowledged leader of the protests:

> We do not have problems with the law, but with the application of the law. This is not the first crime committed in the Rif region and especially in Al Hoceima. Five of our martyred brothers were tortured to death and thrown into a bank; until today no law has been applied. Have the culprits, police officers, been tried? I personally did not see anything. Give us concrete guarantees that we are in a state of law, not in a state of *bbak sahbi* [lit., "your father is my friend"].⁷⁶

The incident recalled Mohamed Bouazizi's death six years earlier in Tunisia. Fearing a similar scenario, the minister of the Interior hastened to Al Hoceima to offer condolences to Fikri's family, conveyed the king's distress with what had happened, and promised a thorough investigation to prevent any further such occurrences. Eleven persons, including security agents and local fisheries officials, were arrested. Seven were eventually convicted, receiving prison sentences ranging from five to eight months; several Interior Ministry–related officials were demoted or transferred to other posts. The failure to probe deeper into the networks that controlled the gathering and distribution of valuable banned fish was disappointing to the activists, to say the least. The fact that the cabinet minister responsible for fisheries was Aziz Akhannouch, a close associate of the king and one of the richest men in the country, was not lost on them.⁷⁷

Although protests took place throughout the country, the regime's fears of a Bouazizi-like scenario were not realized. But in the Rif, the energy unleashed by Fikri's death did not dissipate, and large-scale protests continued for the rest of the year and into the spring of 2017. While the demands for justice, dignity, and rooting out corruption were not separatist, they were underpinned by the region's long history of confrontation and alienation with the state. This ethno-territorial dimension was made clear by references to past abuses and the prominence of the flag of Abdelkrim's Rifian Republic at the demonstrations, alongside the pan-Amazigh flag and an occasional Moroccan flag. On one occasion, an effort to mark the anniversary of Abdelkrim's death (February 6, 1963) was blocked by police, resulting in violent clashes, beatings, and arrests.

As protests continued, they acquired a name—*Hirak al-Sha`bi*—and a leader emerged: the same Nasser Zafzafi who had spoken so passionately on the night of the murder. Born in 1979, his great-grandfather had served as Interior minister in Abdelkrim's government, and his father had been an activist in a leftist party, the National Union of Popular Forces. Zafzafi himself was widely dubbed the *Amghar* ("chief," or "sage" in Tamazight). Zafzafi's condemnation of "Arabizing colonialism," a standard trope of the Amazigh movement, provided additional evidence of the ethnic dimension of the protests. His message was angry, unadorned, and populist, with a dash of religious rhetoric as well. The latter feature made secular Amazigh intellectuals uneasy, and Zafzafi, in turn, harshly attacked one of the leading ones, Ahmed Assid, calling him a puppet of the state. From the opposite direction, he did not hesitate to respond to criticism by a prominent Salafi imam in Tangier who had spent eight years in prison in connection with the 2003 Casablanca bombings, calling him the "Palace preacher."[78]

In January, the *Hirak* leadership produced a list of twenty-one demands to the authorities. They included a major upgrade for the region's health infrastructure, including the ability to treat cancer patients; the establishment of a multidisciplinary university; dropping all legal actions against cannabis growers; reforming the educational system, particularly for the benefit of girls and young women; and the demilitarization of the Rif.[79] The demilitarization demand was unique to the Rif, dating back to the initial uprising following independence: a royal *dahir* in 1958 had decreed Al Hoceima to be a military zone. Although it had been officially frozen for all intents and purposes, the possibility of its reimposition was always on the minds of activists. A government spokesman declared on May 25, 2017, that there was no legal basis or justification for speaking of the region as a military zone; three days earlier, Interior Minister Abdelouafi Laftit led a delegation to Al Hoceima to "speed up a development program."[80]

However, regional political elites failed to play the necessary role of mediating between the *makhzen* and the *Hirak*.[81] And alongside their sympathetic messages, authorities were increasingly taking the rhetorical offensive to delegitimize the *Hirak*. Religious leaders condemned the protests as promoting *fitna* ("sedition," "civil strife"), a word that resonated deeply in traditional Islamic culture. One pro-Palace, anti-Rifian member of parliament reminded her social media audience that King Hasan II had once referred to an earlier iteration of Rifian protesters as "scumbags" (*awbach*).[82] Charges of separatism and acceptance of foreign support (from Algeria) were leveled against Zafzafi, which he denied.[83] They also reinforced his determination to continue on the path of what one scholar called "unruly politics," in which a "continuity of action" maintained mass mobilization. Two of its performative aspects were *chen-ten* (i.e., beating pots at demonstrations) and Zafzafi's delivering an oath at each mass gathering:

> I swear by Allah the very high and the most powerful (three times);
> That we will not betray;
> That we will not bargain;
> That we will not sell; Our cause;
> Even if it costs us our lives; Long live the Rif (three times);
> Let no one live who betrays him (three times).[84]

The breaking point came on May 26, when Zafzafi disrupted an imam's officially dictated Friday prayer sermon at an Al Hoceima mosque, denouncing him for suggesting that the *Hirak* was engaging in *fitna*. "What does *fitna* mean when our people are jobless and have nothing to eat?" he asked. "They want the Rif to kneel down, they want the Gulf puppets to come and rape our women, rape our children. I am asking you, do the mosques belong to Allah or to the *makhzen*?"[85] His harangue, tinged with Islamic populism, was accompanied by chants of "Allahu Akbar!" by his supporters. Zafzafi then left the mosque, mounted the rooftop of his house, and resumed his speech before a crowd of supporters gathered below. The scene was captured on a cell-phone video and widely viewed on social media.[86]

In taking the *Hirak* directly into the mosque, he had crossed the line and gave authorities the excuse that they were looking for. This may have even been their intention.[87] Zafzafi was arrested and spirited away to Casablanca, where he was tortured, including sexually, and held incognito for ten days. Scores of other activists were arrested as well, including the "Voice of the Rif," the twenty-three-year-old singer Silya Ziani.[88] The number of detainees, according to one calculation, eventually reached 798,[89] as the regime sought to decapitate the *Hirak*. The crackdown sparked another wave of protests in the Rif and several other Moroccan cities. The largest—jointly organized in Rabat by the Islamist al-`Adl wal-Ihsan and left-wing and secular groups—including members of the February 20 leadership, drew 50,000 demonstrators.[90] International and domestic human rights groups condemned the crackdown, documenting the abusive treatment of detainees,[91] and Kabylian activists in the cities of Tizi Ouzou and Béjaïa organized solidarity protests.[92] At one demonstration, a protester was killed after being hit by a tear gas canister. Notably, Hamid El Mahdaoui, the director of an important news website and a *Hirak* sympathizer, was arrested and sentenced to three years in prison. Lawyers affiliated with Azetta Amazigh, an organization that worked to advance Amazigh interests within the legal system, quickly stepped in to defend the detainees. However, the die had been cast. Zafzafi and three associates—Nabil Ahmjiq, Ouassim Boustati, and Samir Ighid—were sentenced in July 2018 to twenty years in prison for conspiring to undermine state security; several other senior *Hirak* members received lengthy sentences (five to fifteen years) as well. Scores of others received shorter prison terms. A year later, an appeals court upheld the sentences of fifty-four of them, including Zafzafi. By the summer of 2020, most of those convicted had either served their time or received royal pardons. One prominent *Hirak* leader, Mohamed El Mejjaoui, who had been serving a five-year sentence, was among those pardoned in August 2020. In May 2021, the king pardoned an additional seventeen *Hirak* activists, including Ouassim Boustati. But Zafzafi, Ahmjiq, Ighid, and seven others remained behind bars.

Associational Activism

Social activism and militancy were not the exclusive prerogative of Amazigh activists in the periphery. In fact, the proliferation of Amazigh associations began to blur the center-periphery distinction. Ninety-seven belonged to the National Federation of Amazigh Associations (FNAA), whose coordinator was the Rabat lawyer Ahmed Arrehmouch. In addition to promoting Amazigh culture, including by influencing decision makers, FNAA's mission was to "strengthen internal democracy within member associations, and encourage and support the youth to reinforce their presence and role in the struggle for democracy in general and for the Amazigh culture in particular."[93] Arrehmouch was also the head of Azetta Amazigh. Its twenty-one offices around the country concentrated on documenting and publicizing authorities' detrimental actions and inactions and petitioning for the redress of citizenship grievances according to existing Moroccan law. These complaints, highlighted in a 2013 report, included: continuing difficulties faced by parents seeking to register their newborn children with Amazigh first names; the refusal to allow the use of Tamazight in legal proceedings; arrests of Amazigh students allegedly because of their political opinions; the violation of land and water rights of Amazigh communities; continued discrimination against the Amazigh language in state media organs and the audio-visual field; and the limited allocation of resources devoted to teaching Tamazight in the school system.[94] This last point was especially vexing. According to the FNAA, the number of students learning Tamazight between 2012–2017 declined from 517,000 to 412,000 (less than 10 percent of all those enrolled in primary school and less than 6 percent if including secondary-school students), and the number of education inspectors dropped precipitously, from eighty to fifteen. Moreover, the content of the programs remained weak. The FNAA and Azetta regularly gave detailed information to UN bodies evaluating Morocco's human rights practices, which in turn repeatedly criticized Morocco for its failures to ameliorate Amazigh complaints.[95]

Constitutionalizing Amazighité and Tamazight—Then What?

The 2011 constitution's recognition of Amazighité as an integral part of Morocco's national identity, and the concomitant upgrading of Tamazight to be an official language of the state, alongside Arabic, was a historic achievement for the modern Amazigh identity movement, the culmination of a half-century of uphill struggle. It was also the outcome of an Amazigh-friendly policy pursued by King Mohamed since assuming office twelve years earlier. The official recognition of Tamazight had ramifications throughout the region as well, serving as a model for Amazigh activists and establishing a norm that ruling elites could no longer ignore. To be sure, as already noted, the final version of the text was watered down, to the disappointment of activists, and the confirming referendum was boycotted by Amazigh militants. Nonetheless, the symbolic value was enormous.

The operative question, of course, was how to turn the text into a sociopolitical reality. The new constitution required the establishment of such a mechanism: the passage of an Organic Law that would "define the process of implementation of the official character of this language, as well as the modalities of its integration into teaching and into the priority domains of public life, so that it may be permitted in time to fulfill its function as an official language."[96] In the best of cases, the task would be daunting; in actuality, neither the state authorities nor the coalition governments led by the Islamist PJD saw any urgency in advancing the law. Thus, the drafting of necessary legislation proceeded at a snail's pace—and without the input of Amazigh civil society groups.

Five years passed before a completed draft of the law began to circulate. Amazigh associations immediately criticized it and asked for the king's intervention. The head of Morocco's Royal Institute of Amazigh Culture, Ahmed Boukous, noted that the proposed law had failed to make teaching Tamazight mandatory in secondary schools or commit to supporting Amazigh language departments in higher education institutions.[97] Three more years would pass before the law was finally adopted and published in the *Official Gazette*, bringing it into force. Its final passage may have been facilitated by the fact that

Abdelilah Benkirane, the bête noire of the Amazigh movement, had been forced out of the prime minister's office in 2017 by the Palace, to be replaced by the more sympathetic Saad Eddine El Othmani.

What exactly did the Organic Law entail? It was essentially a roadmap that addressed core complaints tendered by Amazigh associations to authorities and UN bodies. Various target goals were to be implemented gradually, within specified time frames. Many were required to be accomplished within five years: the introduction of Tamazight into most levels of the educational system; the employment of regional linguistic particularities and Arabic to assist this at the primary-school level; integrating Tamazight into informal education and literacy programs; integrating it into parliamentary proceedings, including translation services, and broadcasting them in the Amazigh-language media; upgrading the presence of Tamazight in all audio-visual media; providing services in Tamazight in public institutions and call centers, with trained personnel; and adding Tamazight-language signs to all public facilities, as well as roads, transportation services, gas stations, and airports. The ten-year time frame included the introduction of Tamazight at the higher levels of secondary-school education; its inclusion in news websites of government and public institutions; its incorporation into human resources programs; the creation of specialized research units in higher education institutions; adding Tamazight to all official personal documents (e.g., identity cards, passports, driver's licenses, and marriage certificates) and to bank notes, stamps, and coins; and the integration of Tamazight into the field of litigation, including guarantees of the right to its use at all stages, from initial investigation to court judgments. The state was given up to fifteen years to publish Tamazight-language laws and regulations in the *Official Gazette* and to make other official documents available in Tamazight as well.

Demonstrating a seriousness of intent, the law obligated ministries, as well as educational and other relevant institutions, to formulate plans for implementation within six months with the assistance of the National Council of Moroccan Languages and Culture. A permanent ministerial committee, chaired by the prime minister, was entrusted with the tasks of monitoring and evaluating the law's implementation.[98]

The proof, of course, would be in the pudding. And there was cause for skepticism. Almost before the ink dried, a draft law mandating the issuance of a new biometric ID card for all Moroccan citizens that did not include Tamazight was advanced. Notwithstanding the fierce objections of Amazigh associations, the lower house of parliament passed the bill on July 20, 2020, with officials citing "technical issues" that prevented Tamazight's inclusion alongside

Arabic and French.⁹⁹ More generally, Amazigh activists deemed the timeline for the law's implementation to be far too lengthy and a sign of a lack of commitment. Arrehmouch, for example, thought that universalizing the teaching of Tamazight could be done in one year, assuming there was the political will to do so.¹⁰⁰

How could such political will be created? Efforts more than a decade earlier by the veteran Amazigh militant Ahmed Adghirni to establish the Moroccan Amazigh Democratic Party (Parti Démocrate Amazigh Marocain, or PDAM) had been blocked repeatedly by authorities, on the ground that Moroccan law forbade explicitly ethnic or religious parties. In any case, the idea was seen by many Amazigh movement people as divisive and counterproductive. In 2016, several activists, headed by Mustapha Berhouchi, took steps to establish the Tamunt ("Unity") Party, which would be open to all Moroccans and be dedicated to promoting "the values of justice, freedom, democracy, enlightenment and social justice." However, the Ministry of Interior placed obstacles in its path, and eventually banned it, on the same ground used a decade earlier against PDAM.¹⁰¹

For Arrehmouch and like-minded activists, the answer to the lack of political will was to move beyond the cultural–linguistic–identity sphere of action and open up a new front by engaging directly with political parties and state institutions. This approach was formulated in early 2020 by the Plateforme pour le Front d'Action Politique Amazigh (Inir n Tigawt Tasrtant Tamazight, or NISA). The goal was to "enlarge the space of debate" within Moroccan state institutions and thereby generate a fundamental rethinking about Moroccan identity. The desired result would be "a new social contract that would link the past of the homeland with its present by restoring its identity and the authenticity of its Amazigh and African civilizational roots in order to explore a new Morocco based on pluralism and diversity within the framework of unity ... rejecting the ideologies of exclusion and fanaticism, of all kinds." The task was urgent. In fact, it was a case of now or never. Seeking to implement their strategy, NISA leaders conducted several rounds of meetings with four centrist, pro-Palace political parties: Parti de l'Authenticité et de la Modernité (PAM), Rassemblement National des Indépendants (RNI), Mouvement Populaire (MP), and Parti du Progrès et du Socialisme (PPS). They tendered several requests: modifying the parties' political orientations and platforms in favor of the Amazigh movement; including Amazigh militants on their electoral lists; and integrating members of NISA into party bureaus.¹⁰² By the end of the year, formal agreements to work together with the RNI and MP had been concluded.¹⁰³

Conclusion

The decade covering 2011–2020 was packed with developments affecting Morocco's large and diverse Amazigh community in myriad ways. From the February 20 movement and the propagation of a new constitution that gave official status to Tamazight and Amazigh identity; to the grassroots protests and associational activities on behalf of Amazigh social, economic, and cultural rights; to the Rifian *Hirak* and the struggle over the Organic Law—the Amazigh factor was now an integral part of Morocco's increasingly contested public sphere. It was also an increasingly legitimate part of the country's cultural life. At the same time, the *makhzen* remained in control of the parliamentary political sphere and the economy. F20 had dissipated, local grievances and protest actions remained just that, the *Hirak* had been crushed, and internal divisions over tactics and strategy hampered the ability of the Amazigh movement to advance its agenda.

The dominant mood in the Moroccan Amazigh current at the end of this period was one of pessimism, even malaise. Having finally achieved constitutional recognition of the Amazigh language and culture after decades of efforts, the difficulties of implementation became obvious. Even the passage of the Organic Law, eight years after it had been constitutionally mandated, left a sour taste. The lengthy time frame for implementing its provisions portended the continuation of an underlying status quo that, in itself, posed a threat to the survival of the Amazigh language and culture. The downsizing of IRCAM, through its incorporation into a new and larger body, the National Council of Languages and Culture, seemed to symbolize the decline of the Amazigh project, even for critics who saw it mainly as another tool of the *makhzen*, that is to say, "an instrument of representation rather than a sincere attempt to integrate the language and people into society."[104] The crushing of the *Hirak* served as a reminder of the *makhzen*'s willingness and ability to defend that status quo.

The question, then, was What now? Writing some years earlier, Ahmed Boukous detailed the challenges and possible paths of action facing the Amazigh movement in Morocco. The movement's legitimacy, he said, needed to be claimed on two complementary bases: the historic one, based on Amazigh indigeneity, and the modern one, based on linguistic and cultural rights, as defined by international human rights law. On one side of the fence stood the opponents to Amazigh legitimacy, coming from both the Arab-Islamist perspective that viewed Amazighité as undermining the supremacy of Islam and the Arabic language, and the Westernized one that viewed it as "an anachronistic residue that hinders Morocco from getting access to Modernity." On the other side stood two wings of the Amazigh current: one that focused exclusively on cultural and linguistic issues, and the other, newer one that was more directly political, working simultaneously for "the officialization and the institutionalization of the language and culture, and the socio-economic development of the Amazigh regions within a territorial autonomy." Promoting linguistic and cultural diversity, and particularly a policy of "positive discrimination in favor of the minorized languages and cultures," Boukous said, "could enable them to escape the inevitability of death." No less important was the ability of the Amazigh movement to become more modern (i.e., less communitarian and more of a social movement). This, in turn, required an autonomous leadership that could generate "new mobilizing symbols transcending mechanical solidarity and traditional loyalties."[105]

However, he said that the possibilities of achieving the desired territorial autonomy were severely constrained by the details of the king's "advanced regionalization" project, which did not provide the Amazigh with the "spatial environment suitable for the conditions for sustainability." Boukous's analysis, much like Arrehmouch's, focused on the importance of "effective political will." "Without real commitment from the State and without the consensus of all parties involved in the linguistic and cultural issue," he said, "initiatives to revitalize [the] Amazigh can only be a cautery on a wooden leg or slogans without substance."[106]

In what was perhaps symbolic of the Amazigh current's lack of direction, fall 2020 saw the passing of two of its most senior figures, representing two contrasting perspectives, life experiences, and strategy approaches on how to protect and advance Amazighité: ninety-nine-year-old Mahjoubi Aherdan and seventy-three-year-old Ahmed Adghirni. Aherdan cofounded the Mouvement Populaire in 1957, a loyal promonarchy party representing the interests of rural Berber notables and their followers, as a counterweight to the hegemony-seeking Arab–Islamic Istiqlal Party, and held numerous cabinet positions in subsequent decades. Proud of his Amazigh heritage, this politician/poet/painter was, in the words of the Moroccan Amazigh scholar Moha Ennaji, "a true symbol of cultural diversity and an emblematic figure of the Moroccan culture."[107] Similar praise was tendered by the veteran Kabylian activist-politician Saïd Sadi.[108] In contrast to Aherdan's tight embrace of the monarchy and conservative approach to the place of Amazigh language and culture in modern Morocco, Adghirni ("Dda Hmad" to his followers)[109] was a militant lawyer/activist/author who defended generations of Amazigh detainees, including most recently the detained *Hirak* leadership; was one of the cofounders of the World Amazigh Congress; and had attempted to found an explicitly Amazigh political party, only to have it banned by authorities.

As in Algeria, the COVID-19 crisis caused a temporary halt to political and cultural life in Morocco. Whether or not the timeout was being used wisely by the Amazigh current's various elements in thinking and planning for the future remains to be seen. As for the Rif, one knowledgeable scholar emphasized the importance in Rifian culture of *karama* ("honor," "dignity") and the price of blood, suggesting that people there were licking their wounds while waiting for the next round of confrontation—which could well be more violent than the last one.[110]

Conclusion

The Amazigh question, in all of its diversity, was an integral part of North Africa's increasingly contested politics during the Arab Spring and the decade that followed. Building on its earlier efforts, the Amazigh movement's emphasis shifted from being primarily ethnocultural to more explicitly political and socioeconomic. It did so while further refining its rejection of the hegemonic postcolonial narratives that consigned Amazigh communities to subordinate status. As surviving regimes struggled to recover their fraying legitimacy, and as new ones sought to guarantee power, they could no longer ignore Amazigh demands; the strategies ranged from partial acknowledgment and co-optation to overt repression.

The contexts and dynamics of Amazigh-state relations varied from country to country. Nonetheless, they were characterized by several common themes and focal points, confirming anew that the Amazigh issue transcended state boundaries. In the constitutional sphere, Morocco was compelled to recognize Tamazight as an official language of the state, and the Amazigh component of Moroccan national identity, in 2011. And at the end of the decade, it finally adopted a constitutionally mandated Organic Law laying out the stages of implementation of bringing Tamazight into all phases of Moroccan life. In 2016, Algeria followed Morocco's lead in giving official status to Tamazight, after having long resisted doing so. In Libya, intensive Amazigh efforts to achieve similar recognition fell short, although the 2017 draft constitution formally acknowledged the cultural and linguistic rights of Libya's minorities and defined them as part of the country's heritage and as a "common asset" to all Libyans. Tunisia's new constitution, by contrast, did not address Amazigh demands, despite efforts by activists and sympathetic liberal supporters.

A second common theme was the increasing importance of territory. Kabyles have always been Algeria's most well-defined "Other" and the most modern *ethnie*-like of all Amazigh communities. By the middle of the decade, the notion of autonomy had touched a respondent chord among many of them, who now openly defied the regime. The discourse of Kabyle ethnonationalism had been sharpened and expanded, and the concept of self-determination—whether within a federal and consociational democratic Algeria or through complete independence—was now part of the Kabyle political lexicon. These ideas also filtered into the highly charged situation in the Mzab, where the regime sought to crush a nascent autonomy movement, resulting in the incarceration and death of its head. In Libya, the sudden disappearance of a repressive centralized state and the fractured nature of post-Qaddafi Libya enabled Libyan Amazigh to establish institutions of their own and achieve a measure of agency in their core territories. "Autonomy" and "self-determination" entered into their lexicon as well, even if their meanings remained vague and organically linked to the Libyan state and nation as a whole. Among the Tuareg of Mali, the Azawad moment of independence was unprecedented but ephemeral. However, the underlying conditions that triggered the secession experiment remain extant. As for Morocco, the teaching of Tamazight in Moroccan schools suffered from major deficiencies, and the need for genuine regionalization—one that would enable Amazigh populations in peripheral regions to exert real agency within a democratizing regime—was acute. In its absence, the Rifian *Hirak* protests were impressive in scope, to the point where the regime detected, or perhaps manufactured, a whiff of secession and ultimately crushed it.

A third broad theme was the movement's increasing emphasis on the socioeconomic marginalization, discrimination, and willful neglect toward Amazigh populations in peripheral regions by state authorities. Amazigh associations highlighted state policies, often based on colonial laws, that expropriated collective lands and natural resources, while also pointing to the absence of proper basic infrastructure. Examples abounded in Morocco, from the Imider protests against the poisoning of their water supply by the Managem silver mine and the Zagora "thirst protests" to Rifian complaints of systemic neglect. Much of the tension in the Mzab stemmed from the Algerian state's preferential treatment given to Arab tribes on land questions at the expense of Mzabi Imazighen. Libyan and Tunisian Imazighen had suffered from similar treatment before 2011, and the grievances were still extant. Across the board, Amazigh activists now framed their demands and insistence on their rights as commensurate with their status as the indigenous people of their lands, in line with the 2007 UN Declaration on the Rights of Indigenous Peoples.

A fourth common theme was the difficulty in building durable alliances with other elements in society that would help the Amazigh advance toward their fundamental goals of refashioning the fundamentals of their countries' national identities. Part of the failure of the Azawad project was the gap between the stated intent of building a multiethnic democracy and the understandable perception by Songhay, Fulani, and Arab populations that Azawad was primarily a Tuareg project. Moreover, the repeated Tuareg rebellions against the Malian central government had left a legacy of bad blood and mistrust that was impossible to overcome. The military contribution of Libya's Imazighen to the overthrow of Muammar Qaddafi gave them a measure of legitimacy in their efforts to influence the Tripoli-based government's policies. So did their participation in 2020 in repulsing the forces of General Khalid Haftar. But the strong Islamist influences in both Tripoli and Benghazi, and the correspondingly weak liberal current, limited the possibilities for finding a strategic partner. In Tunisia, the liberal current was stronger, and the unattractiveness of Arab nationalist ideas for Tunisians not affiliated with the Islamist current offered potential for advancing the Amazigh agenda (in combination with other elements). However, Tunisian secular liberals had more pressing matters to deal with, and the established political parties showed scant interest. Of course, the strong Islamist movement in Tunisia viewed the Amazigh movement with opprobrium, as did its counterparts throughout the region.

In Morocco, Amazigh participation in the February 20 movement was considerable, but the alliances forged there do not seem to have been durable. The Palace had always seen the Amazigh movement as a useful tool to help counterbalance its Islamists, but it retained preponderant control over political life, leaving the political parties competing for patronage. An initiative by Ahmed Arrehmouch and like-minded activists to work directly with several political parties to advance the Amazigh agenda produced an agreement with two of the established parties at the end of 2020; whether or not it will have a significant impact remains to be seen. As for the *Hirak*, the state was quick to paint it with a secessionist brush, drawing on anti-Rifian tropes, as well as pushing the *fitna* button, suggesting that the *Hirak* was anti-Islamic. The fact that the officially banned but barely tolerated Islamist al-'Adl wal-Ihsan movement condemned the crackdown against the *Hirak* probably played into the *makhzen*'s hands, confirming the reluctance of other sections of Moroccan society to be associated with the Rifian *Hirak*.

In Algeria, the 2019 *Hirak* suggested new possibilities. Kabyles were prominent in the protests, as was the Amazigh flag. Similar to the Moroccan regime's actions against the Rifian *Hirak*, the Algerian *pouvoir* sought to paint the Amazigh as being antinational and separatist. It was a transparent and unpersuasive move. At the same time, *Hirak* leaders refrained from substantive discussion about a federal framework for a future Second Republic, which would potentially provide Kabyles with a measure of control over their own territory and destiny.

A fifth theme was the increased impact of pan-Amazigh, diaspora-based organizations and communities in bringing the Amazigh agenda to the attention of the international community, particularly UN forums and international NGOs. Social media was an increasingly important tool for mobilizing on behalf of the Amazigh cause, helping to sharpen the collective consciousness of Amazigh in both the homeland and the diaspora. In fact, the distinction often seemed increasingly blurred. This transnational sharpening was also accompanied by more specific ones—Kabyle, Rifian, Libyan, and so on.

The COVID-19 pandemic conferred the Algerian *pouvoir* with an important advantage, bringing a halt to the yearlong *Hirak* protests. In Morocco, too, COVID-19 cast a shadow over political life, reinforcing the uncertainty, and even malaise, that were gripping the Amazigh current. In Libya, the repulsing of Haftar's militia in spring 2020, and the involvement of rival outside countries, pointed to a new equilibrium and continued fractured state. In turn, this suggested that Libyan Amazigh might continue to have the time and space to consolidate and further advance an agenda within their main population areas. In Mali, a military coup in August 2020 was a reminder of the difficulties there in fashioning a stable and consensual polity. The consequences for its Tuareg population remain to be seen.

In the midst of the pandemic, the Amazigh universe was rocked by the death on May 2, 2020, of seventy-year-old Idir (Hamid Cheriet) from pulmonary fibrosis. More than any other artist—perhaps more than any other individual, period—Idir was the beloved symbol of the Amazigh identity movement after having burst on the scene in the early 1970s. His continued exalted status was demonstrated in recent years by his joint performances of "A Vava Inouva" with two of the new voices of Amazigh pride and identity, Libya's Dania Ben Sassi and the Rif's Silya Ziani.

The question of where he would be buried was immediately raised, even though a large funeral was impossible because of pandemic restrictions. Although many Kabyles hoped that he would be interred in his native village of Aït Lahcine in Tizi Ouzou Province, the family announced that Idir had decided to be buried in Paris, where he had lived since the mid-1970s, for the sake of his children, who resided there. For at least one Kabyle militant, the decision was another bitter confirmation of the "curse of exile," for both the living and the dead, that haunts the Kabyles.[1]

But the moving eulogies and swift proliferation of musical homages also pointed to Idir's enduring legacy as an Amazigh cultural icon and symbol, one whose message of pride in one's culture and openness to the values of humanism and mutual tolerance was simultaneously Amazigh and universal. Amid all of the uncertainty and possibilities regarding the Amazigh future, this would surely be comforting to his legions of devotees that crossed generations, as well as to the Amazigh movement in all of its diversity.

Notes

Introduction

1. Nazih N. Ayubi, *Over-stating the Arab State* (London: I. B. Tauris, 1995). "*Sulta*," lit., the "Official Authority" or "Sovereign Power."

2. Marc Lynch, "Obama's 'Arab Spring'?," *Foreign Policy*, January 6, 2011, https://foreignpolicy.com/2011/01/06/obamas-arab-spring. He later wrote that it was a term that "I may have unintentionally coined." Marc Lynch, *The Arab Uprising: The Unfinished Revolutions of the New Middle East* (New York: PublicAffairs, 2012), 9.

3. Marc Lynch, *Voices of the New Arab Public: Iraq, Al-Jazeera and Middle East Politics Today* (New York: Columbia University Press, 2006); and Lynch, *The Arab Uprising*, 8.

4. Fawaz A. Gerges, *The Rise and Fall of Al-Qaeda* (New York: Oxford University Press, 2011).

5. Samuel P. Huntington, *The Third Wave: Democratization in the Late Twentieth Century* (Norman: Oklahoma University Press, 1991).

6. Amr Hamzawy, "Islamists Re-awaken Religious Politics," *Al-Ahram Weekly*, January 3, 2006, https://carnegieendowment.org/publications/index.cfm?fa=view&id=17833.

7. See, e.g., Daniel L. Byman, "After the Hope of the Arab Spring, the Chill of an Arab Winter," Brookings Institute, December 4, 2011, www.brookings.edu/opinions/after-the-hope-of-the-arab-spring-the-chill-of-an-arab-winter; Raphael Israeli, *From Arab Spring to Islamic Winter* (New Brunswick, NJ: Transaction Publishers, 2013).

8. Hussein Agha and Robert Malley, "The Arab Counterrevolution," *New York Review of Books*, September 29, 2011, www.nybooks.com/articles/2011/09/29/arab-counterrevolution; Lynch, *The Arab Uprising*, 131–159.

9. This order is commonly referred to as "Sykes-Picot," the 1916 British-French agreement, later joined by Russia, to partition the remaining territories of the Ottoman Empire. In fact, the postwar order was definitively fashioned by the San Remo conference in April 1920.

10. Steven J. King and Abdeslam M. Maghraoui, *The Lure of Authoritarianism: The Maghreb after the Arab Spring* (Bloomington: Indiana University Press, 2019).

11. Marwan Muasher, "Is This the Arab Spring 2.0?," Carnegie Endowment for International Peace, October 30, 2019, https://carnegieendowment.org/2019/10/30/is-this-arab-spring-2.0-pub-80220; Sarah J. Feuer and Carmit Valensi, "Arab Spring 2.0? Making Sense of the Protests Sweeping the Region," INSS Insight No. 1235, December 1, 2019, www.inss.org.il/publication/arab-spring-2-0-making-sense-of-the-protests-sweeping-the-region.

12. Larbi Sadiki and Layla Saleh, "The Arab Spring Is Not Lost: Moral Protest as the Embodiment of a New Politics," in *The Routledge Handbook to the Middle East and North African State and States System*, Raymond Hinnebusch and Jasmine Gani (eds.) (Abingdon, UK: Routledge, 2019), 178.

13. Sadiki and Saleh, "The Arab Spring Is Not Lost," 179–180.

14. Frederic Volpi, *Revolution and Authoritarianism in North Africa* (Oxford: Oxford University Press, 2017), published to Oxford Scholarship Online, August 2017, DOI:10.1093/oso/9780190642921.001.0001.

15. Amazigh (a neologism meaning "free/noble man"; pl. Imazighen) is "an ethnonym well attested to since antiquity" and has been applied in a variety of contexts, most notably in recent centuries right up until present day to Middle Atlas Berbers, whose dialect is Tamazight. S. Chaker, "Amaziɣ (le/un Berbère)," *Encyclopédie berbère* [En ligne], 4, 1986, document A183, mis en ligne le 01 décembre 2012, consulté le 24 décembre 2020, http://journals.openedition.org/encyclopedieberbere/2465, DOI:https://doi.org/10.4000/encyclopedieberbere.2465. Following the initial impetus from Kabylia in 1945–1950, "Amazigh" has come to be applied to all of the various ethnolinguistic subgroups that make up the Amazigh milieu and has increasingly supplanted the term "Berber," which has a negative connotation ("barbarian," derived from ancient Greek and Latin). I use the terms interchangeably, without prejudice. For a more detailed discussion, see Paul A. Silverstein, "The Amazigh Movement in a Changing North Africa," in *Social Currents in North Africa: Culture and Governance After the Arab Spring*, Osama Abi-Mershed (ed.) (Oxford: Oxford University Press, 2018), 74, n.3.

16. The history of the movement is enumerated in Bruce Maddy-Weitzman, *The Berber Identity Movement and the Challenge to North African States* (Austin: University of Texas Press, 2011).

17. Abdeslam M. Maghraoui, "Introduction: The Lure of Authoritarianism," in King and Maghraoui, *The Lure of Authoritarianism*, 5–6.

18. Paul S. Rowe, "Introduction: Reclaiming 'Minorities' in the Middle East," in *The Routledge Handbook of Minorities in the Middle East*, Paul S. Rowe (ed.) (Abingdon, UK: Routledge, 2018), 6.

19. See, e.g., B. Arredi et al., "A Predominantly Neolithic Origin for Y-Chromosomal DNA Variation in North Africa," *American Journal of Human Genetics* 75(2) (August 2004): 338–345, www.ncbi.nlm.nih.gov/pmc/articles/PMC1216069, published online June 16, 2004, DOI:10.1086/423147. The wiki entry "Genetic Studies on Moroccan" offers a detailed summary of scientific studies on the question: www.wikiwand.com/en/Genetic_studies_on_Moroccans#/Berber_Genetic_Identity_of_Moroccans.

20. For a recent detailed discussion of the origins question, see Michael Peyron, *The Berbers of Morocco: A History of Resistance* (London: I. B. Taurus, 2020), 5–8.

21. The degree of fluency in Tamazight is another matter. A 2004 official Moroccan census found that only 28 percent of Moroccans used the language in their daily lives, down from 34 percent ten years earlier. This figure was contested by Amazigh activists. Michael Brett and Elizabeth Fentress had already suggested in 1996 that the accepted percentages of Amazigh in the population, presumably defined primarily by those who actively used the language and thus defined themselves as such, were "decades out of date." Michael Brett and Elizabeth Fentress, *The Berbers* (Oxford: Blackwell, 1996), 276–277.

22. Ramzi Roughi, *Inventing the Berbers: History and Ideology in the Maghrib* (Philadelphia: University of Pennsylvania Press, 2019), 15–20.

23. Roughi, *Inventing the Berbers*.

24. Patricia M. E. Lorcin, *Imperial Identities: Stereotyping, Prejudice and Race in Colonial Algeria* (London: I. B. Tauris, 1999); Edmund Burke III, *The Ethnographic State: France and the Invention of Moroccan Islam* (Oakland: University of California Press, 2014).

25. Ernest Gellner, "Introduction," in *Arabs and Berbers: From Tribe to Nation in North Africa*, Ernest Gellner and Charles Micaud (eds.) (Lexington, MA: D. C. Heath, 1972), 13.

26. John Waterbury, *Commander of the Faithful: The Moroccan Political Elite—A Study in Segmented Politics* (London: Weidenfeld & Nicolson, 1970).

27. Clifford Geertz, *The Interpretation of Cultures* (New York: Basic Books, 1973); Joel S. Migdal, *Peasants, Politics and Revolution: Pressures toward Political and Social Change in the Third World* (Princeton: Princeton University Press, 1974). For a detailed discussion of Amazigh traditional leadership structures and the degree of their salience today, see Mohamed Chtatou, "The Evolution of Amazigh Activism in Morocco," *Amazigh World News*, July 24, 2020, https://amazighworldnews.com/the-evolution-of-amazigh-activism-in-morocco.

28. Benedict Anderson, *Imagined Communities*, 2nd ed. (London: Verso, 1991), 5–7.

29. Anthony D. Smith, *Nations and Nationalism in a Global Era* (Cambridge: Polity Press, 1995), 59.

30. Miroslav Hroch, "Social and Territorial Characteristics in the Composition of the Leading Groups of National Movements," in Miroslav Hroch, *Social Preconditions of National Revival in Europe: A Comparative Analysis of the Social Composition of Patriotic Groups Among the Smaller European Nations* (New York: Columbia University Press, 2000), 257–275.

31. Fouad Ajami, "The End of Pan-Arabism," *Foreign Affairs* 52(1) (Winter 1978–1979): 355–373.

32. Doug McAdam, Sidney Tarrow, and Charles Tilly, *Dynamics of Contention* (Cambridge: Cambridge University Press, 2001); Maddy-Weitzman, *The Berber Identity Movement*, 69–84.

33. Maddy-Weitzman, 84–101.

34. For a thorough discussion of the term, its application, and the surrounding controversies, see Cressida Heyes, "Identity Politics," in *The Stanford Encyclopedia of Philosophy* (Fall 2018 ed.), Edward N. Zalta (ed.), https://plato.stanford.edu/archives/fall2018/entries/identity-politics.

35. Roughi, *Inventing the Berbers*.

36. Bernard Lewis, *History—Remembered, Recovered, Invented* (Princeton: Princeton University Press, 1976).

37. Martin Evans and John Phillips, *Algeria: Anger of the Dispossessed* (New Haven, CT: Yale University Press, 2008), photo insert between pages 176 and 177.

38. McAdam et al., *Dynamics of Contention*.

39. Benjamin Stora, *Algérie Maroc, Histoires parallèles, destin croisés* (Paris: Maisonneuve et Larose Zellige, 2002).

40. "Long used to refer to the obscure nature of the Algerian regime, indicating a general uncertainty of who runs what." Muriam Haleh Davis, Hiyem Cheurfa, and Thomas Serres, "A Hirak Glossary: Terms from Algeria and Morocco," Jadaliyya.com, June 13, 2019, https://www.jadaliyya.com/Details/38734.

41. David Crawford, "How 'Berber' Matters in the Middle of Nowhere," *Middle East Report*, no. 219 (Summer 2001): 20–25.

42. The Saghru band's version of "Ekker a Mmis Umazigh" can be heard at https://soundcloud.com/azawanamazigh/kker-a-mmis-umazigh; "Ulaç Smah" can be heard at https://soundcloud.com/khaled-oualarbi/saghru-band-ulac-s.

43. The Amazigh narrative, particularly its Moroccan iteration, includes the Western Sahara within its purview, even though its population speaks the Hassaniya Arabic dialect.

44. For the French translation of the text, see "Debout fils d'Amazigh!," WikiSource, https://fr.wikisource.org/wiki/Debout_fils_d%27Amazigh_!.

45. Daniela Merolla, "Cultural Heritage, Artistic Innovation, and Activism on Amazigh Berber Websites," *Journal of African Cultural Studies* 32(1) (2020): 42–59, DOI:10.1080/13696815.2019.1624153. She also makes the point that the internet has served as a tool to reinforce local Amazigh identities as well.

Chapter 1: Toward a Second Republic?

1. The economic data is taken from BTI 2012, "Algeria Country Report," www.bti-project.org/en/meta/downloads.html?content=country&country=DZ; Transparency International, "Corruption Perceptions Index 2011," www.transparency.org/cpi2011/results.

2. FM AMEMBASSY ALGIERS [Robert Ford] TO RUEHC/SECSTATE WASHDC PRIORITY 5295, February 8, 2008, https://web.archive.org/web/20110118195427/http://wikileaks.ch/cable/2008/02/08ALGIERS198.html.

3. Hugh Roberts, "Algeria's National 'Protesta,'" *Foreign Policy*, January 10, 2011, https://foreignpolicy.com/2011/01/10/algerias-national-protesta.

4. Roberts, "Algeria's National 'Protesta.'"

5. Azzedine Layachi, "Algeria: Economic Austerity, Political Stagnation and the Gathering Storm," in *The Lure of Authoritarianism: The Maghreb After the Arab Spring*, Stephen J. King and Abdeslam M. Maghraoui (Bloomington: Indiana University Press, 2019), 320 [pp. 308–333].

6. "Algeria leader Bouteflika pledges constitutional reform," BBC News, April 16, 2011, www.bbc.com/news/world-africa-13102157.

7. Layachi, "Algeria," 308.
8. Interview with Mustapha Benfodil, "Algerian Elections and the Barakat Movement: 'We Are Saying No to Submission,'" Opendemocracy.net, April 2, 2014, www.opendemocracy.net/en/5050/algerian-elections-and-barakat-movement-we-are-saying-no-to-s.
9. Layachi, "Algeria," 323.
10. Layachi, 322.
11. A recent study by one scholar had a lower estimate of those who identify themselves as Berber, about 15 percent, two-thirds of whom are Kabyles. Mohamed Benrabah, "Tensions Between Arabophones and Berberopohones in Algeria," *Multiculturalism and Democracy in North Africa: Aftermath of the Arab Spring*, in Moha Ennaji (ed.) (Abingdon, UK: Routledge, 2014), 58.
12. Patricia M. E. Lorcin, *Imperial Identities: Stereotyping, Prejudice and Race in Colonial Algeria* (London: I. B. Tauris, 1999), 146–195.
13. Mohand Tilmatine deconstructs the notion that France (and Spain) actually gave priority to their Berber populations, showing how the two colonial powers empowered Arabic as an imperial and dominant language, thereby contributing to a different myth that North Africa was "Arab and Muslim." Mohand Tilmatine, "French and Spanish Colonial Policy in North Africa: Revisiting the Kabyle and Berber Myth," *International Journal of the Sociology of Language*, no. 239 (2016): 95–119.
14. On the latter, see Hugh Roberts, *Berber Government: The Kabyle Polity in Precolonial Algeria* (London: I. B. Tauris, 2017).
15. Ratiba Hadj-Moussa and Mohand Tilmatine, "Cultures minoritaires en Algérie: la Kabylie et le Mzab aux limites de l'impensé politique," in *Cultures de résistance: Peuples et langues minorisés*, Jacques Guyot (dir.) (Paris: Presses des Mines, Collection Matérialismes, 2020), 111–126.
16. For details, see Bruce Maddy-Weitzman, *The Berber Identity Movement and the Challenge to North African States* (Austin: University of Texas Press, 2011), 79–84, 184–188.
17. Didier Le Saout "Les associations amazighes au défi de l'institutionnalisation au Maroc et en Algérie," in *Les revendications Amazighes dans la tourmente des "Printemps Arabes,"* Mohand Tilmatine and Thierry Desrues (eds.) (Rabat: Centre Jacques Berque, 2017), 171, https://books.openedition.org/cjb/1360.
18. Hugh Roberts argues forcefully that the FFS bears a measure of responsibility for failing to achieve its goal, for it was not genuinely a party of democratic reform, but one of dissidence derived from a sense of entitlement: it was concerned, he said, not with how Algeria should be governed but more with the question of legitimacy, i.e., on who held the right to rule. Roberts, "The Calculus of Dissidence: How the Front Des Forces Socialistes Became What It Is," LSE Middle East Centre Paper Series, 26 October 2018 8, http://eprints.lse.ac.uk/id/eprint/90418.
19. *Al-Sharq al-Awsat*, January 14—Foreign Broadcast Information Service (FBIS), Near East and South Asia, Daily Report, January 18 1995.
20. "*Amazighité—Communique De La Presidence*," issued by the Embassy of Algeria, Washington, D.C., April 23 1995; for an analysis, see *Annuaire de l'Afrique du Nord* 34 (1995) (Paris, CNRS Editions, 1997), 583–590.
21. For details, see Maddy-Weitzman, *The Berber Identity Movement*, 114–115.

22. World and Universal Academy, "ÉLISEZ LES MEILLEURS PRÉSIDENTS OU CHEFS DE GOUVERNEMENTS DE L'AFRIQUE ET DU MONDE," www.wuacademia.org/politicien2-afrique-algerie.php.

23. The International Crisis Group report on the events, the most thorough and nuanced account made, speaks of 123 dead and many more injured, with some maimed for life. See International Crisis Group, "Algeria: Unrest and Impasse in Kabylia," *Middle East/North Africa Report No. 15*, June 10, 2003, www.crisisgroup.org/middle-east-north-africa/north-africa/algeria/algeria-unrest-and-impasse-.

24. Maddy-Weitzman, *The Berber Identity Movement*, 194.

25. Lyes Aflou, "Amazigh Language Teaching in Algeria Lacks Standardisation, Qualified Teachers," Maghrebia.com, December 10, 2006, http://listserv.linguistlist.org/pipermail/lgpolicy-list/2006-December/004063.html; "L'enseignement du Tamazight en Algérie piétine," December 6, 2006, www.algerie-dz.com/article7301.html; "Algérie, stagnation de l'enseignement de la langue amazighe," interview reported on www.LeMonde.fr, www.bladi.net/forum/83062-algerie-stagnation-lenseignement-langue-amazighe.

26. Bahbouh Lehsene, "Haut Commissariat à l'Amazighité, 13 ans après," cited in Bruce Maddy-Weitzman, *The Berber Identity Movement*, 251, n.32; the relevant text in the book is at page 193.

27. Abderrezak Dourari, "Cultural Multiplicity and Unity Dialects," in *Multiculturalism and Democracy in North Africa: Aftermath of the Arab Spring*, Moha Ennaji (ed.) (Abingdon, UK: Routledge, 2014), 47.

28. Benrabah, "Tensions," 77–78.

29. Ferhat Mehenni, *Algérie: la question kabyle* (Paris: Éditions Michalon, 2004), 141–149, and annex, "Proposition D'Un Projet Pour L'Autonomie De La Kabylie," 181–186.

30. Lina Murr Nehmé, "Farhat Mehenni: 15 ans après, on ne dit toujours pas qui a assassiné mon fils," Causeur.com, June 19, 2019, www.causeur.fr/farhat-mehenni-mohamed-mediene-assassinat-162413.

31. "Projet pour l'autonomie de la Kabylie," www.autonomiahazi.eu/sahara-occidental-grand-rif-berberes-amazighs-kabylie.

32. Interview with Mohamed Benfodil, "Algerian Elections and the Barakat Movement."

33. Reliably-sourced data on the elections can be found at "2014 Algerian Presidential Election," https://en.wikipedia.org/wiki/2014_Algerian_presidential_election#Results.

34. Yahia Zoubir, "The Algerian Crisis: Origins and Prospects for a 'Second Republic,'" Al Jazeera Center for Studies, May 20, 2019, https://studies.aljazeera.net/en/reports/2019/05/algerian-crisis-origins-prospects-republic-190520100257161.html. Transparency International: Algeria, www.transparency.org/country/DZA.

35. Rachid Tlemcani, "Algeria: Inventing New Political Rules," Arab Reform Initiative, April 9, 2009, www.arab-reform.net/publication/algeria-inventing-new-political-rules.

36. Mohand Tilmatine, "Des revendications linguistiques aux projets d'autodétermination: le cas de la Kabylie (Algérie)," in *Les revendications Aamzighes dans la tourmente des "Printemps Arabes,"* Mohand Tilmatine and Thierry Desrues (eds.) (Rabat:

Centre Jacques Berque, 2017), 138–139, 142–149, https://books.openedition.org/cjb/1359.

37. Fatma Oussedik, "L'Algérie, une société en guerre contre elle-même," *NAQD* 32(1) (2015): 131, www.cairn.info/article.php?ID_ARTICLE=NAQD_032_0105#pa1.

38. Holding the meeting in the Soummam Valley carried considerable symbolic weight. It was there in 1956, in the midst of the war of independence, that the FLN leadership met secretly to draw up a new strategic plan to combat the French colonial regime and reorganize its leadership. Primacy was to be given to the internal leadership, in which Kabyles played an outsized role, over the external one. Eventually, the external leadership gained the upper hand. Martin Evans, *Algeria: France's Undeclared War* (Oxford: Oxford University Press, 2012), 177–181. For Kabylian ethnonationalists, this constituted a betrayal and set the stage for the postindependence years of repression.

39. The text of the "Projet pour un Etat Kabyle" can be found at www.makabylie.org/index.php/toute-la-documentation-du-mak-en-un-clic.

40. To that end, Mehenni made a very public visit to Israel in 2012, drawing much opprobrium from a variety of directions, within Algeria and beyond. "Algerian Separatist Leader's Visit to Israel Stirs Controversy," *Al-'Arabiyya*, May 22, 2012, www.alarabiya.net/articles/2012/05/22/215732.html.

41. Personal communication from the lexicographer Amazigh Tazaghart, March 22, 2020.

42. Karina Direche-Slimani, *Chrétiens de Kabylie, 1873–1954* (Paris: Editions Bouchene, 2004), 73–112.

43. See, e.g., U.S. Department of State, "2018 Report on International Religious Freedom: Algeria," www.state.gov/reports/2018-report-on-international-religious-freedom/algeria.

44. Carmen Garratón Mateu, "Religion et identité amazighe: réflexions sur le rôle de l'islam en Kabylie (Algérie)," in *Les revendications Amazighes dans la tourmente des "Printemps Arabes,"* Mohand Tilmatine and Thierry Desrues (eds.) (Rabat: Centre Jacaues Berque, 2017), 93–103, https://books.openedition.org/cjb/1359.

45. For an insightful look into the expression of religious sensibilities among the Kabyles, see Judith Scheele, "Recycling *Baraka*: Knowledge, Politics, and Religion in Contemporary Algeria," *Comparative Studies in Society and History* 49(2) (2007): 304–328.

46. Garratón Mateu, 108–110; Frederic Wehrey and Anouar Boukhars, *Salafism in the Maghreb: Politics, Piety, and Militancy* (Oxford: Oxford University Press, 2019), 70, 74.

47. Personal communiqué.

48. For the text of the *Manifeste*, see www.elwatan.com/edition/contributions/manifeste-pour-la-reconnaissance-constitutionnelle-dun-statut-politique-particulier-de-la-kabylie-07-12-2014.

49. "Pour une convention politique des autonomistes kabyles ouverte et rassembleuse," *El Watan*, January 11, 2017, www.elwatan.com/edition/contributions/pour-une-convention-politique-des-autonomistes-kabyles-ouverte-et-rassembleuse-11-01-2017.

50. Djaffar Benmesbah, "'Manifeste Kabyle': le leurre autonomiste," *Siwel*, January 20, 2017, www.siwel.info/manifeste-kabyle-le-leurre-autonomiste_361.html.

51. Aït Oumalou carried symbolic resonance, having been an area of heavy fighting during the war of independence, which touched every village.

52. Mokrane Aït Ouarabi, "Le RPK, nouveau mouvement autonomiste pour la Kabylie," *El Watan*, February 26, 2017 www.elwatan.com/actualite/le-rpk-nouveau-mouvement-autonomiste-pour-la-kabylie-26-02-2017-340040_109.php.

53. Tilmatine, "*Des revendications,*" 150–151.

54. Benjamin Stora, "Algérie: Les retours de la mémoire de la guerre d'indépendance," *Modern & Contemporary France* 10(4) (2002): 461–473.

55. Lounis Aggoun, "Hocine Aït-Ahmed, l'Albatros Deplume," March 3, 2013, http://etudescoloniales.canalblog.com/archives/2013/03/03/26575854.html; Roberts, "The Calculus of Dissidence," 7.

56. Roberts, 24–26.

57. "The Constitution of the People's Democratic Republic of Algeria," Edition 2016, www.conseil-constitutionnel.dz/pdf/Constitutioneng.pdf; Layachi, "Algeria," 327; "New Algerian Constitution Enacted But Reforms Not Celebrated," Fanack.com, May 5, 2016, https://fanack.com/algeria/governance-and-politics-of-algeria/new-algerian-constitution/?gclid=CjwKCAjwkPX0BRBKEiwA7THxiAaQskf9Rb5XgjgXm7CnugZCyy9YKLF8DqY8B1LqJ2eAiEXMbCQCrRoCIpEQAvD_BwE.

58. Salem Chaker, "Tamazight dans la Constitution Algérienne: un Leurre! Une Analyse de Salem Chaker," February 15, 2016, http://tamazgha.fr/Tamazight-dans-la-constitution.html.

59. *Journal Officiel De La Republic Algerienne*, No. 14, 7 March 2016, www.joradp.dz/FTP/jo-francais/2016/F2016014.pdf; the official Arabic text, issued in tandem, can be found at www.premier-ministre.gov.dz/ressources/front/files/pdf/texts-fondamentaux/nouvelle-constitution-2016-arabe.pdf.

60. The currently moribund five-nation Arab Maghrib Union (*Ittihad al-Maghrib al-`Arabi*), established in 1989, was an institutional expression of the ideological construct of the Maghrib being an "Arab" region. For its establishment, see Bruce Maddy-Weitzman, "Inter-Arab Relations," in *Middle East Contemporary Survey* 13 (1989), Ami Ayalon (ed.) (Boulder: Westview, 1991), 144–147.

61. Chaker, "Tamazight dans la Constitution Algérienne."

62. "Boycott of the Arabic Language in Kabylia Schools," Kabylia Blog, October 21, 2018, https://kabylia.wordpress.com/2018/10/21/boycott-of-arabic-language-in-all-schools-of-kabylia; "Des Collégiens Et des Lycéens Boycottent La Langue Arabes En Kabylie," *Le Monde Amazigh*, no. 213 (October 2018), 7.

63. Wehrey and Boukhars, *Salafism in the Maghreb*, 80.

64. Sana Elouzi, "Algeria to Celebrate Officially Amazigh New Year 'Yennayer' on January 12," *Morocco World News*, December 28, 2017, www.moroccoworldnews.com/2017/12/237378/algeria-amazigh-new-year-yennayer. For a discussion of modern day Yennayer celebrations as an "invented tradition," and the motivations behind its recognition by the Algerian state, see Yassine Temlali, "Algeria's Berber New Year Aims to Show State's Approval for 'Invented Tradition,'" *Middle East Eye*, January 15, 2018, www.middleeasteye.net/opinion/algerias-berber-new-year-aims-show-states-approval-invented-tradition.

65. Kamal Louadj, "Vers la criminalisation du discours raciste et régionaliste en Algérie," Sputnik News, January 14, 2020, https://fr.sputniknews.com/maghreb

/202001141042900390-vers-la-criminalisation-du-discours-raciste-et-regionaliste-en-algerie.

66. Hadj-Moussa and Tilmatine, "Cultures minoritaires en Algérie," 114.

67. M. Rouvillois-Brigol and M. Mercier, "Mzāb," in *Encyclopaedia of Islam, 2nd ed.*, P. Bearman, Th. Bianquis, C. E. Bosworth, E. van Donzel, and W. P. Heinrichs (eds.), http://dx.doi.org/10.1163/1573-3912_islam_SIM_5696, first published online 2012, first print edition ISBN: 9789004161214, 1960–2007; E. A. Alport, "The Mzab," in *Arabs and Berbers: From Tribe to Nation in North Africa*, Ernest Gellner and Charles Micaud (eds.) (Lexington, MA: Lexington Books, 1972), 141–152; Fatma Oussedik, "The Rites of Baba Merzug: Diaspora, Ibadism, and Social Status in the Valley of the Mzab," in *Saharan Frontiers: Space and Mobility in Northwest Africa*, Judith Scheele and James McDougall (eds.) (Bloomington: Indiana University Press, 2012), 93–108; Fatma Oussedik, "L'Algérie, une société en guerre contre elle-même," *NAQD* 32(1) (2015): 105–134, www.cairn.info/article.php?ID_ARTICLE=NAQD_032_0105#pa1.

68. Hadj-Moussa and Tilmatine, "Cultures minoritaires en Algérie," 112.

69. "Algeria's South: Trouble's Bellwether," International Crisis Group, Middle East and North Africa, Report No. 171, November 21, 2016, 7, www.crisisgroup.org/middle-east-north-africa/north-africa/algeria/algeria-s-south-trouble-s-bellwether.

70. "Algeria's South: Trouble's Bellwether," 7; Wehrey and Boukhars, *Salafism in the Maghreb*, 74–75.

71. The latter descend from the Banu Sulaym tribe that more than a thousand years earlier migrated from the Medina area in Arabia first to northern Egypt, then farther west and south in North Africa.

72. "Algeria's South: Trouble's Bellwether," 8–11. A subsequent inquiry by Human Rights Watch into the status of its complaint about the actions of the torturers in 2013 drew no response. Human Rights Watch, "Algeria: Pro-Autonomy Activists Detained," August 25, 2015, www.hrw.org/news/2015/08/25/algeria-pro-autonomy-activists-detained; Oussedik, "L'Algérie, une société en guerre contre elle-même"; the article is accompanied by an excerpt of a statement by Mozabite notables on the situation in Ghardaïa, "Stop Provocations," *El Watan*, June 24, 2015.

73. Oussedik, "L'Algérie."

74. "Algeria's South: Trouble's Bellwether," 9.

75. Congres Mondial Amazigh, "Algérie: "La communauté Mozabite en danger," January 1, 2014 (document provided to the author by Belkacem Lounes).

76. Congres Mondial Amazigh, "Algérie: agressions criminelles contre les Mozabites," June 27–July 9, 2015 (document provided to the author by Belkacem Lounes).

77. "Algerian PM Accuses Morocco of Fomenting Sectarian Clashes in Ghardaia," *Morocco World News*, July 14, 2015, www.moroccoworldnews.com/2015/07/163204/algerian-pm-accuses-morocco-of-fomenting-sectarian-clashes-in-ghardaia.

78. See dialogue with Hamid A`dush (in Arabic), *Le Monde Amazigh*, July 20, 2016, 6–7, https://amadalamazigh.press.ma/archivesPDF/186.pdf?fbclid=IwAR1zokWYROMobs5pIOosWR4YkT8sbFwT3NubMDDuUQNsTlWmWKUoWUiasSA.

79. Amnesty International, "Algeria: Ensure Fair Trial for Minority Rights Activists," May 29, 2017, www.amnesty.org/en/latest/news/2017/05/algeria-ensure-fair-trial-for-minority-rights-activists-fekhar-and-other-amazigh-rights-advocates-held-since-july-2015.

80. U.S. Department of State, "2019 Country Reports on Human Rights Practices: Algeria," www.state.gov/reports/2019-country-reports-on-human-rights-practices /algeria.

81. Tamba François Koundouno, "Death of Algerian Activist Kamel Eddine Fekhar Sparks Human Rights Questions," *Morocco World News*, May 29, 2019, www.moroccoworldnews.com/2019/05/274532/death-algerian-activist-kamel -fekhar-human-rights; "Funeral of Algerian Activist Draws Thousands after Prison Death," *The Arab Weekly*, https://thearabweekly.com/funeral-algerian-activist-draws -thousands-after-prison-death; BBC News, "Anger over Death of Algeria Hunger-striking Activist Kamel Eddine Fekhar," www.bbc.com/news/world-africa-48444664.

82. Yahia Zoubir, "The Algerian Crisis: Origins and Prospects for a 'Second Republic,'" Al Jazeera Center for Studies, May 20, 2019, https://studies.aljazeera.net/en /reports/2019/05/algerian-crisis-origins-prospects-republic-190520100257161.html; Transparency International: Algeria, www.transparency.org/country/DZA.

83. Reserves plummeted in five years by half, from $178 billion in 2014 to roughly $75 billion in 2019, with the budget deficit in 2018 amounting to 10.2 percent of the country's GDP. Yahia H. Zoubir, "Introduction: The Making of a New Republic?" in *The Politics of Algeria: Domestic Issues and International Relations*, Yahia H. Zoubir (ed.) (London: Routledge, 2020), xxxiv.

84. Zoubir, "Introduction: The Making of a New Republic?"

85. Muriam Haleh Davis, Hiyem Cheurfa, and Thomas Serres, "A Hirak Glossary: Terms from Algeria and Morocco" (Part One), *Jadaliyya*, June 13, 2019, www.jadaliyya .com/Details/38734.

86. For an insightful analysis of the moment in which "*Yetnaḥāw gāʿ*" became a rallying cry, indicating how language and a desire for dialect validation and pride remain significant issues in Algeria today, see Ziad Bentahar, "'*Ytnahaw ga*'': Algeria's Cultural Revolution and the Role of Language in the Early Stages of the Spring 2019 Hirak," *Journal of African Cultural Studies* (2020), DOI:10.1080/13696815.2020.1788517.

87. Abdelbaqi Ghorab, "Hirak Glossary: Terms from Algeria" (Part Two), *Jadaliyya*, February 25, 2020, www.jadaliyya.com/Details/40741/Hirak-Glossary-Terms -from-Algeria-Part-2.

88. Two years earlier, he had been questioned in a drug-trafficking case that had resulted in two former ministers being sent to prison. "Algeria: Inner-clan Warfare Continues Inside the Regime, Ex-head of Police Gets Stiff Prison Sentence," *North Africa Journal*, April 1, 2020, http://north-africa.com/2020/04/algeria-inner-clan-warfare -continues-inside-the-regime-ex-head-of-police-gets-stiff-prison-sentence.

89. *Casbah Tribune*, "Amnesty International demande l'annulation de la condamnation de Karim Tabbou," March 25, 2020, http://casbah-tribune.com/amnesty -international-demande-lannulation-de-la-condamnation-de-karim-tabbou.

90. Committee to Protect Journalists, "Journalist and RSF Correspondent Khaled Drareni Imprisoned in Algeria," March 27, 2020, https://cpj.org/2020/03/rsf -correspondent-khaled-drareni-sentenced-to-inde.php; "Algeria: Inner-clan Warfare Continues," *North Africa Journal*, April 1, 2020; VOA News, "Media Watchdog: Algeria Arrests Independent Journalist," March 27, 2020, www.voanews.com/press-freedom /media-watchdog-algeria-arrests-independent-journalist.

91. For the English language text of the draft constitution, see www.constitute project.org/constitution/Algeria_2020D?lang=en.

92. Tabbou was from the commune of Ouadhia in Tizi Ouzou Province. Aït Ahmed had catapulted him in 2007 to the position of first secretary of the FFS, a position he held between 2007–2011. His radical critique of the regime led to a rupture with the party, and while refusing to give up his seat in parliament, which he won in 2012, he formed a new party in 2013, the Union Démocratique et Sociale (UDS). He retained his seat in 2017, winning 33,372 votes. "Karim Tabbou lance officiellement L'UDS qui opte pour une «opposition radicale»," http://udsalgerie.politicien.fr, September 2, 2013; www.wikiwand.com/en/2017_Algerian_legislative_election.

93. The Chaoui were historically less self-contained and collectively defined than the Kabyles. In April 2018, Chaoui Amazigh activists declared May 2 the date of the statue's erection, a "national day of celebration for the Chawii people." "The Chawi People: All People Have a Date to Their Nation, Which Refers to Its History." Mergueze.info, https://mergueze.info/the-chawi-people-all-people-have-a-date-to-their-nation-which-refers-to-its-history.

94. Martin Evans, *Algeria: France's Undeclared War*, 82, 85–88, 91–95; Alistair Horne, *A Savage War of Peace*, rev. ed. (Harmondsworth, Middlesex, UK: Penguin Books, 1987), 23–28; James McDougall, *A History of Algeria* (Cambridge: Cambridge University Press, 2017), 179–181.

95. Mohand Tilmatine, "Interdiction des emblèmes berbères et occupation des espaces symboliques: amazighité versus algérianité?," *L'Année du Maghreb* 21 (2019): 151, https://journals.openedition.org/anneemaghreb/5435.

96. Marc Daou, "Arrests of Algerian Protestors Show Desire to 'Strangle' Popular Movement," France24, July 4, 2019, www.france24.com/en/20190704-arrests-algeria-protesters-berbers-bouteflika-gaid-salah; Boualem Goumrass, "Algerian Authorities Arrest Protestors Carrying Amazigh Flags," *Alsharq Alawsat*, June 23, 2019, https://aawsat.com/english/home/article/1780746/algerian-authorities-arrest-protesters-carrying-amazigh-flags; Tilmatine, "Interdiction des emblèmes berbères," 151–153.

97. Tilmatine, 156, 158.

98. Ghorab, "Hirak Glossary: Terms from Algeria" (Part Two); Arezki Metre, "Algeria's Massive Movement for Change," *Le Monde Diplomatique*, December 2019, https://mondediplo.com/2019/12/03algeria.

99. "A Party Leader and an Elected to the Assembly of the Algerian Republic Calls to Exterminate the Kabyle," Mergueze.info, December 2019, https://mergueze.info/a-party-leader-and-an-elected-to-the-assembly-of-the-algerian-republic-calls-to-exterminate-the-kabyle.

100. Agence France Presse, "Algeria Presidential Vote Faces Brick Wall of Berber Opposition," December 11, 2019, www.france24.com/en/20191211-algeria-presidential-vote-faces-brick-wall-of-berber-opposition; Naïma Ameur, "'No more talk of voting': Algeria's Kabylia Boycotts Presidential Election," *Middle East Eye*, December 12, 2020, www.middleeasteye.net/news/no-more-talk-voting-algeria-kabylia-boycotting-presidential-elections; Boukhelifa Zahir, "Kabylie, vers un boycott massif des élections du 12 décembre," Kab News, September 24, 2019, https://web.archive.org/web/20191102231750/https://kab-news.com/kabylie-vers-un-boycott-massif-des-elections-du-12-decembre.

101. "Présidentielle: le taux de participation par wilayas annoncé à 17h," www.aps.dz/algerie/98902-taux.

102. Hadj-Moussa and Tilmatine, "Cultures minoritaires en Algérie," 122–123, drawing on the work of Guy Di Méo, "Patrimonialization Process and Construction of Territories," in *Colloquium Heritage and industry in Poitou-Charentes: to know to enhance,* September 2007 (Poitiers-Châtellerault, France: Geste Éditions, 2008), 87–109.

103. Amar Benhamouche, "L'infanticide du régime algérien," Kablye.com, March 5, 2020, https://kabyle.com/linfanticide-du-regime-algerien.

Chapter 2: Obscure No Longer

1. David Andersen, Jørgen Møller, and Svend-Erik Skaaning, "The State-Democracy Nexus: Conceptual Distinctions, Theoretical Perspectives, and Comparative Approaches," *Democratization* 21(7) (2014): 1205; J. P. Nettl, "The State as a Conceptual Variable," *World Politics* 20(4) (1968): 559–592.

2. Tunisia's existence as a distinct political unity stretches back to the seventeenth century as an Ottoman regency. Regarding the degree of social cohesion, Ernest Gellner succinctly described Tunisians as "feeling quite at home in their own cultural skin." Ernest Gellner, *Muslim Society* (Cambridge: Cambridge University Press, 1981), 95.

3. Anna Baldenetti, *The Origins of the Libyan Nation* (Abingdon, UK: Routledge, 2010), 143–144.

4. Dirk VandeWalle, *A History of Modern Libya* (Cambridge: Cambridge University Press, 2006), 50.

5. "Rapport alternatif de Tamazgha au Comité pour l'Élimination de la Discrimination Raciale (CERD)," Nations Unies Conseil Economique et Social Convention internationale sur l'élimination de toutes les formes de discrimination raciale, 64eme session du Comité pour l'élimination de la discrimination raciale, Genève, 23 février au 12 mars 2004, www.tamazgha.fr/Imazighen-en-Libye-rapport-de-Tamazgha-au-CERD,541.html; an earlier 1998 estimate by "Ethnologue" placed the number at only 240,000, leading UNESCO to classify "Nafusi" as a "severely endangered language." *UNESCO Atlas of the World's Languages in Danger*, www.unesco.org/culture/languages-atlas/en/atlasmap/language-id-1970.html.

6. Salem Chaker et Masin Ferkal, "Berbères de Libye: un paramètre méconnu, une irruption politique inattendue,' *Politique Africaine 2012/1 (No. 125)*, 109, www.cairn.info/article.php?ID_ARTICLE=POLAF_125_0105; interview with Amazigh activist, Tripoli, June 12, 2020. (Interviews with the author were generally conducted by Skype or Facebook; the physical location of interviewees was not always confirmed.)

7. Chaker et Ferkal, "Berbères de Libye," 120, citing H. Bleuchot, "Chronique politique Libye," *Annuaire de l'Afrique du Nord* 19 (1981): 550. This number does not include the tens of thousands of Tuareg who had migrated from Mali and Niger during the 1960s and 1970s. Ines Kohl, "Libya's 'Major Minorities.' Berber, Touareg and Tebu: Multiple Narratives of Citizenship, Language and Border Control," *Middle East Critique* 23(4) (2014): 429–430.

8. Chiara Pagano, "Shall We Speak of an Arab-Berber Libya? Towards an Interconnected History of Tripolitania's Social Groups (1911–1918)," in *Libya Between History and Revolution: Resilience, New Opportunities and Challenges for the Berbers,* Anna Maria Di Tolla and Valentina Schiattarella (eds.), Studi Africanistici Quaderni di Studi Berberi e Libico-berberi no. 7 (Napoli: Unior Press, 2020), 60.

9. Vandewalle, *A History of Modern Libya*, 28–30; Wolfram Lacher and Ahmed Labnouj, "Factionalism Resurgent: The War in the Jabal Nafusa," in *The Libyan Revolution and Its Aftermath*, Peter Cole and Brian McQuinn (eds.) (Oxford: Oxford University Press, 2015), 259, www.oxfordscholarship.com/view/10.1093/acprof:oso/9780190210960.001.0001/acprof-9780190210960-chapter-12.

10. On the concept of legibility, see James Scott, "Seeing Like a State: A Conversation with James C. Scott," Cato Institute, September 2010, https://www.cato-unbound.org/print-issue/487.

11. Chia-Lin Pan, "The Population of Libya," *Population Studies* 3(1) (June 1949): Table 7, 121, www.jstor.com/stable/2172494.

12. Anna Baldinetti, "Languages in Libya: Building Blocks of National Identity and Soft Power Tools," *Journal of North African Studies* 23(3) (2018): 423–426. The choice of Zuwara, the Berber coastal enclave, was obviously deliberate. Karlos Zurutuza, "The Amazigh: Libya's Third Actor?," *Nationalia*, May 23, 2019, www.nationalia.info/dossier/11217/the-amazigh-libyas-third-actor.

13. Quoted in K. Lee, "The Amazigh's Fight for Cultural Revival in the New Libya: Reclaiming and Establishing Identity Through Antiquity," *Seattle Journal for Social Justice* 11(1) (July 1, 2012): 301.

14. Bruce Maddy-Weitzman, *The Berber Identity Movement and the Challenge to North African States* (Austin: University of Texas Press, 2011), 141.

15. "Berberism and Berber Political Movements," www.temehu.com/imazighen/berberism.htm.

16. Frederick Wehrey, *The Burning Shores* (New York: Farrar, Straus & Giroux, 2018), 79–80, 92, 209.

17. Lacher and Labnouj, "Factionalism Resurgent," 261–262.

18. Interview with Zorgh Madi, May 5, 2020; the US State Department Human Rights Report for 1993 stated that the regime was seeking to dilute Berber identity by ensuring Berber-Arab marriages. Cited in International Crisis Group, "Popular Protest in North Africa and the Middle East (V): Making Sense of Libya," *Middle East/North Africa Report* No. 107, June 6, 2011, 22, www.crisisgroup.org/middle-east-north-africa/north-africa/libya/popular-protest-north-africa-and-middle-east-v-making-sense-libya. Some Libyan Amazigh living in Europe stated that Qaddafi's hostility toward the Amazigh stemmed from the refusal of a Zuwara family to allow him to marry their daughter. "Rapport alternatif de Tamazgha."

19. George Joffé, "Minorities in the New Libya," in *Multiculturalism and Democracy in North Africa*, Moha Ennaji (ed.) (London: Routledge: 2014), 300.

20. "Rapport alternatif de Tamazgha"; a detailed account of Amazigh assertion and Qaddafi's actions against it during the 1970s and 1980s can be found at "Berberism and Berber Political Movements."

21. Senem Aslan, *Nation-Building in Turkey and Morocco: Governing Kurdish and Berber Descent* (Cambridge: Cambridge University Press, 2015).

22. Ofra Bengio, "Ankara Erbil Baghdad: Relations Fraught with Dilemmas," in *Conflict, Democratization and the Kurds in the Middle East*, David Romano and Mehmet Gurses (eds.) (New York: Palgrave Macmillan, 2014), 267–282.

23. Madghis Buzakhar, Mazigh Buzakhar, and Nasser Buzakhar, "The Role of Amazigh Libyan Civil Society in the Tamazgha Spring," in *Studi Magrebini*, "Emerging Actors in Post Revolutionary North Africa," vol. 2, "*Berber Movements in North Africa:*

Identity, New Issues, New Challenges," Anna Maria Di Tolla and Ersilia Francesca (eds.), Volumi XIV–XV (Napoli: 2016–2017), 189, fn.4.

24. Lacher and Labnouj, "Factionalism Resurgent," 261–262.

25. "Said Sifaw El Mehroug," www.mondeberbere.com/sifaw_en.html; "Berberism and Berber Political Movements."

26. Yehudit Ronen, *Qaddafi's Libya in World Politics* (Boulder: Lynne Rienner, 2008), 41–79.

27. Baldinetti, "Languages in Libya," 429; Anna Baldinetti, "*Le istanze amazigh in Libia: la nascita di una società civile?*," in *Processi politici nel Mediterraneo: dinamiche e prospettive*, Anna Baldinetti and Amina Maneggia (eds.) (Perugia, Italy: Morlacchi, 2009), 242–246.

28. Maddy-Weitzman, *The Berber Identity Movement*, 159–164.

29. A link to the text of the founding manifesto is located at "The Libyan National Tamazight Congress," www.temehu.com/imazighen/alt.htm.

30. Aisha al-Rumi, "Libyan Berbers Struggle to Assert their Identity Online," *Arab Media and Society*, Spring 2009, www.arabmediasociety.com/libyan-berbers-struggle-to-assert-their-identity-online.

31. It has since been reopened and redeveloped and contains a large collection of material. See www.tawalt.com.

32. Interviews with Zorgh Madi and an anonymous Amazigh activist, May 5, 2020.

33. Of Kabylian origin, Lounes has been since 2019 a member of the UN Human Rights Council's Consultative Group on the rights of Indigenous peoples.

34. Maddy-Weitzman, *The Berber Identity Movement*, 140–143; Frédéric Volpi, Revolution and Authoritarianism in North Africa (Oxford: Oxford University Press, 2017), 87, www.oxfordscholarship.com/view/10.1093/oso/9780190642921.001.0001/oso-9780190642921-chapter-004#pageid_87.

35. Lacher and Labnouj, "Factionalism Resurgent," 262.

36. Masin Ferkal, "Tamazgha orientale: émergence/renaissance du combat amazigh après 2011," in Di Tolla and Francesca, eds., *Emerging Actors in Post-revolutionary North Africa*, 217, https://unora.unior.it/retrieve/handle/11574/176357/39967/estratto%20Di%20Tolla%20introduction.pdf; Thierry Desrues, "Le surgissement de la cause Amazighe en Libye: des espoirs de reconnaissance aux déconvenues de la realpolitik," in *Les revendications Amazighes dans la tourmente des "Printemps Arabes*," Mohand Tilmatine and Thierry Desrues (eds.) (Rabat: Centre Jacques Berque, 2017), 239–241, https://books.openedition.org/cjb/1367.

37. Lacher and Labnouj, "Factionalism Resurgent," 264–265. Based primarily on interviews with the participants, the authors present an invaluable, detailed account of the dynamics of the rebellion in the region.

38. Desrues, "Le surgissement de la cause Amazighe en Libye," 239, fn.22.

39. Minority Rights Group International, *World Directory of Minorities and Indigenous Peoples—Libya: Imazighen*, July 2018, www.refworld.org/docid/5b9fb61e7.html; Katherine E. Hoffman, "Berbers, Borders and Breakdown in the 2011 Libyan Civil War," in *On the Ground: New Directions in Middle East and North African Studies*, Brian T. Edwards (ed.) (Doha: Akkadia Press, 2014), http://ontheground.qatar.northwestern.edu/uncategorized/chapter-9-berbers-borders-and-breakdown-%E2

%80%A8in-the-2011-libyan-civil-war; and Katherine E. Hoffman, "Navigating the Border: Amazigh Minorities from Libya in Tunisia during the 2011–2012 Uprisings," in *Mobility and Minorities in Africa*, Giovanni Sistu and Michele Carboni (eds.) (Rome: Aracne Editrice, 2018), 149–171, DOI:10.4399/97888548934058.

40. Lacher and Labnouj, "Factionalism Resurgent," 274. For an additional detailed account of the fighting town by town, see M. Cherif Bassiouini, *Libya: From Repression to Revolution* (Leiden: Brill, 2013), 641–701.

41. Wehrey, *The Burning Shores*, 55.

42. Luca D'Anna, "nəḥne kull-na yad wāḥda: The Mobilization of Amazigh Libyans in Revolutionary Rap," in *Libya Between History and Revolution*, Di Tolla and Schiattarella (eds.), 235–255. For later versions of the songs and accompanying film, with Spanish subtitles, see "The Western Mountains" ("al-Jabal al-Gharbi"), www.youtube.com/watch?v=6QI6wp0xGbQ; and "Libya Is" ("Libya Hiya"), www.youtube.com/watch?v=_VRF2fbN-Tw.

43. For a detailed discussion of the song's origins and path to a wide audience, see Leila Tayeb, "Our Star: Amazigh Music and the Production of Intimacy in 2011 Libya," *Journal of North African Studies* 23(5) (2018): 834–850.

44. A somewhat grainy video can be found at www.youtube.com/watch?v=G8zz5qGp_DQ.

45. See www.youtube.com/watch?v=BOMAgmsa254.

46. Jane Goodman, *Berber Culture on the World Stage* (Bloomington: Indiana University Press, 2005), 49–68. Their performance can be found at www.youtube.com/watch?v=RhWBrOyZnuE; an earlier, more intimate version can be found at www.youtube.com/watch?v=YBdSlsmN-XE.

47. See www.youtube.com/watch?v=5IB5Ut_2Qdk.

48. Tayeb, "Our Star," 840.

49. Ferkal, "Tamazgha orientale," 217–219.

50. Ashour S. Abdulaziz, "The First Libya News in Tamazight in Libya: Examining the Consequences of Libya's Past Language Policies," paper delivered at American Institute for Maghrib Studies Workshop, "Berber Societies: New Approaches to Space, Time, and Social Process," Tangier, Morocco, June 29–July 2, 2012.

51. Moez Zeiton, "In liberated Libya in the Year 2961," *The Guardian*, August 6, 2011, www.theguardian.com/commentisfree/2011/aug/06/libya-berber-amazagh.

52. Thierry Portes, "Le printemps des Berbères libyens," *Le Figaro*, July 20, 2011, www.lefigaro.fr/international/2011/07/20/01003-20110720ARTFIG00551-le-printemps-des-berberes-libyens.php; Baldinetti, *Origins of the Libyan Nation*, 56–58; Anna Baldinetti, "Italian Colonial Rule and Muslim Elites in Libya: A Relationship of Antagonism and Collaboration," in *Guardians of Faith in Modern Times: Ulama' in the Middle East*, Meir Hatina (ed.) (Leiden: Brill, 2008), 91–108; Federico Cresti, "Sulayman al-Baruni in Italy (1919–1920): From the Dream of the Berber Principality to the Italo-Tripolitanian Brotherhood," in *Libya Between History and Revolution*, Di Tolla and Schiattarella (eds.), 67–98. For a brief summary of his career, including the obvious (albeit simplistic) parallel with Mohamed bin Abdelkrim's short-lived Rifian Republic in northern Morocco, see the page titled "Libya" on the Libyan Amazigh website Temehu.com: www.temehu.com/imazighen/berberism.htm. See also Todd M. Thompson and Youcef Bouandel, "The Amazigh in Post-Revolution Libya: A Century

of Struggle," in K. Scott Parker and Tony E. Nasrallah (eds.), *Middle Eastern Minorities and the Arab Spring: Identity and Community in the Twenty-first Century* (Piscataway, NJ: Gorgias Press, 2017), 48–51 [45–77].

53. Derek Henry Flood, "Special Commentary from Inside Western Libya—On the Precipice: Libya's Amazigh in Revolt," Jamestown Foundation, July 25, 2011, https://jamestown.org/program/special-commentary-from-inside-western-libya-on-the-precipice-libyas-amazigh-in-revolt.

54. Lacher and Labnou, "Factionalism Resurgent," 278; Abdulaziz, "The First Libya News."

55. Karlos Zurutuza, "Libya's Tuareg Find a New Home in Coastal Amazigh enclave," *Middle East Eye*, November 30, 2018, www.middleeasteye.net/news/libyas-Touareg-find-new-home-coastal-amazigh-enclave.

56. For the official Arabic language text, see www.temehu.com/NTC/tnc-constitutional-declaration-in-arabic.pdf.

57. See www.temehu.com/imazighen/berberism.htm; Desrues, "Le surgissement de la cause Amazighe en Libye," 240.

58. "Comment le Mouvement amazigh libyen voit la Libye de demain," August 12, 2011, in "Pour le mouvement Amazigh, la Libye est un Etat laïc qui ne peut exister sans Tamazight," Tamazgha.fr, August 30, 2011, www.tamazgha.fr/Pour-le-mouvement-amazigh-la-Libye.html; Desrues, "Le surgissement de la cause Amazighe en Libye," 242.

59. For the Arabic-language text of the Open Letter, see *Libya Almostaqbal*, http://archive2.libya-al-mostakbal.org/news/clicked/13365; for a summary of the main points in English, see "Open Letter to the TNC," www.temehu.com/imazighen/alt.htm.

60. See www.youtube.com/watch?v=X0O10LxQSW0; www.youtube.com/watch?v=wbiYC9s5Ahs, beginning at 4 minutes, 30 seconds.

61. "First Libyan National Amazigh Congress (LNAC)," www.temehu.com/imazighen/alt.htm; Joseph Logan, "Libya Amazigh Demand Recognition in New Constitution," Reuters, September 26, 2011, https://uk.reuters.com/article/uk-libya-berber-language/libya-amazigh-demand-recognition-in-new-constitution-idUKTRE78P4RJ20110926; for the text of the declaration, see http://tamazgha.fr/Le-Congres-national-amazigh-libyen.html.

62. "Berberism and Berber Political Movements, Libya, 23–27 November 2011," www.temehu.com/imazighen/berberism.htm; Ferkal says he had an Amazigh flag draped around his shoulders. Ferkal, "Tamazgha orientale," 225.

63. "Communiqué du Congrès national amazigh libyen," November 24, 2011, in Ferkal, "Tamazgha orientale," Annexe 5, 235–236.

64. Benkhalifa interview with *De Weil* (dw.com), "Libya's Berbers Feel Rejected by Transitional Government," November 8, 2011, www.dw.com/en/libyas-berbers-feel-rejected-by-transitional-government/a-15515687.

65. "Même après Kadhafi, les Amazighs demeurent toujours marginalisés," *Le Matin d'Algérie*, December 1, 2011, www.lematindz.net/news/6446-meme-apres-kadhafi-les-amazighs-demeurent-toujours-marginalises.

66. See, e.g., interview with AmazighTimes.nl, July 13, 2014, www.youtube.com/watch?v=mPSC2TLhM2Q.

67. International Crisis Group, "Divided We Stand: Libya's Enduring Conflicts," Report 130/Middle East & North Africa, September 14, 2012, 5–7, https://d2071andvip0wj.cloudfront.net/130-divided-we-stand-libya-s-enduring-conflicts.pdf.

68. For a dramatic and detailed account of the episode, see Wehrey, *The Burning Shores*, 124–143.

69. Buzakhar et al., "The Role of Amazigh Libyan Civil Society in the Tamazgha Spring," 184–185.

70. Buzakhar et al., 185.

71. Eva Pföestl and Will Kymlicka, "Minority Politics in the Middle East and North Africa: The Prospects for Transformative Change," *Ethnic and Racial Studies* 38(14) (2015): 2489–2498.

72. "Berbers' Constitutional Recognition," www.temehu.com/constitutions.htm?tab=5.

73. "Berbers' Constitutional Recognition"; English translation of Quranic verses in `Abdullah Yusuf `Ali, *The Holy Qur'an: Text, Translation and Commentary*, new rev. ed. (Brentwood, MD: Amana Corp., 1409 A.H./1989), 1013, 1343. For the full texts of the statement in Tamazight and Arabic, see www.temehu.com/imazighen/berberdownloads/constitution-rights-forum-for-amazigh-people.pdf.

74. "Version anglaise du communiqué du Haut Conseil des Amazigh de Libye," Ferkal, "Tamazgha Oriental," Annexe 10, 240–242.

75. The Arabic language text and its English translation can be found at Temehu.com, "Berber Constitution Update (1)Law 18 (2013): On The Rights of Cultural & Linguistic Components of The Libyan People. Issued by the GNC," www.temehu.com/constitutions.htm ("Amazigh").

76. BBC News, "Libyan Berbers Demanding Recognition Storm Parliament," August 13, 2013, www.bbc.com/news/world-africa-23690797.

77. Ghaith Shennib and Ulf Laessing, "Libyan Berbers Shut Gas Pipeline to Italy, Cut Major Income Source," Reuters, November 11, 2013, www.reuters.com/article/us-libya-gas/libyan-berbers-shut-gas-pipeline-to-italy-cut-major-income-source-idUSBRE9AA0UT20131111.

78. "The Mourning Day (*'As N Tkerkas'*): 20 February 2014," Temhu.com, www.temehu.com/constitutions.htm ("Amazigh").

79. Wehrey, *The Burning Shores*, 86–87.

80. Karlos Zurutuza, "Libya's Berbers Fear Ethnic Conflict," *Al Jazeera English*, January 6, 2015, www.aljazeera.com/news/middleeast/2014/12/libya-berbers-fear-ethnic-conflict-2014123065353199495.html; Nicolas Pelham, "Libya Against Itself," *New York Review of Books*, February 19, 2015, www.nybooks.com/articles/2015/02/19/libya-against-itself.

81. Desrues, "Le surgissement de la cause Amazighe en Libye," 246.

82. Amazigh Supreme Council, "Final Report of the Elections of the Amazigh Supreme Council That Took Place on 08–30–15," September 14, 2015, www.facebook.com/media/set/?set=a.760928497362501&type=3&__cft__[0]=AZV5xrfG0onn6 TBALFjq37TnEg5WtmBXHS3eaY7MFefrhfxEGLO8XVKaLfuHuL2Tjwf7Cpr dHAJsZC9UYE2fxnzxwOK5k8JLsbrWbV8ElCmmuvhn8zEOwb_EEourqMJCX _1Udk0Tj0FobXudcUvT6CbglW_ZOj5i70qiNi3M72xU2lNOmvNZvvLRrZhfT 0F3X8yrgdYvXXnoI_hYLELp2kE4&__tn__=-R.

83. The controversial mufti of Libya, Saïd al-Ghariani, had issued a strong statement two months earlier opposing the officialization of Tamazight. Baldinetti, "Languages in Libya," 432.

84. International Commission of Jurists, "Libya: Revised Draft Constitution to Ensure Compliance with International Standards," December 2015, www.icj.org/libya-revise-draft-constitution-to-ensure-compliance-with-international-standards; "Constitution Drafting Assembly CDA," www.temehu.com/constitutions.htm?tab=6.

85. Abdulkader Assad, "Tamazight Declared Official Language in Amazigh-peopled Districts," February 22, 2017, www.libyaobserver.ly/life/tamazight-declared-official-language-amazighpeopled-districts.

86. Jamie Prentis, "Amazigh Council Describe LNA as Terrorist Militia," *Libya Herald*, July 31, 2017, www.libyaherald.com/2017/07/31/amazigh-council-describe-lna-as-terrorist-militia.

87. Statement by Amazigh Supreme Council, July 30, 2017 (supplied to the author by Madghis Buzakher, Tira Center for Research and Studies, June 5, 2020).

88. Abdullah BenIbrahim, "Amazigh Activist Abducted in Benghazi and Accused of Espionage Because of His Language," *Libya Observer*, January 3, 2018, www.libyaobserver.ly/news/amazigh-activist-abducted-benghazi-and-accused-espionage-because-his-language.

89. Valerie Stocker, "Citizenship on Hold: Undetermined Legal Status and Implications for Libya's Peace Process," European Institute of Peace, July 2019, 22, www.eip.org/publication/citizenship-on-hold-in-libya-an-eip-policy-paper.

90. For an English translation of the constitution, see www.temehu.com/CDA/final-draft-libya-constitution-29-july-2017-english-translation.pdf.

91. Fathi Ben Khalifa, "The Political Situation of the Imazighen in Libya Before and after 2011," in *Libya Between History and Revolution,* Di Tolla and Schiattarella (eds.), 31.

92. For the chain of events and various statements aimed at containing the crisis, see "GNA's Western Zone Commander Attacks Ras Ajdir & Abukemmash," January 5, 2018, www.temehu.com/news-Libya.htm.

93. Abdulkader Assad, "Libyan Amazigh Supreme Council Accuses Audit Bureau of Jeopardizing National Unity," *Libya Observer*, April 21, 2016, www.libyaobserver.ly/news/libyan-amazigh-supreme-council-accuses-audit-bureau-jeopardizing-national-unity; Safa Alharty, "Protesters in Zuwara Accuse Education Minister of Marginalizing Amazigh Language," *Libya Observer*, March 28, 2019, www.libyaobserver.ly/inbrief/protesters-zuwara-accuse-education-minister-marginalizing-amazigh-language. The government denied such intent. Abdelkader Assad, "Libya's Education Ministry Denies Removing Amazigh language from Syllabus amid Accusations of Racism," *Libya Observer*, June 27, 2018, www.libyaobserver.ly/education/libya%E2%80%99s-education-ministry-denies-removing-amazigh-language-syllabus-amid-accusations.

94. Text provided to the author by Fathi Benkhalifa.

95. Buzakhar et al., "The Role of Amazigh Libyan Civil Society in the Tamazgha Spring," 188–201.

96. Buzakhar et al. (quote from 198).

97. "Giving a Voice to Minority Women in Libya: An Interview with Asma Khalifa and Inas Miloud," *al-Mufaqira*, December 22, 2016, https://jusoor.ly/2016/12/22

/giving-a-voice-to-minority-women-in-libya-an-interview-with-asma-khalifa-and-inas-miloud; interview with Zorgh Madi, May 5, 2020.

98. Zurutuza, "The Amazigh: Libya's Third Actor?"

99. Emily Burchfeld, "How the Exclusion of Women Has Cost Libya," November 26, 2019, www.atlanticcouncil.org/blogs/menasource/how-the-exclusion-of-women-has-cost-libya.

100. Tamazight Women Movement, www.euromedwomen.foundation/pg/en/profile/ermwf.twm.

101. Zurutuza, "The Amazigh: Libya's Third Actor?"

102. Asma Khalifa, "Libya's Forgotten Half: Between Conflict and Pandemic, Women Pay the Higher Price," Open Democracy, May 14, 2020, www.opendemocracy.net/en/author/asma-khalifa.

103. Charlotte de Harder, "A Polarised Nation during a Global Pandemic: The Libyan Predicament," Civil Society Platform for Peacebuilding and Statebuilding (CSPPS), n.d., https://cspps.org/Polarised-Nation-covid19-libya?fbclid=IwAR2LFQS4qu221VTsjZx4ZapFtIEpth0fEgHhDo3X5iHEcAENw5I5GjU3FaY; "Transforming Our World: The 2030 Agenda for Sustainable Development," https://sustainabledevelopment.un.org/post2015/transformingourworld.

104. The organization's website is located at http://tira.ly.

105. USAID, "Libya Elections and Legislative Strengthening Activity (LELSA)—NDI," www.usaid.gov/libya/fact-sheets/elections-and-legislative-strengthening-activity-lelsa-ndi.

106. USAID, "Libya Elections and Governance Support Program—NDI," www.usaid.gov/libya/fact-sheets/libya-elections-and-governance-support-ndi; USAID, "Libya Elections and Legislative Strengthening Activity"; USAID, "Breaking Down Language Barriers in Education," May 27, 2020, www.usaid.gov/libya/program-updates/may-2020-breaking-down-language-barriers-education; National Democratic Institute, "NDI, Tebu Activists Bring Indigenous Languages to Classrooms in southern Libya," June, 9, 2020, www.ndi.org/our-stories/ndi-tebu-activists-bring-indigenous-language-classrooms-southern-libya.

107. Interview with Asma Khalifa, June 3, 2020.

108. For a detailed discussion on the origins and strength of madkhalism in Libya, see Frederic Wehrey and Anouar Boukhars, *Salafism in the Maghreb* (Oxford: Oxford University Press, 2019), 107–135; and International Crisis Group, "Addressing the Rise of Libya's Madkhali-Salafis," Middle East & North Africa Report No. 200, April 25, 2019, www.crisisgroup.org/middle-east-north-africa/north-africa/libya/addressing-rise-libyas-madkhli-salafis.

109. A. Azergui, "Libye: une milice salfiste pro-Haftar meanace les Berbères d'extermination," April 7, 2020, http://tamazgha.fr/LIBYE-une-milice-salafiste-pro.html; Masin Ferkal, "L'autre guerre des Amazighs des Libye," April 20, 2019, www.tamazgha.fr/L-autre-guerre-des-Amazighs-de.html.

110. "In Libya, the Amazighs Fight for Their Rights, but Risk Getting Caught in the Country's Ongoing and Bloody Conflict," fanack.com, September 12, 2019, https://fanack.com/libya/population/libya-amazighs-fight-for-their-rights; Karlos Zurutuza, "'Autonomy is a right': Amazigh Minority Fights for Rebirth amid Libyan Chaos," Middle East Eye, January 16, 2018, www.middleeasteye.net/news/autonomy-right-amazigh-minority-fights-rebirth-amid-libyan-chaos.

111. Déclaration du Haut Conseil des Amazighs de Libye (HCAL), May 18, 2020, http://tamazgha.fr/Le-HCAL-se-felicite-de-la-victoire.html.

112. Masin Ferkal, "Tweet en Tifingah du GNA: clarifications de Fethi Khlifa," April 23, 2020, http://tamazgha.fr/Fethi-n-Khlifa-s-adresse-au-GNA.html.

113. Stéphane Arrami, "La langue amazighe officialisée en Libye," Amazigh24, June 1, 2020, https://amazigh24.com/la-langue-amazighe-officialisee-en-libye; Madghis Bouzakher, private communiqué, July 24, 2020.

114. Al-Marsad, "US Ambassador Expresses Support for the Activities of the Amazigh Supreme Council," June 16, 2020, https://almarsad.co/en/2020/06/16/us-ambassador-expresses-support-for-the-activities-of-the-amazigh-supreme-council/lish.

115. Interview with Asma Khalifa, June 4, 2020.

116. The term is from Nazih N. Ayubi, *Over-Stating the Arab State* (London: I. B. Tauris, 1995). "*Dawlat mukhabarat*" ("state of the internal security agencies") is an appropriate synonym. For a lengthy discussion of the term and its interpretations, see Steven Heydemann, "Beyond Fragility: Syria and the Challenges of Reconstruction in Fierce States," Brookings Institution, June 2018, fn.11, www.brookings.edu/wp-content/uploads/2018/06/FP_20180626_beyond_fragility.pdf.

117. Baldinetti, "Languages in Libya," 431.

118. State of Libya, Ministry of Education, *Adlis Nnu* ("My Book"), sixth grade of primary level, prepared by Muhammed Madi and reviewed by Nuha Loasi, Abed Arrahman Billush, and Mahmud Abekkush, 2968/2969, 2018/2019, 33, 37 (thanks to Wail Moammer for providing me with an electronic version of the book).

119. Desrues, "Le surgissement de la cause Amazighe en Libye," 171.

120. See, e.g., "Statement by Amazigh Supreme Council, November 28, 2017," provided to the author by TIRA Research and Studies, Tripoli. Responding to complaints against the African migrant community in Libya, the statement emphasized that the Amazigh were "one of the Indigenous Peoples of Africa," with "deeply rooted ties to its African brothers and sisters."

121. Eden Almasude and Mazigh Buzakhar, "From Failed State to Regional Autonomy: Amazigh Self-determination in Libya," *Nationalia*, April 14, 2016, www.nationalia.info/opinion/10760/from%20-failed-state-to-regional-autonomy-amazigh-self-determination-in-libya; Zurutuza, "'Autonomy is a right'"; Zurutuza, "The Amazigh: Libya's Third Actor?"

122. Zayid Hadaya, "Amidst the Libyan War, Berbers Are Demanding Recognition of Their Identity, Language and Culture" (in Arabic), *Independent Arabiyya*, November 5, 2020, https://www.independentarabia.com/node/166031.

Chapter 3: Azawad

1. The name apparently derives from "Azawagh," a Tuareg-dialect word meaning "basin." Within what is now Mali, it referred to the expansive plain north of the Niger River between Bourem and Timbuktu, but it has now been expanded to cover all of northeastern Mali. Niger's Tuareg leaders also used the name during the 1940s and 1950s in demanding independence from the French, as did the rebels during the early 1990s; it continues to be employed today, although it has no official adminis-

trative meaning. E. Bernus, "Azawad," *Encyclopédie berbère* 8, 1990, document A339, http://journals.openedition.org/encyclopedieberbere/197; Charles Grémont, "Villages and Crossroads," in *Saharan Crossroads*, James McDougall and Judith Scheele (eds.) (Bloomington: Indiana University Press, 2012), 145, n.22.

2. "Moor," in this case, is a synonym for "Arabs," often applied to the Arab population of neighboring Mauritania. MNLA, "Political Platform," September 5, 2020, https://kabylia.wordpress.com/2012/10/05/mnla-politiske-plattform.

3. International Crisis Group, "Mali: Avoiding Escalation," Africa Report No. 189, July 18, 2012, 11, https://d2071andvip0wj.cloudfront.net/189-mali-avoiding-escalation.pdf.

4. This was done at the Congress's seventh gathering, in 2015, held in Agadir, Morocco.

5. E. Baldaro and L. Raineri, "Azawad: A Parastate Between Nomads and Mujahidins?" *Nationalities Papers* 48 (2020): 100–115, DOI:10.1017/nps.2019.62.

6. Baz Lecocq and Georg Klute, "Tuareg Separatism in Mali," *International Journal* 68(3) (2013): 425.

7. K.-G. Prasse, "Ṭawārik," in *Encyclopaedia of Islam, 2nd ed.*, P. Bearman, Th. Bianquis, C. E. Bosworth, E. van Donzel, and W. P. Heinrichs (eds.), http://dx.doi.org/10.1163/1573-3912_islam_COM_1200, first published online 2012, first print edition ISBN: 9789004161214, 1960–2007.

8. *CIA World Factbook*, May 2021, "Niger," https://www.cia.gov/the-world-factbook/countries/niger.

9. The higher figure comes from L. Bossard, ed., *An Atlas of the Sahara Sahel*, Organisation for Economic Co-operation and Development, Sahel and West Africa Club, 2015, 191, cited in Grégory Chauzal and Thibault van Damme, "The Roots of Mali's Conflict: Moving Beyond the 2012 Crisis," Clingendael, Netherlands Institute of International Relations, CRU Report, March 2015, 35, www.clingendael.org/sites/default/files/pdfs/The_roots_of_Malis_conflict.pdf.

10. George Joffé, "Minorities in the New Libya," in *Multiculturalism and Democracy in North Africa: Aftermath of the Arab Spring*, Moha Ennaji (ed.) (London: Routledge, 2014), 298.

11. Hélène Claudot-Hawad, "'Libérer l'Azawad': La reformulation des luttes politiques touarègues," *Studi Magrebini*, "Emerging Actors in Post Revolutionary North Africa," vol. 2, "Berber Movements in North Africa: Identity, New Issues, New Challenges," Anna Maria Di Tolla and Ersilia Francesca (eds.), Volumi XIV–XV (Napoli: 2016–2017), 155–178.

12. Charles Grémont, "Mali et Sahel: Nous sommes tous Sahéliens. Origines et perspectives des conflits menés par des Touaregs au Mali," *Rena Hors Les Murs,* January/February 2017, no. 467, www.aaeena.fr/medias/editor/files/Origines_et_perspectives_des_conflits_men%C3%A9s_par_des_Touaregs_au_Mali_-_Charles_Gr%C3%A9mont.pdf.

13. Thomas K. Seligman, "The Art of Being Touareg," in *The Art of Being Touareg*, Thomas K. Seligman and Kristyne Loughran (eds.) (Los Angeles: UCLA Fowler Museum, 2006), 213, cited by Cynthia Becker, "Matriarchal Nomads and Freedom Fighters: Transnational Amazigh Consciousness and Moroccan, Algerian, and Nigerien Artists," *Critical Interventions* 5 (Fall 2009): 79.

14. Grémont, "Mali et Sahel: Nous sommes tous Sahéliens," 133–137.

15. E. Baldaro and L. Raineri, "Azawad: A Parastate Between Nomads and Mujahidins?," 102. The letter actually begins by referring to an earlier petition sent in October 1957. For the original French text, see https://fr.solidaritenordsud.net/res/site107721/res793954_DU-58.pdf. According to Charles Grémont, the letter was sent by the chief of Timbuktu and was opposed by his rivals. Also according to Grémont, the region's main tribal chiefs categorically rejected the plan in 1959, the reason apparently being that by then it was clear to all that the French plan was a nonstarter and therefore something to distance themselves from. Grémont, "Mali et Sahel: Nous sommes tous Sahéliens."

16. Claudot-Hawad, "'Libérer l'Azawad,'" 158–159, fn.2.

17. Alexander Thurston, "Tuareg Rebellions," in *Encyclopaedia of Islam Three Online*, Kate Fleet, Gudrun Krämer, Denis Matringe, John Nawas, and Everett Rowson (eds.), http://dx.doi.org/10.1163/1573-3912_ei3_COM_40353.

18. Grémont, 137–140.

19. Baz Lecocq, *Disputed Desert: Decolonisation, Competing Nationalisms and Tuareg Rebellions in Northern Mali* (Leiden: Brill, 2010), 227–228.

20. Ines Kohl, "Modern Nomads, Vagabonds, Or Cosmopolitans? Reflections on Contemporary Touareg Society," *Journal of Anthropological Research* 66(4) (Winter 2010): 450. "'Borderliner' (or 'border crosser') 'designates groups of people who live on state borders and who specialize in benefiting from crossing these borders on a regular basis" (460, n.2).

21. Lecocq, *Disputed Desert*, 229–230.

22. Ironically, the term *evolués* belongs originally to the Algerian colonial context, referring to the thin layer of Algerian Muslims who had received modern French education and sought to fashion a "third way" between continued colonial domination and complete rejection of any association with France.

23. Lecocq and Klute, "Tuareg Separatism in Mali," 426–428.

24. Charles Grémont, "Mobility in Pastoral Societies of Northern Mali: Perspectives on Social and Political Rationales," *Canadian Journal of African Studies/La Revue canadienne des études africaines* 48(1) (2014): 36–37.

25. Grémont, "Mobility in Pastoral Societies," 3; Stephanie Pezard and Michael Shurkin, *Achieving Peace in Northern Mali* (Santa Monica, CA: RAND Corporation, 2015), 17–18, www.rand.org/pubs/research_reports/RR892.html; Andy Morgan, "The Causes of the Uprising in Northern Mali," Think Africa Press, February 6, 2012, https://thinkafricapress.com/causes-uprising-northern-mali-Touareg.

26. Jeremy Keenan, *Lesser Gods of the Sahara* (London: Routledge, 2007), 75. Keenan states (at page 77) that the Tuareg have been a minority of the population of Ahaggar and Tassili since the 1940s.

27. Yehudit Ronen, "Libya, the Tuareg and Mali on the Eve of the 'Arab Spring' and in Its Aftermath: An Anatomy of Changed Relations," *Journal of North African Studies* 18(4) (2013): 544–559, DOI:10.1080/13629387.2013.809660.

28. Andy Morgan, "Tinariwen—Sons of the Desert," 2009, www.andymorganwrites.com/tinariwen-sons-of-the-desert.

29. Rollo Romig, "Rebel Music: The Touareg Uprising in 12 Songs by Tinariwen," *The New Yorker*, April 2, 2012, www.newyorker.com/culture/culture-desk/rebel-music-the-Touareg-uprising-in-12-songs-by-tinariwen.

30. "Andy Morgan on Touareg Music and History," Afropop Worldwide, April 1, 2016 https://afropop.org/articles/andy-morgan-on-Touareg-music-and-history.

31. Susan Rasmussen, "The People of Solitude: Recalling and Reinventing Essuf (the Wild) in Traditional and Emergent Tuareg Cultural Spaces," *Journal of the Royal Anthropological Institute* (N.S.) 14 (2008): 609.

32. Remarks to an Algerian journalist, cited in Romig, "Rebel Music."

33. Masin Ferkal, "Tinariwen: un combat pour l'existence," Tamazgha.fr, January 31, 2012, http://tamazgha.fr/Tinariwen-un-combat-pour-l-existence,1871.html.

34. On the dynamic revival of ancient Libico-Berber scripts on the basis of *tifinagh*, see Mohammed Aghali, "Libyco-Berber Scripts from Antiquity to the 21st Century," in *About the Berbers: History, Language, Culture and Socio-Economic Conditions*, Bo Issakson and Marianne Laanatza (eds.) (Uppsala: Uppsala University, 2004), 66–72.

35. On Mammeri, see Bruce Maddy-Weitzman, *The Berber Identity Movement and the Challenge to North African States* (Austin: University of Texas Press, 2011), 74–79.

36. Becker, "Matriarchal Nomads," 92.

37. See, e.g., www.facebook.com/temoust; www.instagram.com/explore/tags/Touareg/?hl=en; www.instagram.com/amazigh_nation/?hl=en.

38. Hsen Larbi, "The Amazigh World Congress," *The Amazigh Voice*, December 1995–March 1996, https://user.eng.umd.edu/~sellami/DEC95/congress.html.

39. Maddy-Weitzman, *The Berber Identity Movement*, 135–136.

40. John Ahni Schertow, "World Amazigh Congress Reviews the State of Amazigh Rights," Intercontinental Cry, January, 7, 2011, WORLD, https://intercontinentalcry.org/world-amazigh-congress-reviews-the-state-of-amazigh-rights.

41. Andy Morgan, "The Causes of the Uprising in Northern Mali," Think Africa Press, February 6, 2020, https://thinkafricapress.com/causes-uprising-northern-mali-Touareg.

42. Morgan, "The Causes of the Uprising in Northern Mali."

43. "Andy Morgan on Touareg Music and History," Afropop Worldwide, April 1, 2016, https://afropop.org/articles/andy-morgan-on-Touareg-music-and-history.

44. Morgan, "The Causes of the Uprising in Northern Mali."

45. Andy Morgan, "What do the Tuareg Want?," Al Jazeera, January 9, 2014, www.aljazeera.com/indepth/opinion/2014/01/what-do-Touareg-want-20141913923498438.html.

46. Yvan Guichaoua, "Mali: the Fallacy of Ungoverned Spaces," February 14, 2013, https://matsutas.wordpress.com/2013/02/14/mali-the-fallacy-of-ungoverned-spaces-by-yvan-guichaoua.

47. Alex Thurston, "Mali's Tragic But Persistent Status Quo," RLS Research Papers on Peace and Conflict Studies in West and Central Africa, January 2018, 20–23, http://rosalux.sn/wp-content/uploads/2019/05/RLS_DAKAR_PC_01_2018-3-alex-thosten.pdf.

48. Déclaration d'indépendance de l'Azawad, April 6, 2012, www.webcitation.org/6BTul59wU?url=www.mnlamov.net/component/content/article/169-declaration-dindependance-de-lazawad.html.

49. MNLA, "Political Platform," September 5, 2012, https://kabylia.wordpress.com/2012/10/05/mnla-politiske-plattform.

50. Mike McGovern, "Understanding Conflict Drivers and Resilience Factors in

the Sahel: Desk Study," Navanti Group, USAID/USSOCOM Joint Sahel Assessment, 2011–2013, 34, https://sahelresearch.africa.ufl.edu/files/USAID-USSOCOM-Sahel-Desk-Study-7-Jun-13.pdf.

51. Baba Ahmed, "Mali—Bilal Ag Achérif (MNLA): 'Ansar Eddine peut obtenir qu'Aqmi quitte l'Azawad,'" *Jeune Afrique*, June 13, 2012, www.jeuneafrique.com/175643/politique/mali-bilal-ag-ach-rif-mnla-ansar-eddine-peut-obtenir-qu-aqmi-quitte-l-azawad.

52. MNLA, "Political Platform," September 5, 2012.

53. Judd Devermont, "Why Mali Needs a New Peace Deal," Center for Strategic and International Studies, April 15, 2020, www.csis.org/analysis/why-mali-needs-new-peace-deal.

54. "Agreement for Peace and Reconciliation in Mali Resulting from the Algiers Process," www.un.org/en/pdfs/EN-ML_150620_Accord-pour-la-paix-et-la-reconciliation-au-Mali_Issu-du-Processus-d'Alger.pdf.

55. For the reasons behind these developments, see Pezard and Shirkin, *Achieving Peace in Northern Mali*, 59–87; "Can Niger Offer Mali Lessons on the Tuareg?," The New Humanitarian, November 25, 2016, www.thenewhumanitarian.org/news/2013/04/11/can-niger-offer-mali-lessons-Touareg.

56. Chris Elliot, "On Targuite, Nomadism and the Nation: The Origins of Tuareg Militant Nationalism in North Africa," *Small Wars Journal*, June 12, 2013, https://smallwarsjournal.com/jrnl/art/on-targuit%C3%A9-nomadism-and-the-nation-the-origins-of-Touareg-militant-nationalism-in-north-afr.

Chapter 4: Tunisia

1. Stéphanie Pouessel, "Les marges renaissantes: Amazigh, Juif, Noir. Ce que la révolution a changé dans ce 'petit pays homogène par excellence' qu'est la Tunisie," *L'Année du Maghreb* [En ligne], VIII, 2012, mis en ligne le 01 janvier 2013, consulté le 28 décembre 2020, http://journals.openedition.org/anneemaghreb/1432; DOI:https://doi.org/10.4000/anneemaghreb.1432.

2. Sebag, P., "Tūnis," in *Encyclopaedia of Islam, 2nd ed.*, P. Bearman, Th. Bianquis, C. E. Bosworth, E. van Donzel, and W. P. Heinrichs (eds.), http://dx.doi.org/10.1163/1573-3912_islam_SIM_7630, first published online 2012, first print ed. ISBN: 9789004161214, 1960–2007.

3. W. Vycichl, "Africa," *Encyclopédie berbère* 2 (1985), document A79, mis en ligne le 01 décembre 2012, http://journals.openedition.org/encyclopedieberbere/888.

4. Michael Brett and Elizabeth Fentress, *The Berbers* (Oxford: Blackwell, 1996), 24–80.

5. Brett and Fentress, 81–153.

6. Brett and Fentress, 150–151.

7. Ernest Gellner, "Introduction," in *Arabs and Berbers: From Tribe to Nation*, Ernest Gellner and Charles Micaud (eds.) (Lexington, MA: D. C. Heath, 1972), 13–14.

8. Belgacem Hamza, "Berber Ethnicity and Language Shift in Tunisia" (doctoral thesis, Sussex University, 2006), 21–25.

9. Ricard González, "A Timid Amazigh Awakening in Tunisia," *Nationalia*, September 19, 2019, www.nationalia.info/dossier/11240/a-timid-amazigh-awakening-in

-tunisia#:~:text=Also%20called%20Berbers%2C%20the%20Amazigh,Romans%2C%20Ottomans%2C%20and%20Arabs. (This number, if accurate, would seem to be referring to monolingual Tamazight speakers only.)

10. Sam Kimball, "Amazigh languish in underserved pockets of southeast Tunisia," *Al-Monitor*, July 8, 2020, www.al-monitor.com/pulse/originals/2020/07/tunisia-amazigh-politics-minorities-taoujout-marginalized.html#ixzz6RnemF6Xt.

11. Hédi Abdelkefi, "The Tunisian Constitution: The Evolution of a Text," 2, https://www.arabstates.undp.org/content/rbas/en/home/library/Dem_Gov/the-constitution-of-tunisie-/the-process-of-the-constitution.html.

12. Interview with Stéphanie Pouessel, "Pluralism and Minorities in Post-Revolutionary Tunisia," *Middle East Law and Governance* 6 (2014): 55.

13. Stéphanie Pouessel "The Democratic Turn in Tunisia: Civic and Political Redefinition of Canons of Cultural Diversity," *Nationalism and Ethnic Politics* 22(1) (2016): 53–54.

14. On the concept of legibility, see James Scott, "Seeing Like a State: A Conversation with James C. Scott," Cato Institute, September 2010, https://www.cato-unbound.org/print-issue/487.

15. Kimball, quoting Ahmed Gwirah, "Amazigh Languish in Underserved Pockets of Southeast Tunisia."

16. Marisa Fois, "Relire l'histoire. La Tunisie entre revendications berbères et enjeux identitaires," *Studi Magrebini*, "*Emerging Actors in Post Revolutionary North Africa*," vol. 2, "*Berber Movements in North Africa: Identity, New Issues, New Challenges*," Anna Maria Di Tolla and Ersilia Francesca (eds.), Volumi XIV–XV (Napoli: 2016–2017), 115.

17. Hamza, "Berber Ethnicity and Language Shift in Tunisia," 221.

18. Mohamed Errihani, "Language Attitudes and Language Use in Morocco: Effects of Attitudes on 'Berber Language Policy,'" *Journal of North African Studies* 13(4) (December 2008): 411–428.

19. Hamza, "Berber Ethnicity and Language Shift in Tunisia," 28, 221.

20. Mohamed Daoud, "The Language Situation in Tunisia," *Current Issues in Language Planning* 2(1) (2001): 39–40.

21. *UNESCO Atlas of the World's Languages in Danger*, www.unesco.org/culture/languages-atlas/en/atlasmap/language-id-718.html.

22. "Les Amazighs (Berbères) de Tunisie: Marginalisation, négation, occultation," Conseil des Droits de l'Homme des Nations Unies Examen Périodique Universel 2° cycle, 13ème session, Genève, 21 mai–1er juin 2012, Contribution du CMA à l'EPU concernant la Tunisie, https://lib.ohchr.org/HRBodies/UPR/Documents/session13/TN/CMA_UPR_TUN_S13_2012_CongresMondialAmazigh_F.pdf.

23. Hamza, "Berber Ethnicity and Language Shift in Tunisia," 28.

24. Hamza, 136–137.

25. Stéphanie Pouessel, "Le revendication amazighe en Tunisie: la tunisianité au défi de la transition politique," in *Les revendications Amazighes dans la tourmente des "Printemps Arabes,"* Mohand Tilmatine and Thierry Desrues (eds.) (Rabat: Centre Jacques Berque, 2017), 215–232, https://books.openedition.org/cjb/1365.

26. United Nations Human Rights, Office of the High Commissioner, "Committee on Elimination of Racial Discrimination Concludes Review of Tunisia's Periodic Report, CERD 62nd session, 7 March 2003," https://newsarchive.ohchr.org/en/NewsEvents/Pages/DisplayNews.aspx?NewsID=588&LangID=E.

27. United Nations Human Rights, Office of the High Commissioner, "Committee on Elimination of Racial Discrimination Considers Report of Tunisia," February 17, 2009, https://newsarchive.ohchr.org/en/NewsEvents/Pages/DisplayNews.aspx?NewsID=8940&LangID=E.

28. "Les Berbères en Tunisie," Rapport de Tamazgha Présenté au Comité pour l'élimination de la discrimination raciale, Nations Unies, Conseil des droits de l'homme, 74ème session du Comité pour l'élimination de la discrimination raciale (CERD), Genève, 16 février au 6 mars 2009, http://berberi.org/Documenti/Rapport_Tamazgha_Tunisie_CERD_2009.pdf.

29. United Nations, Committee on the Elimination of Racial Discrimination, Seventy-fourth Session, February 16–March 6, 2009, "Consideration of Reports Submitted by States Parties under Article 9 of the Convention, Concluding observations of the Committee on the Elimination of Racial Discrimination, TUNISIA," https://undocs.org/CERD/C/TUN/CO/19.

30. Christopher Alexander, *Tunisia: From Stability to Revolution in the Maghreb*, 2nd ed. (London: Routledge, 2016), 82–105.

31. CMA Report, "Les Amazighs (Berbères) de Tunisie: Marginalisation, négation, occultation," Contribution du CMA à l'EPU concernant la Tunisie, Conseil des Droits de l'Homme des Nations Unies, Examen Périodique Universel 2° cycle, 13ème session, Genève, 21 mai–1er juin 2012, https://lib.ohchr.org/HRBodies/UPR/Documents/session13/TN/CMA_UPR_TUN_S13_2012_CongresMondialAmazigh_F.pdf.

32. The first Moroccan Amazigh associations had confronted the same obstacles in the 1960s. At that time, they couldn't even use the word "Amazigh" or "Berber" in their names.

33. Alexander, *Tunisia*, 87–88; interview with Stéphanie Pouessel, "Pluralism and Minorities in Post-revolutionary Tunisia"; Emily Parker, "Tunisia's Preamble: Space for Minorities Within an "Arab-Islamic Identity?," Fikra Forum, July 26, 2012, http://fikraforum.org/?p=2455.

34. Pouessel, "The Democratic Turn in Tunisia," 56; Parker, "Tunisia's Preamble."

35. Interview with Omar Fasstaoui, July 15, 2020.

36. Katherine E. Hoffman, "Berbers, Borders and Breakdown in the 2011 Libyan Civil War," in *On the Ground: New Directions in Middle East and North African Studies*, Brian T. Edwards (ed.) (Doha: Akkadia Press, 2014), http://ontheground.qatar.northwestern.edu/uncategorized/chapter-9-berbers-borders-and-breakdown-%E2%80%A8in-the-2011-libyan-civil-war; and Katherine E. Hoffman, "Navigating the Border: Amazigh Minorities from Libya in Tunisia during the 2011–2012 Uprisings," in *Mobility and Minorities in Africa*, Giovanni Sistu and Michele Carboni (eds.) (Rome: Aracne editrice, 2018), 149–171, DOI:10.4399/97888548934058.

37. Hoffman, "Navigating the Border," 151, n.4.

38. CMA Report, "Les Amazighs (Berbères) de Tunisie: Marginalisation, négation, occultation."

39. Silvia Quattrini, "Identity and Citizenship in Tunisia: The Situation of Minorities After the 2011 Revolution," Minority Rights Group International, November 2018, https://minorityrights.org/publications/identity-and-citizenship-in-tunisia-the-situation-of-minorities-after-the-2011-revolution; "Tunisia: Alternative report by Congrès Mondial Amazigh, Economic, social and cultural exclusion of the Amazighs

of Tunisia," CMA, June 2016, https://tbinternet.ohchr.org/Treaties/CESCR/Shared%20Documents/TUN/INT_CESCR_CSS_TUN_24718_E.pdf.

40. For the English language version of the 2014 constitution, see www.constituteproject.org/constitution/Tunisia_2014.pdf.

41. Ricard González, "Across the Maghreb, the Imazighen Are Pressing for Rights and Cultural Recognition," *Equal Times*, February 5, 2020, www.equaltimes.org/across-the-maghreb-the-imazighen?lang=en#.XxLNoSgzY2x; Ricard González, "A Timid Amazigh Awakening."

42. "Tunisia: Alternative report by Congrès Mondial Amazigh."

43. Nations Unies, Conseil économique et social, Comité des droits économiques, sociaux et culturels, "Observations finales concernant le troisième rapport périodique de la Tunisie," E/C.12/TUN/CO/3, November 14, 2016, http://docstore.ohchr.org/SelfServices/FilesHandler.ashx?enc=4slQ6QSm1BEDzFEovLCuW1l-HU172P161pGVYxuGhhIwkzwoWmqP2KpW6segLmb%2Bl%2BjzluVdIPU519%2FhEFo6QoKNUZq8mLh1HhRWAbOZkaCyRLpsgp1IOTUwvSo11MCp9.

44. Organic Law no. 2018-50 of October 23, 2018, on the elimination of all forms of racial discrimination, www.legislation.tn/sites/default/files/news/tf2018501.pdf; interview with Omar Fasstaoui, July 15, 2020.

45. Belkacem Lounes, "Indigenous World 2020: Tunisia," www.iwgia.org/en/tunesia/3595-iw-2020-tunisia.html.

46. Minority Rights Group International in partnership with the Anti-Discrimination Points Network: Damj, Association pour la Promotion du Droit à la Différence, Association Tunisienne de Prevention Positive, By Lhwem, Danseurs Citoyens Sud, Mawjoudin, Mnemty, "Review of the 6th Periodic Report of Tunisia," UN Human Rights Committee, Session no. 128, Geneva, 2—27 March 2020, https://minorityrights.org/wp-content/uploads/2020/02/CCPR128_Tunisia_MRG.pdf; "Contribution de la societe civile a l'examen du sixieme (vi)rapport de la Tunisie pour l'application du pacte international relatif aux droits civils et politiques," Comité des droits de l'Homme Session no. 128 Genève 2–27 Mars 2020, https://tbinternet.ohchr.org/Treaties/CCPR/Shared%20Documents/TUN/INT_CCPR_CSS_TUN_41625_F.pdf.

47. Belkacem Lounes, "Indigenous World 2020: Tunisia," www.iwgia.org/en/tunesia/3595-iw-2020-tunisia.html.

48. Lounes, "Indigenous World 2020: Tunisia"; Belkacem Lounes, "Indigenous World 2019: Tunisia," www.iwgia.org/en/tunesia/3476-iw2019-tunisia.html.

49. González, "A Timid Amazigh Awakening in Tunisia."

50. González, "A Timid Amazigh Awakening in Tunisia."

51. Communicated to me by Samir Nefzi, July 19 2020.

52. Amel al-Hilali, "Tunisia's Indigenous Amazighs Launch Their First Political Party," *Al-Monitor*, May 19, 2019, www.al-monitor.com/pulse/originals/2019/05/amazigh-tunisia-presidential-elections-political-party.html#ixzz6SYASHYED.

53. Nefzi, personal communication.

54. Nefzi, personal communication.

55. Nora Gharyéni, "Takrust," July 5, 2019, www.youtube.com/watch?v=NvKym0vumYU&fbclid=IwAR3bmhtlMFngBxm7_noLJD6XoA-LtHjoQ0OjQVn5_gjXvxIYBi7TNdFF5sA.

56. "Nur al-Gharyéni, A Tunisian Singer Who Loves Amazigh Music, Dialogue with Moh Lahcen," (in Arabic), Ahdath.info, September 8, 2019, https://ahdath.info/511901?fbclid=IwAR0O3q6FI99o6FjyoYu2wh3C0XPJdiailX4ProfRxvF0r7GYyjF_zIidtsI.

57. Pouessel, "The Democratic Turn in Tunisia."

Chapter 5: Moroccan Imazighen and the *Makhzen*

1. Morocco, Human Development Indictors, http://hdr.undp.org/en/countries/profiles/MAR; Morocco, Human Development Report 2019, Inequalities in Human Development in the 21st Century, Briefing Note for Countries on the 2019 Human Development Report, http://hdr.undp.org/sites/all/themes/hdr_theme/country-notes/MAR.pdf; "La jeunesse, grande oubliée de la croissance marocaine," *Le Monde*, August 10, 2018, https://www.lemonde.fr/afrique/article/2018/08/10/la-jeunesse-grande-oubliee-de-la-croissance-marocaine_5341269_3212.html; "4 Marocains sur 10 cherchent à quitter le Maroc," *Telquel*, November 15, 2018, https://telquel.ma/2018/11/15/4-marocains-sur-10-cherchent-a-quitter-le-maroc_1618079.

2. In 2018, the killing of a nineteen-year-old female student on a boatload of would-be emigrants by Moroccan coast guard units sparked angry protests in her home city of Tetouan. Safaa Kasraoui, "Hundreds of Football Fans March in Tetouan to Condemn Tragic Death of Hayat," Morocco World News, September 28, 2018, www.moroccoworldnews.com/2018/09/254240/hundreds-of-football-fans-march-in-tetouan-to-condemn-tragic-death-of-hayat; Ahlam Ben Saga, "Video: Hayat Risked Her Life to Support Impoverished Family," Morocco World News, September 28, 2018, www.moroccoworldnews.com/2018/09/254207/hayat-support-impoverished-family; Ali Attar, "Colère Au Maroc en mémoire d'Hayat, L'hymne nationale sifflè sur les stades de football," LeNouvelAfrik.com, October 1, 2018, www.afrik.com/colere-au-maroc-pour-la-mort-d-hayat-abattue-par-la-royal-navy; "Tetouan Football Stadium Crowd Booing during the Playing of the Moroccan National Anthem," https://youtube/IR2b7Q3LGfc.

3. See, e.g., "Fi Bladi Dalmouni" ("In my country I suffer from injustice"), sung by the supporters of Raja Casablanca F.C. "We live under a heavy cloud . . . talented people have been destroyed by the drugs you give them. You robbed the state treasures you shared with strangers. . . . Who can you complain to? Only to God, the Supreme, the only one who knows." The song is a regular part of the team's games and serves as the soundtrack to many protest videos on YouTube; see, e.g., www.youtube.com/watch?v=lQGPMRMMz_8 and www.youtube.com/watch?v=ub_PPa8Adpc. Supporters of other groups created and adopted their protest songs. For example, Ittihad Tangier fans sing against "injustice" and ask for "ships that will save us from this country." "Hadi Bled Lhogra," www.youtube.com/watch?v=2338LKs-n3c&list=PLK1lcEGJo2gJPOtjPT-sCNpVcBgtlBvZS&index=4&t=0s; and https://twitter.com/middleeasteye/status/1179072320817844224?lang=en.

4. Transparency International, "Global Corruption Barometer Middle East & North Africa, Citizens' Views and Experiences of Corruption," https://images.transparencycdn.org/images/2019_GCB_MENA_Report_EN.pdf.

5. "Palace Coercion Plagues Morocco's Real Estate Sector," Wikileaks, December 11, 2009, https://wikileaks.org/plusd/cables/09CASABLANCA226_a.html.

6. "The Top 16 Richest World Leaders and Their Net Worth," *Slice*, n.d., www.slice.ca/money/photos/richest-world-leaders/#!4aabbe4eafd8a764152da2b441bcc509.

7. Catherine Graciet and Éric Laurent, *Le Roi prédateur* (Paris: Éditions Du Seuil, 2012), 131–144, 201–207, https://archive.org/details/LeRoiPredateur/page/n197/mode/2up.

8. Abdelilah Essatte, "Social Protests in Morocco may Shift to Political Claims due to the Socio-Economic Exclusion of some Regions," Moroccan Institute for Policy Analysis, August 2, 2018, https://mipa.institute/584.

9. Tahar Ben Jelloun, "Partir, Hélas!," Le360, October 1, 2018, http://fr.le360.ma/blog/le-coup-de-gueule/partir-helas-175435.

10. "Tamazight"/"Amazigh" have long been terms that were applied specifically to the Middle Atlas tribes. In recent decades, they have taken on broader meaning (see introduction), n. 15.

11. Michael Peyron, *The Berbers of Morocco: A History of Resistance* (London: I. B. Taurus, 2020), 101–239.

12. Peyron, *The Berbers of Morocco*, 127–130.

13. Peyron, 243–245.

14. Remy Leveau, *Le fellah marocain: Défenseur du trône* (Paris: Presses De La Fondation Nationale Des Sciences Politiques, 1985).

15. Bruce Maddy-Weitzman, *The Berber Identity Movement and the Challenge to North African States* (Austin: University of Texas Press, 2011), 118–119.

16. Maddy-Weitzman, *The Berber Identity Movement*, 120–123.

17. The English translation was made from the Arabic-language text, with some modifications; see www.amazighworld.org/human_rights/morocco/manifesto2000.php.

18. Maddy-Weitzman, *The Berber Identity Movement*, 164–167.

19. Abdeslam Maghroui, "Morocco's Reforms After the Casablanca Bombings," https://carnegieendowment.org/sada/21592.

20. Maddy-Weitzman, "Women, Islam and the Moroccan State: The Struggle over the Personal Status Law," *Middle East Journal* 59(3) (Summer 2005): 393–410.

21. John Waterbury, *Commander of the Faithful* (London: Weidenfeld & Nicholson, 1970); for an analysis on how the rituals of power have enabled the monarchy to dominate the opposition, see Mohammed Daadaoui, *Moroccan Monarchy and the Islamist Challenge* (New York: Palgrave, 2011).

22. "The 'February 20' Movement," Project on Middle East Democracy, https://pomed.org/wp-content/uploads/2011/06/Press_Kit_June2011.pdf.

23. Merouan Mekouar, *Protest and Mass Mobilization: Authoritarian Collapse and Political Change in North Africa* (Abingdon, Oxon, UK: Routledge, 2016), 95, quoted by Noureddine Jebnoun, "Public Space Security and Contentious Politics of Morocco's Rif Protests," *Middle Eastern Studies* 56(1) (2020): 51, DOI:10.1080/00263206.2019.1597347.

24. John Chalcraft, *Popular Politics in the Making of the Modern Middle East* (Cambridge: Cambridge University Press, 2016), 22–29.

25. Daniele Rossi-Doria, "'Le Printemps Démocratique': Amazigh Activism in the February 20 Movement in Southern Morocco," *Contemporary Levant* 1(1) (2016): 68.

26. Jebnoun, "Public Space Security," 51–52.

27. "King Mohammed VI's Speech to the Nation," March 9, 2011, www.voltairenet.org/article168894.html.

28. Interview with Lahcen Oulhaj, Rabat, September 2011, who provided me with the draft text.

29. The original draft had spoken about "reinforcing the ties of solidarity with Arab and Muslim states."

30. Hassan Masiky, "Maghreb Union: Polemic About 'Arab,'" Morocco Tomorrow, February 29, 2012, www.moroccotomorrow.org/maghreb-union-polemic-about-arab.

31. *Le Monde Amazigh,* no. 133, July 2013, 9–13.

32. S. I. Bergh and D. Rossi-Doria, "Plus ça change? Observing the dynamics of Morocco's 'Arab Spring' in the High Atlas," *Mediterranean Politics* 20(2) (2015): 1–19.

33. Eva Pföstl and Will Kymlicka, "Minority Politics in the Middle East and North Africa: The Prospects for Transformative Change," *Ethnic and Racial Studies* 38(14) (2015): 2489–2498, DOI:10.1080/01419870.2015.1061132.

34. Rossi-Doria, "'Le Printemps Démocratique,'" 68–69.

35. GDP (PPP) per capita data ranking is as of 2017. "GDP Per Capita," Worldometers, www.worldometers.info/gdp/gdp-per-capita; Borgen Project, "The 10 Most Important Facts about Poverty in Morocco," February 25, 2018, https://borgenproject.org/10-facts-about-poverty-in-morocco; CIA World Factbook, "Infant Mortality Rate," www.cia.gov/library/publications/the-world-factbook/rankorder/2091rank.html, and "Maternal Mortality Rate," www.cia.gov/library/publications/the-world-factbook/rankorder/2223rank.html.

36. Moha Ennaji, "The Rural World Today: Development Is a National Need" (in Arabic), January 2, 2013, www.hespress.com/writers/69382.html.

37. Othman Skalli, "Anfgou. Les damnés du froid," *TelQuel*, March 12, 2014, http://telquel.ma/2014/03/12/anfgou-les-damnes-du-froid_132766.

38. Moha Moukhlis, "La Tragedie D'Anfgou: Des amazighes enterrés vivants," April 6, 2007, http://amazighrightswatch.blogspot.co.il/2007/04/la-tragedie-danfgou-des-amazighes.html.

39. Reported to me by a journalist who was present at the scene.

40. Safaa Kasraoui, "Ouarzazate Court of Appeal Jails 5 Demonstrators over 'Thirst Protests' in Zagora," Morocco World News, November 18, 2017, www.moroccoworldnews.com/2017/11/234173/ouarzazate-court-of-appeal-demonstrators-thirst-protests-zagora-water-scarcity; "Wave of 'Thirsty Protests' Hit Morocco After Water Shortages," The New Arab, October 15, 2017, www.alaraby.co.uk/english/society/2017/10/15/wave-of-thirsty-protests-hit-morocco-after-water-shortages.

41. Lit., "storehouse." The term essentially means "deep state," centering on the Palace and allied elites in the Moroccan political lexicon.

42. Paul A. Silverstein, "The Pitfalls of Transnational Consciousness: Amazigh Activism as a Scalar Dilemma," *Journal of North African Studies* 18 (2013): 768–778; Rossi-Doria, "'Le Printemps Démocratique.'"

43. Paul A. Silverstein, "The Amazigh Movement in a Changing North Africa," in *Social Currents in North Africa: Culture and Governance After the Arab Spring*, Osama Abi-Mershed (ed.) (Oxford: Oxford University Press, 2018), 87–88.

44. Larbi Arbaoui, "Amazigh Activist Killed by Pro-Polisario Students in Marrakech," Morocco World News, January 28, 2016, www.moroccoworldnews.com/2016/01/178494/amazigh-activist-killed-by-pro-polisario-students-in-marrakech; Safaa Kasraoui, "Morocco Sentences Pro-Polisario Sahrawi to 12 Years in Murder Case," Mo-

rocco World News, November 27, 2019, www.moroccoworldnews.com/2019/11/287693/morocco-pro-polisario-sahrawi-murder-case; Amazigh World News, "Omar Khaleq's Tomb Destroyed in Tinghir," October 1, 2018, https://amazighworldnews.com/omar-khaleqs-tomb-destroyed-in-tinghir.

45. Interview with Hamid ʾOudeh (in Arabic), *Le Monde Amazigh*, July 20, 2016, 6–7, https://amadalamazigh.press.ma/archivesPDF/186.pdf?fbclid=IwAR2XguiH6P-xu2MBu7w-jO_tIj9RC7y2rlunf1XYcj9QL12HNmwfFW4_VHY; Mustafa Usay, *The Road to Tamazgha: Memoirs of a Prisoner [adhering to] the Amazigh Idea* (in Arabic) (Rabat: Infobaranet, 2016).

46. "Recommandations de la conférence internationale sur les droits à la terre et aux ressources dans les pays de Tamazgha," July 21–22 2017, Congres Mondial Amazigh, February 26, 2018, www.congres-mondial-amazigh.org/2018/02/26/recommandations-de-la-conf%C3%A9rence-internationale-sur-les-droits-%C3%A0-la-terre-et-aux-ressources-dans-les-pays-de-tamazgha.

47. Sarah Ryser, "The Anti-Politics Machine of Green Energy Development: The Moroccan Solar Project in Ouarzazate and Its Impact on Gendered Local Communities," *Land* (spec. 100th issue) 8(6) (2019): 19, www.mdpi.com/2073-445X/8/6/100; Fabíola Ortiz, "Is the World's Largest Solar Project a 'Green Megawatt' or a 'Green Grab?,'" *Equal Times*, December 23, 2016, www.equaltimes.org/is-the-world-s-largest-solar?lang=en#.X-ZXN9gzY2x.

48. Yasmine Berriane, "Bridging Social Divides: Leadership and the Making of an Alliance for Women's Land-use Rights in Morocco," *Review of African Political Economy* 43(149) (2016): 350–364, DOI:10.1080/03056244.2016.1214118; ATTAC Maroc, "The Right to Land and the Modalities of Dispossession: A Focus on the Soulaliyate Movement," War on Want, August 14, 2020, https://waronwant.org/news-analysis/soulaliyate-movement-moroccan-women-fighting-land-dispossession?fbclid=IwAR1qcgw-_ZO8hQE8oGZWQhML2ief3v3dufWB-kyLosiNOaU8Z_Y6vYw321M. *Soulaliyate* "refers to the patrilineal tie that links each member to its community of origin and by extension to the land this tribe owns collectively" (Berriane, "Bridging Social Divides," n.1).

49. Mohamed Benidir, "Exploitation minière, mobilisation villageoise et pouvoir local: Le cas de la mine d'argent d'Imiter," AIMS International Workshop, "Berber Societies: New Approaches to Space, Time and Social Processes," Tangier, June 28–July 2, 2012 (23 pp.).

50. In 2012, the company's consolidated turnover was 53 billion MAD and its net income was 5 billion MAD; see "Al Mada (Holding)," http://en.wikipedia.org/wiki/Soci%C3%A9t%C3%A9_Nationale_d'Investissement; Environmental Justice Atlas, "Imider Silver Mine, Morocco," 2017-03-06, https://ejatlas.org/conflict/imider-silver-mine-morocco.

51. Quoted in Koenraad Bogaert, "Imider vs. COP22: Understanding Climate Justice from Morocco's Peripheries," *Jadaliyya*, November 21, 2016 www.jadaliyya.com/Details/33760/Imider-vs-COP22-Understanding-Climate-Justice-from-Morocco%E2%80%99s-Peripheries.

52. Benidir, "Exploitation minière," 14–16.

53. See https://m.facebook.com/Amussu.96Imider.

54. Aida Alami, "On Moroccan Hill, Villagers Make Stand Against a Mine," *New York Times*, January 25, 2014.

55. Margot Eliason, "Amazigh Land and Water Rights Documentary Wins

FIDADOC Grand Prix," *Morocco World News*, June 25, 2019, www.moroccoworld news.com/2019/06/276704/amazigh-documentary-fidadoc-grand-prix.

56. See www.facebook.com/Amussu.96Imider/photos/a.264942610188876.86775 .264059770277160/1156342587715536/?type=1&theater.

57. Koenraad Bogaert, "The Revolt of Small Towns: The Meaning of Morocco's History and the Geography of Social Protests," *Review of African Political Economy* 42(143) (2014): 124–140.

58. Wendy Wolford, "Families, Fields, and Fighting for Land: The Spatial Dynamics of Contention in Rural Brazil," *Mobilization* 8(2) (2003): 201–215.

59. "3rd Anniversary of the Mustapha Ochtouban Detention: The Imam Forbids the Prayer," Facebook page titled "Movement on the Road '96 Imider shared Amussu :Xf ubrid n 96 (Imider)," October 6, 2014.

60. Wolford, "Families, Fields, and Fighting for Land"; Mounia Bennani-Chraïbi and Olivier Fillieule, "Towards a Sociology of Revolutionary Situations: Reflections on the Arab Uprisings," *Revue française de science politique* (English) 62(5) (2012): 1–29, DOI:10.3917/rfspe.625.0001.

61. Bouhmouch's film contained impressive scenes from the *Agraw*. See www .idfa.nl/en/film/0d6b54ab-62d2-4ca4-9abc-6785fa7173f7/amussu?gclid=Cj0KCQjw 4f35BRDBARIsAPePBHwKjhJSspSO5EZXOJzW3aFAcCjlQIKQy-JL6ahDzh0 BfOEDRCISqccaAhpVEALw_wcB.

62. Boegaert, "The Revolt of Small Towns," 124–125, 133–136.

63. A. Azergui, "The Seven Plagues of Imider," posted on Facebook pages titled "Movement on the Road '96 Imider" and "Amussu :Xf ubrid n 96 (Imider)," September 23, 2014.

64. Sebastian Balfour, *Deadly Embrace: Morocco and the Road to the Spanish Civil War* (Oxford: Oxford University Press, 2002), 61–75; Daniel Woolman, *Rebels in the Rif* (Stanford: Stanford University Press, 1968), 83–102; C. R. Pennell, *A Country with a Government and a Flag: The Rif War in Morocco, 1921–1926* (Wisbech, UK: Menas Press, 1986); Peyron, *The Berbers of Morocco*, 149–160.

65. Nabil Mouline, "Reconsidering the Rif Revolt (1958–59)," *Jadaliyya*, January 28, 2015, www.jadaliyya.com/Details/31718; Maati Monjib, "Le Rif, Mohammed V et l'Istiqlal," *Le Journal Hebdomadaire*, no. 368 (October 2008): 25–31; Monjib, "Moulay Hassan et le Rif," *Zamane*, no. 20 (June 2012); Monjib, "Le Nord: La Memoire Oubliee," *Zamane*, no. 27 (February 2013); David M. Hart, "Rural and Tribal Uprisings in Post-Colonial Morocco, 1957–1960: An Overview and a Reappraisal," in David M. Hart, *Journal of North African Studies (Special Issue on Tribe and Rural Society in Morocco)* 4(2) (Summer 1999): 93.

66. "Top 50 World Container Ports," www.worldshipping.org/about-the-industry /global-trade/top-50-world-container-ports.

67. Angela Suárez Collado, "Territorial Stress in Morocco: From Democratic to Autonomist Demands in Popular Protests in the Rif," *Mediterranean Politics* 20(2) (2015): 221–224.

68. Collado, "Territorial Stress in Morocco," 226–227; Jebnoun, "Public Space Security," 52.

69. Anthony D. Smith, *Nations and Nationalism in a Global Era* (Cambridge: Polity Press, 1995), 146.

70. Mohamed Nadrani, *Al-Amir, Ibn ʿAbd al-Karim* (Casablanca: Al-Ayyam, 2008).

71. Amnesty International, Testimony of Mohamed Nadrani, in "Morocco: Breaking the Walls of Silence: 'The Disappeared,'" April 13, 1993, www.amnesty.org/en/library/info/MDE29/001/1993/en.
72. "Mohammed Nadrani: le dessin ou la Folie," interview by Christophe Cassiau-Haurie, June 7, 2009, www.bdzoom.com/spip.php?article3884.
73. Swordfish fishing was banned by law during that time of the year.
74. See www.youtube.com/watch?v=5fEMrepVTds.
75. Zakaria Rhani, Khalid Nabalssi, and Mariam Benalioua, "'The Rif again! Popular Uprisings and Resurgent Violence in Post-transitional Morocco," *Journal of North African Studies* (2020): 2–3, DOI:10.1080/13629387.2020.1780921.
76. Rhani et al., "'The Rif again!," 2.
77. Abderrahim Chalfaouat, "Al-Hoceima Protests Mirror Morocco's Political Fragility," *Mideast Monitor*, May 16, 2017, www.middleeastmonitor.com/20170516-al-hoceima-protests-mirror-moroccos-political-fragility.
78. Mohamed Amine Harmach, "Qui est vraiment Nasser Zefzafi?," H24info, May 29, 2017, www.h24info.ma/maroc/politique/vraiment-nasser-zefzafi; Yassine Benargane and Latifa Babas, "Rif: El Fizazi Replies to Zefzafi and Calls Him a 'Scavenging' Leader," *Yabiladi*, May 28, 2017, https://en.yabiladi.com/articles/details/54097/fizazi-replies-zafzafi-calls-scavenging.html.
79. A fuller list of the demands can be found in Jebnoun, "Public Space Security," 55.
80. Youssef Igrouane, "Militarization of Al Hoceima 'Without Legal Basis': Govt Spokesperson," Morocco World News, May 26, 2017, www.moroccoworldnews.com/2017/05/217739/militarization-al-hoceima-without-legal-basis-govt-spokesperson.
81. Jabnoun, "Public Space Security," 55–56.
82. "Pour Avoir Traité les Rifains de 'Racailles,' la Députée Khadija Ziyani Suspendue," bladi.net, November 3, 2016, www.bladi.net/khadija-ziyani-racailles-rifains,46578.html.
83. Anne Wolf, "Morocco's Hirak Movement and Legacies of Contention in the Rif," *Journal of North African Studies* 24(1) (2019): 4–5, DOI:10.1080/13629387.2018.1538188.
84. Ghally Rhannou, "Powerful Assemblages in the Rif," *Emancipations*, http://taharour.org/?powerfulassemblages-In-the-rif, cited by Jabnoun, "Public Space Security," 57.
85. Jabnoun, 21; "The Video That Got Rif Protests Activist Nasser Zafzafi Arrested," Morocco World News, June 1, 2017, www.moroccoworldnews.com/2017/06/218468/video-got-rif-protests-activist-nasser-zefzafi-al-hoceima.
86. Zafazafi videos, in Al-Hoceima mosque, at https://youtu.be/_0TOOo6FYDg; on rooftop of house, https://youtu.be/IWsI3AAL2_; "Actualité—La tension monte d'un cran à Al Hoceima, Zefzafi provoque et l'État vient de réagir … (Vidéos)," Article19.ma. May 26, 2017, http://article19.ma/accueil/archives/73612.
87. Maati Monjb, "The Relentless Tide of Morocco's Rif Protests," *Sada Journal*, June 21, 2017, https://carnegieendowment.org/sada/71331#:~:text=The%20Moroccan%20authorities%20are%20unsuccessfully,against%20protesters%20in%20the%20Rif.
88. Her incarceration was brief, albeit traumatic. It also enhanced her symbolic status as a struggler for Rifian and Amazigh rights. As was the case with Dania Ben Sassi, the "voice of the Libyan revolution," she was subsequently invited to perform "A

Vava Inouva," with the iconic Idir, at a 2018 Amazigh Yennayer celebration in Holland; see www.youtube.com/watch?v=toeJCsxlifM.

89. Jabnoun, "Public Space Security," 24.

90. Monjib, "The Relentless Tide of Morocco's Rif Protests."

91. "Morocco: Protest Leader Alleges Police Beat Him," Human Rights Watch, June 22, 2017, www.hrw.org/news/2017/06/22/morocco-protest-leader-alleges-police-beat-him; "Morocco: Rif Protesters Punished with Wave of Mass Arrests," Amnesty International, June 2, 2017, www.amnesty.org/en/latest/news/2017/06/morocco-rif-protesters-punished-with-wave-of-mass-arrests; Association Marocaine des Droits Humains Section de Rabat, "Rapport sur les Violations des Droits Humains à Hoceima le 20/07/201," www.scribd.com/document/355995820/Rapport-Hoceima-200717-Fr.

92. "Protests in Bejaia and Tizi-Ouzou Express Solidarity with the Rif Movement and Denounce Arrests" (in Arabic), *Le Monde Amazigh*, no. 197, July 2017, 12.

93. National Federation of Amazigh Associations (FNAA), "Shadow Report of the National Federation of Amazigh Associations in Morocco Under the Third Cycle of the Universal Periodic Review of Morocco 27th Session of the Universal Periodic Review Working Group/May 2017," www.upr-info.org/sites/default/files/document/morocco/session_27_-_may_2017/js20_upr27_mar_e_main.pdf.

94. Annual statement of the Amazigh Network for Citizenship—AZETTA AMAZIGHE—"On the situation of Amazigh linguistic and cultural rights through 2013 on the occasion of the 65th anniversary of the Universal Declaration of Human Rights," www.amazighworld.org/eng/human_rights/index_show.php?id=141.

95. FNAA, "Shadow Report"; UN Human Rights Council, "Summary of Stakeholders' Submissions on Morocco," May 1–12, 2017, https://documents-dds-ny.un.org/doc/UNDOC/GEN/G17/036/33/PDF/G1703633.pdf?OpenElement; "Report of the Working Group on the Universal Periodic Review, Morocco," September 11–29, 2017, https://documents-dds-ny.un.org/doc/UNDOC/GEN/G17/190/71/PDF/G1719071.pdf?OpenElement; UN Human Rights Office of the High Commissioner, "End of Mission Statement of the Special Rapporteur on Contemporary Forms of Racism, Racial Discrimination, Xenophobia and Related Intolerance at the Conclusion of Her Mission to the Kingdom of Morocco," December 21, 2018, www.ohchr.org/EN/News Events/Pages/DisplayNews.aspx?NewsID=24043&LangID=E; Juliette Owen-Jones, "UN Special Rapporteur Calls on Morocco to Take Action Against Racism," Morocco World News, July 11, 2019, www.moroccoworldnews.com/2019/07/277919/un-rapporteur-racism-report.

96. English-language text of the 2011 constitution is at www.constituteproject.org/constitution/Morocco_2011.pdf?lang=en.

97. Reda Zaireg, "370 Associations Contre la Loi Organique sur l'Amazighe," *HuffPost Maghreb*, September 9, 2016, www.huffpostmaghreb.com/2016/09/09/memorandum-roi-amazigh_n_11933782.html, and Reda Zaireg, "Ahmed Boukous Plaide Pour un Plan Stratégique pour l'Officialisation de l'Amazighe," *HuffPost Maghreb*, July 28, 2016, www.huffpostmaghreb.com/2016/07/28/ahmed-boukous-officialisa_n_11240978.html.

98. Organic Law 26-16, September 12, 2019, http://bdj.mmsp.gov.ma/Ar/Document/10396-Loi-organique-n-26-16-promulgu%C3%A9e-par-le-dahir-n-.aspx?KeyPath=594/596/595/10396.

99. Yahia Hatim, "Exclusion of Tamazight on Morocco's New Identity Cards Re-

ignites Debate," Morocco World News, June 15, 2020, www.moroccoworldnews.com/2020/06/305863/exclusion-of-tamazight-on-moroccos-new-identity-cards-reignites-debate; "Amazigh Excluded from Moroccan ID Cards Despite Being Official Language," *Nationalia*, July 27, 2020, www.nationalia.info/brief/11332/amazigh-excluded-from-moroccan-id-cards-despite-being-official-language.

100. Jassim Ahdani, "Ahmed Arahmouch: Observations autour de la circulaire d'El Otmani sur l'Amazigh," *Hespress*, December 13, 2019, https://fr.hespress.com/114301-ahmed-arahmouch-observations-autour-de-la-circulaire-del-otmani-sur-lamazigh.html?fbclid=IwAR3yt-GXrRkPuOMczGHm9kO05EtJp6yk3EccvWo8RHpQFuilSXZsutfB8nA.

101. "The 'Tamunt' Party in Morocco: Can It Accomodate Non-Amazigh?," Maghreb Voices (in Arabic), April 17, 2018, https://www.maghrebvoices.com/2018/04/17/%D8%AD%D8%B2%D8%A8-%D8%AA%D8%A7%D9%85%D9%88%D9%86%D8%AA-%D8%A8%D8%A7%D9%84%D9%85%D8%BA%D8%B1%D8%A8-%D9%8A%D8%B3%D8%AA%D9%88%D8%B9%D8%A8-%D8%BA%D9%8A%D8%B1-%D8%A7%D9%84%D8%A3%D9%85%D8%A7%D8%B2%D9%8A%D8%BA%D8%9F; "Ban of Amazigh Party Raises Controversy in Morocco," *Al-`Araby al-Jadid* (in Arabic), September 13, 2018, https://www.alaraby.co.uk/%D9%85%D9%86%D8%B9-%D8%A5%D9%86%D8%B4%D8%A7%D8%A1-%D8%AD%D8%B2%D8%A8-%D8%A3%D9%85%D8%A7%D8%B2%D9%8A%D8%BA%D9%8A-%D9%8A%D8%AB%D9%8A%D8%B1-%D8%AC%D8%AF%D9%84%D8%A7%D9%8B-%D9%81%D9%8A-%D8%A7%D9%84%D9%85%D8%BA%D8%B1%D8%A8.

102. Ahmed Arrehmouch, personal communication, July 28, 2020; "Dossier de l'amazighité: Une plateforme d'action politique voit le jour," Perspectives Med, January 22, 2020, www.perspectivesmed.ma/dossier-de-lamazighite-une-plateforme-daction-politique-voit-le-jour/?fbclid=IwAR0rY67SFXeT0LUbOz51cKLhL15wrpbc2gqArnIJC3IzlV46tnoBqz0av8E.

103. Mohamed Chakir Alaoui et Yassine Benmini, "Vidéo. Le RNI scelle une alliance avec une ong Amazighe, voici pourquoi," le360.ma, November 18, 2020, https://fr.le360.ma/politique/video-le-rni-scelle-une-alliance-avec-une-ong-amazighe-voici-pourquoi-227524; and "Vidéo. En vue des élections 2021 et après le RNI, entente entre le MP et le front Amazigh," le360.ma, December 31, 2020, https://fr.le360.ma/politique/video-en-vue-des-elections-2021-et-apres-le-rni-entente-entre-le-mp-et-le-front-amazigh-230477.

104. Mohamed Chtatou, "The Evolution of Amazigh Activism in Morocco," Amazigh World News, n.d., https://amazighworldnews.com/the-evolution-of-amazigh-activism-in-morocco, and Mohamed Chtatou, "Amazigh Cultural Revival in North Africa," Amazigh World News, July 3, 2020, https://amazighworldnews.com/amazigh-cultural-revival-in-north-africa.

105. For a detailed discussion of traditional leadership structures in Amazigh society, and the extent of their relevance today, see Mohamed Chtatou, "Leadership among the Amazigh People in Morocco," Amazigh World News, June 15, 2020, https://amazighworldnews.com/leadership-among-the-amazigh-of-morocco.

106. Ahmed Boukous, "Amazigh Constitutionalization in Morocco: Stakes and Strategies," in *Studi Magrebini*, "*Emerging Actors in Post Revolutionary North Africa*," vol. 2, "*Berber Movements in North Africa: Identity, New Issues, New Challenges*," Anna Maria

Di Tolla and Ersilia Francesca (eds.), Volumi XIV–XV (Napoli: 2016–2017), quotes on 268, 271–272, 275.

107. Moha Ennaji, "A Tribute to Mahjoubi Aherdan," *Morocco World News*, November 25, 2020, www.moroccoworldnews.com/2020/11/327007/a-tribute-to-mahjoubi-aherdan.

108. Saïd Sadi, "Mahjoubi Aherdane: un amazigh debout," *Algerie Cultures*, November 16, 2020, https://algeriecultures.com/actualite-culturelle/mahjoubi-aherdane-un-amazigh-debout/?fbclid=IwAR2NHKkZRY1m1Z48ZztKIK0nazBgphWJysEeopipU6SQwt_-i4FFi_T-Si4.

109. "Dda" is an honorific title, meaning "wise man" or "sage."

110. Mohamed Chtatou, personal communiqué, August 1, 2020.

Conclusion

1. S. Nadir, "Idir n'est pas enterré en Kabylie, comme Hasnaoui, Azem et Zerrouki," Tamurt.info, https://tamurt.info/fr/2020/05/14/idir-nest-pas-enterre-en-kabylie-comme-hasnaoui-azem-et-zerrouki/154349, May 14, 2020.

Index

Note: Page numbers in *italics* indicate map images.

Abdeljalil, Moustapha, 71–72
Abdelkrim al-Khattabi, Mohamed bin, 144–148
Abu Kammash, Libya, 79
Abusahmen, Nouri, 74
Abu Zakhar, Fathi Salem, 70
Académie Berbère, 49, 58, 97
Achérif, Billal Ag, 100–101
Adghirni, Ahmed, 153, 155
African Union, 89, 138–139
Agadir Charter for Linguistic and Cultural Rights, 129–130
Ag Najm, Mohammed, 99
Agraw, 33, 142, 194n61
"*Agrawli Itri Enegh*" ("The Rebel Is Our Star"), 65
Aherdan, Mahjoubi, 155
Ahmjiq, Nabil, 150
Aït Ahmed, Hocine, 25, 37–39, 52, 173n92
Aït Atta tribe, 139, 142–143
Aït Bouknifen clan, 139
Aït Lahcine (village), 160
Aït Oumalou commune, 37
Aït Waryaghar tribe, 144
Aït Willut tribe, 58
Akal ("Land") political party, 120–121
Akhannouch, Aziz, 146
al-'Adl wal-Ihsan ("Justice and Beneficence"), 131, 133, 149, 159

Algeria: Amazigh movement prior to Arab Spring, 16; and Amazigh nationalism in Libya, 57; Amazigh political dynamics in, 4, 23–30; and Amazigh-Tuareg relationship, 97; and Arab Spring protests, 1, 3, 21–23, 30–31, 51; and Azawad autonomy movement, 89; and Berber identity, 7; contrasted with Morocco, 125; and democratic reforms, 39–41, 167n18; demographics of Imazighen in, 23–24; distribution of Amazigh-speaking groups, *8*; history of civil conflict, 13; and Imazighen of Libya, 58–61; impact of *Hirak* protests, 51–53; impact of reforms in Libya, 83; independence, 9–10, 14; indigenous Tamazight-speaking peoples, 6, 7, *8*; influence in Tunisian politics, 120; Kabyle-Amazigh dimension of the *Hirak* protests, 48–51; and Kabylian radicalization, 31–39; and nationalist anti-colonial movements, 9; origins of *Hirak* protests, 45–48; and scope of Amazigh identity movement, 3–4, 17, 158, 159; tensions in Mzab Valley, 41–45; Tunisia contrasted with, 105
Algerian Academy of the Amazigh Language, 41

Algerian League for the Defense of Human Rights, 44
Algerian War of Liberation, 46
Alhabib, Ibrahim Ag, 95–96
Al Hoceima, Morocco, 131–132, 135, 144, 146–149
al-Jamil, Libya, 72
Al Khadra Hospital, 81
al-Qaeda of the Islamic Maghreb (AQIM), 93–94, 100, 102
Amazigh calendar, 58
Amazigh Culture Movement, 137
"Amazigh" ethnonym, 164n15
Amazigh Flag Day, 76
Amazigh language. *See* Tamazight language
Amazigh Supreme Council, 75–79, 82, 84, 85
Amir, Ibn Abdelkrim, The (graphic novel), 146
Amnesty International, 45, 48
Amussu (film), 141
Ansar al-Din, 100, 102, 103
Ansar al-Shari`a, 72
anticolonial movements, 9, 144. *See also* colonial legacy in North Africa; French colonialism; Italian colonialism
antidiscrimination efforts, 119
Aoudia, Dalila, 97
Arab culture and identity: and Algeria's Imazighen, 25, 27; and Amazigh activism in Tunisia, 117, 123; and Amazigh culture in Tunisia, 6, 108, 109, 113–114, 121; Arab Awakening, 1–2; Arabism, 26, 33, 40, 69, 71; Arab nationalism, 15, 18–19, 60, 79; and ethnic groups of Libya, 59, 59–60; and Imazighen of Libya, 57, 58–62; and independence era, 9–13; pan-Arabism of Nasser, 57; and political background of Tunisia, 108–111; promotion of Arabic language, 7, 9, 39–40, 68, 76, 78, 132–133, 151, 154; and Rifian autonomy movement, 148
Arab-Israeli conflict, 110

Arab League, 125, 134
Arab Maghrib Union, 133, 170n60
Arab Socialists, 60
Arab Spring: in Algeria, 1, 3, 21–23, 30–31, 51; Amazigh movement prior to, 14–16; authoritarian responses to, 2–3; and Berber collective identity, 13; in Egypt, 1, 2, 55, 63; and independence era, 13; in Libya, 1, 55–56, 63–65, 65–67; in Morocco, 1, 2, 22, 131–135; origins of, 14–16; and scope of Amazigh identity movement, 1–5, 157; self-immolations as precipitating event, 22; in Tunisia, 1, 2, 63, 105
"Arab Winter," 2
Arrehmouch, Ahmed, 150, 153, 155, 159
Assid, Ahmed, 148
associational activism, 150–151. *See also* civil society
Association des Amazighs de Tunisie, 115
Association Tunisienne de la Culture Amazighe (ATCA), 115–118, 120–121
Attatürk, Kemal, 109
authoritarianism, 4, 37, 51–52. *See also specific countries*
autonomy and self-determination: and Kabyle activism in Algeria, 29–30; and the Kabyle Project, 32–35, 52; and pan-Amazigh institutions, 98; and regionalization in Morocco, 145, 155; and scope of Amazigh identity movement, 4, 158; and UN indigenous rights movement, 85. *See also* ethnonationalism
"A Vava Inouva" (song), 66, 160
Azawad autonomy movement: Azawagh dialect, 184n1; background and context of, 87–89, 89–94, 99–103, 104; extent of, *88*; and scope of Amazigh identity movement, 4, 18, 158–161
Azawagh dialect, 182n1
Azetta Amazigh, 149–150, 150–151

Ba`th Party, 10
Bahanga, Ibrahim Ag, 99, 100
Bahrain, 2

Baldinetti, Anna, 62
Ban Ki-moon, 44
"Barbary" term, 7
Baruni, Sulayman al-, 67
Battle of Anoual, 144
Becker, Cynthia, 97
Bedouin Arabs, 43
Ben Ali, Zine El Abidine, 1, 18, 106, 109, 111, 115–116, 123
ben-Askar, Khalifa, 67
Benghazi, Libya, 64, 72
Ben Jelloun, Taher, 126
Benkhalifa, Fathi, 69, 71–73, 78–79, 83
Benkirane, Abdelilah, 152
Ben Mahfoudh, Mohamed Fadhel, 119
Benmesbah, Djaffar, 37
Bensalah, Abdelkader, 47
Ben Salah, Ahmed, 47
Ben Sassi, Dania, 65, 121, 160, 195n88
Ben Youssef, Salah, 111
Berbers and Berber identity: and Algerian constitutional reforms, 39, 41; and Amazigh culture in Algerian society, 23–27, 29, 52; and Amazigh movements prior to Arab Spring, 14–16; Berber Culture Movement, 26; Berber language, 27, 60–61, 109, 111–115, 164n15 (*see also* Tamazight language); Berber Manifesto, 130; Berber Spring, 10, 13, 16, 25, 26, 61, 129; and borders of Amazigh identity, 6–7, 9; and ethnic groups of Libya, 59, *59*; and Hirak protests, 49; and Imazighen of Libya, 62; and independence era politics, 9–13; and indigenous Tamazight-speaking peoples, 6; and nationalist anticolonial movements, 9; rate of self-identification, 167n11; and tensions in Mzab Valley, 41–43, 45; and Tifinagh script, 52, 64, 66, 72, 83–84, 97, 119, 122
Berhouchi, Mustapha, 153
Bessaoud, Mohand Arav, 49
Black Spring (2001), 13, 25, 29, 146
Bogaert, Koenraad, 141
Bordj Bou Arréridjis, Algeria, 49
Bouazizi, Mohamed, 1, 22, 131, 146
Bouhired, Djamila, 46
Bouhmouch, Nadir, 141
Boukhars, Anouar, 34
Boukous, Ahmed, 151, 154–155
Bourguiba, Habib, 10, 109, 110–111
Boustati, Ouassim, 150
Bouteflika, Abdelaziz, 13, 22, 27, 30–31, 39, 41, 46, 94
Bouteflika, Saïd, 31, 46, 47
boycotts, 28, 31, 48, 51, 133
Brett, Michael, 108, 165n21
Burke, Edmund, 74
Burkina Faso, *8*, 89

Canary Islands, 11
cannabis cultivation, 148
Catalans, 15
Catholic Church, 34, 141
census data, 59, 109, 165n21
Center for Strategic and International Studies, 103
center-periphery relations, 3, 15, 105–106, 126–127, 144, 150
Central Intelligence Agency (CIA), 58, 89
Chad, *8*, 79
Chaker, Salem, 39, 40
Chaouis, *8*, 23, 49, 173n93
charitable endowments, 110
Chengriha, Saïd, 48
Chenouas, *8*, 23, 29
Cheriet, Hamid ("Idir"), 66
Christianity, 34, 84
citizenship issues, 150. *See also* elections
civil society: and advanced regionalization in Morocco, 145; and Amazigh activism in Libya, 80–82; and Amazigh activism in Tunisia, 119, 121, 123–124; and Arab Spring successes in Tunisia, 105; and Azawad autonomy movement, 101; and constitutional reforms in Morocco, 151; and Imazighen of Libya, 62; and origins of Arab Spring, 16; and "patrimonialization" in Algeria, 52; and regime change in Algeria, 47; and women's rights movements, 80–81

class divisions and politics, 15, 27, 105, 135–139
Claudot-Hawad, Hélène, 90
Club de la Culture Amazigh à Sfax, 123
collective discrimination, 61
colonial legacy in North Africa, 34, 49, 60, 105, 138, 167n13. *See also* French colonialism; Italian colonialism
Committee to Protect Journalists, 48
consociational democracy, 36–37
Constituent Assembly (Tunisia), 117
Constitutional Assembly (Libya), 75
constitutional reforms: in Algeria, 39–41; in Libya, 67–78; in Morocco, 125, 127, 132–134, 138, 145, 151–153, 154, 157; in Tunisia, 115, 117
Constitution Drafting Assembly (CDA; Libya), 77
contraband trade, 90
Coordination des Mouvements de l'Azawad (CMA), 103
Coordination Inter-wilayas des 'Aarch, Dairas et Communes (CIADC' "Citizens' Movement"), 28
corruption: and Azawad autonomy movement, 93, 103; and Kabylian activism in Algeria, 36, 37, 39; and political structure of Algeria, 21–22, 31, 51–52; and regime change in Algeria, 46, 47; and social protest in Morocco, 126, 131; and social protest in Rif region, 147
Corruption Perception Index, 21
COVID-19 pandemic, 17, 48, 51, 81, 156, 160
cultural rights, 17, 68, 84, 115, 118, 129, 154. *See also* language and linguistics

decentralization, 102. *See also* autonomy and self-determination
Declaration on the Rights of Indigenous Peoples, 5, 33, 77, 100–101, 138, 158
decolonization, 9–14, 91
demilitarization, 148
democracy and democratic reforms: in Algeria, 25–26, 28–29, 35, 46–47, 167n18; and Azawad autonomy movement, 93; in Libya, 68; in Morocco, 130; and the Projet pour un état Kabyle, 32–33; and radicalism of Kabylian intellectuals, 32–33, 35–37, 51–53; and Republic of Azawad, 101; and "stateness" concept, 56; in Tunisia, 124. *See also* constitutional reforms
Democracy Spring protests (Morocco), 125, 142
Department of Amazigh Studies, 84
diaspora Amazigh groups, 16–17
Djerba, Tunisia, 41, 58, 69, 106, 113, 116–117
Drareni, Khaled, 48
droughts, 92
DRS (Algerian intelligence services), 30, 31

Economic Community of West African States (ECOWAS), 89
economic marginalization, 114
education: and Azawad autonomy movement, 102; and Libyan politics, 59–60, 74–75, 79, 81–82; and Moroccan politics, 126–127, 130, 150–151, 152–153; and student activism, 14, 25, 27–28, 50, 137–138, 140, 150; and Tunisian politics, 105, 110, 117, 118, 120. *See also* language and linguistics
Egypt: and Arab Spring protests, 1, 2, 55, 63; and borders of Amazigh identity, 7; contrasted with Morocco, 125; distribution of Amazigh-speaking groups, 8; influence on Algerian politics, 22; intervention in Libya, 56; Mubarak's removal from power, 47; and pan-Arabism, 10, 57, 110; and "stateness," 56
Eid al-Adha, 142
"Ekker a Mmis Umazigh" ("Rise Up Son of Amazigh"), 16
El-Alia cemetery, 38
elections: and Algerian politics, 23, 26–28, 30–31, 39, 45–48, 51; Islamist gains after Arab Spring, 2; and Libyan politics, 70, 72–78, 82, 84; and

Moroccan politics, 133–134; and Tunisian politics, 55, 115–116, 120, 121. *See also* democracy and democratic reforms
Ennahda Party, 2, 115
Ennaji, Moha, 155
environmentalism, 140
Eritrea, 88
ethnicity and ethnic tensions: and Azawad autonomy movement, 103; the Kabyle Project, 35; and political background of Morocco, 143; and Tunisian politics, 105, 113–114, 115–116, 120, 124. *See also* ethnonationalism; *specific ethnicities*
ethnolinguistic groupings and minorities, 23, 76, 77–78
ethnonationalism: and authoritarian responses to Arab Spring, 2; and Azawad autonomy movement, 93, 104; and independence era, 13; influence of Kurdish activism, 2, 15, 57, 61, 120; Kabyle ethnonationalism in Algeria, 31–39, 52–53, 158, 169n38; and origins of Arab Spring, 15; and scope of Amazigh identity movement, 17. *See also* autonomy and self-determination
EuroMed Rights, 45
European culture, 7–9. *See also* French colonialism; Italian colonialism
European Union (EU), 30, 73, 98

Facebook, 97, 131
Fajr Libya ("Libyan Dawn"), 75, 79
family codes, 130
Fassis, 144
fatwas, 41, 77
February 20 protests (F20), 131–135, 137, 154, 159
federalism, 29, 56
Fekhar, Kemal Eddine, 44–45
female literacy, 105
Fentress, Elizabeth, 108, 165n21
"Fi Bladi Dalmouni" (song), 190n3
Fikri, Mohcen, 146–147
film festivals, 98
flag symbolism: and Amazigh activism in Libya, 65, 66, 70–71, 76; and Amazigh activism in Morocco, 131, 146, 147, 159; and Amazigh activism in Tunisia, 123; and Kabylian activism in Algeria, 30, 49–50, 53; and scope of Amazigh identity movement, 17
floods, 136
Ford, Robert, 21
French colonialism: and Azawad autonomy movement, 90, 92; and borders of Amazigh identity, 7–9; and human insecurity in Morocco, 137–138; and independence era, 9–10; and origin of Azawad autonomy movement, 100; and political background of Morocco, 127–129, 143; and political background of Tunisia, 109; political legacy in Algeria, 24, 33, 35, 46, 49, 50, 169n38; and Republic of the Rif, 144; Tuareg resistance to, 87, 90. *See also* colonial legacy in North Africa
French Sahara, 91
French West Africa, 90
Front de Libération Nationale (FLN), 25–26, 38, 169n38
Front des Forces Socialistes (FFS), 25–26, 32, 38, 44, 167n18, 173n92
Front Line Defenders, 45
Fulas, 101

Gaïd Salah, Ahmed, 47–48, 50, 53
Garratón Mateu, Carmen, 34
Gaulle, Charles de, 91
Gellner, Ernest, 9, 109
gender-based violence, 80–81
gender norms, 97, 105, 123, 139
general assembly *(Agraw)*, 142
General National Congress (GNC; Libya), 72–73, 74
general trade union (UGTA), 31
Generation Y, 131
Gerges, Fawaz, 1–2
Ghadames, Libya, 67
Ghali, Iyad Ag, 95, 100
Ghardaïa Province, 43, 44
Gharyéni, Nora, 121–123, 124
Glaoui, Thami el-, 127–129

Government of National Accord (GNA), 56, 79, 83
"Greater Maghrib," 40
Great Man Made River project, 61
Greenstream gas pipeline, 75
Grémont, Charles, 184n15
grievance theories, 141
Guanches, 11
guerrilla warfare, 144
Gwirah, Ahmed, 109

habous institution, 110
Hadj-Moussa, Ratiba, 52
Haftar, Khalid, 18, 56, 75, 77–85, 159–160
Hamel, Abdelghani, 47
Hamza, Belgacem, 109, 111–112, 124
Hamzawy, Amr, 2
Hanoune, Louisa, 47
Hasan II, King of Morocco, 14, 26, 129, 144, 148
Hassi Messaoud oil field, 43
Haut Commissariat a l'Amazighité (HCA), 26, 40
Hawad, Mahmudan, 92
haybat al-sulta ("fear of the regime"), 1
Himma, Fouad Ali El, 126
Hinshir, al-Hadi, 72–73
Hirak al-Sha`bi ("People's Movement") protests, 46–51, 53, 143–144, 148–149, 158
hirak "peoplehood," 3, 4, 17, 19
Ho Chi Minh, 144
Hoffman, Katherine, 116
Human Development Index, 21
human rights activism: and Amazigh activism in Tunisia, 115, 117; and associational activism in Morocco, 151; and Azawad autonomy movement, 101; and constitutional reforms in Libya, 68, 74, 77; and Declaration on the Rights of Indigenous Peoples, 5, 33, 77, 100–101, 138, 158; and human insecurity in Morocco, 135–139; and Imazighen of Libya, 62; and Imider mine protests, 140, 143; and Kabylian activism in Algeria, 37; and Libo Party in Libya, 79–80; and origins of Arab Spring, 16; and Rifian autonomy movement, 149–151; Universal Declaration of Human Rights, 33, 113
Human Rights Watch, 30, 45
hunger strikes, 45
Husayn, Saddam, 136

Ibn Khaldun, 113
Ibn Thabit, 65
Idbalkassm, Hassan, 138
Idir (Hamid Cheriet), 66, 160–161
Idris I, King of Libya, 10, 56
Ifogha Tuareg, 100
Ighid, Samir, 150
Imider protests, 139–143, 158
independence movements, 6, 9–14, 18. See also autonomy and self-determination
indigenous rights, 6, 85
infant mortality, 135
Inir n Tigawt Tasrtant Tamazight (NISA), 153
Institut Royal de la Culture Amazighe (IRCAM), 116, 130, 151, 154
International Commission of Jurists, 76
International Crisis Group, 27, 43, 72
International Day of Indigenous Peoples, 75
International Federation for Human Rights, 30
International Women's Day, 140
Iraq, 2, 3
irrigation canals *(khettaras)*, 140. See also water resources
Ishelhin, 8
ishumar generation, 92, 100
Islam and Islamism: and Algeria's Imazighen, 26, 29–30; and Azawad autonomy movement, 93–94, 102, 103; and Berber activism in Algeria, 129; and conflict with Algerian military, 22; and constitutional reforms in Algeria, 40; and constitutional reforms in Libya, 71, 72, 73–74, 75; and elements of Libyan identity, 69; Ibadi Islam, 41, 43, 58, 61, 67, 77, 82, 108–109, 116; influence in Egypt, 2;

"Islamic Winter," 2; Islamist political parties, 2; Islamization efforts, 6, 7, 9–10, 13–14, 108, 117, 148–149; and Kabylian activism in Algeria, 33, 37; Kharijite Islam, 108; Maliki school of, 41, 108; and Muslim Brotherhood, 2, 55, 74; and origins of Arab Spring, 15; and political conflict in Libya, 79, 159; political influence in Morocco, 2, 9, 125, 133–134, 154–155; and political tensions in Tunisia, 106; and post-Ben Ali political landscape, 115; Salafism, 34, 41, 43, 70, 82, 102, 104, 148; and scope of Amazigh identity movement, 18–19; Sufism, 34, 109; Sunni Islam, 35, 41, 43, 60, 70, 108, 109; and terrorist attacks in Morocco, 130; and Tunisian constitution, 110
Islamic Salvation Front (FIS), 26
Islamic State (ISIS), 2, 3, 75, 82
Islamist Justice and Development Party (PJD), 133–134, 151
Israel, 32
Istiqlal Party, 134, 155
Italian colonialism, 56, 67
Izri, Khalid, 66

Jacobinism, 35
jamahiriya ("polity of the masses"), 60
Japonais, 95
Jayasha, Rabea, 77
Jewish community, 50, 84, 106
jihadists, 55, 75
Jordan, 1, 2, 125
judicial oversight, 119

Kabyles and Kabilia: activism in Mzab Valley, 41–45; and Amazigh activism in Libya, 66; and Amazigh activism in Tunisia, 117; and Amazigh music in Tunisia, 121; and Amazigh-Tuareg relationship, 97; and Azawad autonomy movement, 87–88, 94, 103; and Berber activism in Morocco, 131; and constitutional reforms in Algeria, 39–41; and distribution of Amazigh-speaking groups, *8*; Imazighen of Algeria, 23–30, 129; and Imazighen of Libya, 61; and independence era, 10, 13; Kabyle-Amazigh dimension of the *Hirak*, 48–51; Kabyle collective identity, 25; Kabyle language, 52; Kabylian activism in Algeria, 31–32, 32–35, 35–37, 37–39, 169n38; and origins of "Amazigh" term, 164n15; and origins of Arab Spring, 14, 16; political status of, in Algeria, 51–53; population estimates, 167n11; and Rifian autonomy movement, 147–148; and scope of Amazigh identity movement, 4–5, 6, 17, 157–160
Kahina (mythical Berber queen), 49
Karameh ("Dignity"), 75
Keib, Abdurrahim Abdulhafiz El-, 71
Keita, Modibo, 91
Kel Adagh confederation, 92–93
Kel Aïr confederation, 91
Kel Ajjer confederation, 58
Kel Tagelmust ("veiled people"), 89
Kel Tamasheq/Tamajaq, 89
Khaleq, Omar, 137
Khalifa, Asma, 81
Khattabi, Mohamed bin Abdelkrim al-, 127
Kherrata, Algeria, 49
Kohl, Ines, 92
Kurds, 2, 15, 57, 61, 120
Kymlicka, Will, 73, 134

Laftit, Abdelouafi, 148
land rights, 150
language and linguistics: and borders of Amazigh identity, 6–9; distribution of Amazigh-speaking groups, *8*; and educational curricula in Libya, 74–75; promotion of language rights, 70; Tamazight in Algeria, 13; Tifinagh script, 52, 64, 66, 72, 83, 84, 97, 119, 122. *See also* official languages; Tamazight language
Law No. 18, 74
Layachi, Azzedine, 22
League of Arab States, 110
Lebanon, 1, 3

Lecocq, Baz, 92
Le Printemps Noir (the "Black Spring," or *Tafsut Taberkant*), 27
Le Roi prédateur (Graciet and Laurent), 126
LGBTQ+ community, 118
Libo Party, 79
Libya: Amazigh communities of, 57–63; and Amazigh movement prior to Arab Spring, 15; and Amazigh political identity, 4, 78–83, 83–85; Amazigh refugees in Tunisia, 116; and Arab Spring protests, 1, 55–56, 63–65, 65–67; and Azawad autonomy movement, 89; constitutional and institutional battles, 67–78; contrasted with Morocco, 125; distribution of Amazigh-speaking groups, *8*; ethnic groups of, *59*; independence, 9, 10; influence on Algerian poltics, 22-23; influence of Islamist movements, 2; influence of Mali rebellion, 87; Nafusa region, *8*, 58–61, 64, 66–67, 72, 82–83, 85, 122; and pan-Amazigh institutions, 98; political background, 55–57; Qaddafi's influence in North Africa, 94; and scope of Amazigh identity movement, 17–18, 157, 158; and Tuareg migrants, 95; Tunisia contrasted with, 105; Zuwara region, *8*, 58, 72, 79, 85
Libya Free People TV, 66
Libyan List for Freedom and Development, 72
Libyan National Amazigh Congress, 69–71
Libyan National Army, 56
Libyan Pharaonic Dynasties, 58
Libyan T'mazight Congress (Agraw a'Libi n'Tmazight), 62, 68, 69
Libyan Writers Union, 61
literacy, 84, 135. *See also* education; language and linguistics
Lounes, Belkacem, 63
Lure of Authoritarianism: The Maghreb After the Arab Spring, The (King and Maghraoui), 3, 4
Lynch, Marc, 1

Macron, Emmanuel, 77
Madi, Abderrazaq, 63
Madi, Salem, 63
Madi, Zorgh, 63, 81
Magariaf, Mohamed, 73, 74
Maghreb unity, 117
Mahdaoui, Hamid El, 149
Mahroug, Saïd ("Sifaw") El, 61
Majidi, Mounir, 126
makhzen, 136, 144, 147–149, 154, 159
Mali: and Amazigh movements prior to Arab Spring, 15, 16; and Amazigh political identity, 4; context of Tuareg conflict in, 89–93; distribution of Amazigh-speaking groups, *8*; mercenary forces from, 79; and origins of "Azawad" name, 182n1; and pan-Amazigh institutions, 98–99; and the Republic of Azawad, 87–89, 99–103, 104; and scope of Amazigh identity movement, 17, 18, 158, 159, 160; Tuareg independence movement, 6; Tuareg migrants in Libya, 55; Tuareg performing arts in, 95
Mammeri, Mouloud, 25, 97
Managem silver mine, 140, 143, 158
Mandefication, 92
Mandela, Nelson, 30
Manifeste Kabylie, 34, 35–37
Manouba University, 112
Mao Tse-tung, 144
March for Democracy on Algiers, 28
Martyr's Square, Tripoli, 65, 70
Marxism, 146
maternal mortality, 135
Matoub, Lounes, 27
matrilineal descent, 97
Mauritania, *8*, 9, 90
Médiene, Mohamed "Toufik," 30, 31, 47
Mediterranean Union Summit, 30
Mehenni, Améziane, 30, 41
Mehenni, Ferhat, 29–30, 32, 44
Mejjaoui, Mohamed El, 150
mercenaries, 79
middle class, 105
Mill, John Stuart, 74
Miloud, Inas, 80
mining industry, 139–142, 158

Ministry of Municipal Affairs (Tunisia), 119
Minority Rights Group International, 118, 119
Moatassim, Mohammed, 132
Mohamed V, King of Morocco, 127, 145
Mohamed VI, King of Morocco, 14, 22, 125–126, 129–132, 139, 141, 144–146
Moors, 101
Morgan, Andy, 94, 96
Moroccan Amazigh Democratic Party (PDAM), 153
Morocco: and Algeria's Imazighen, 26; and Amazigh movement prior to Arab Spring, 14–15, 16; and Amazigh political identity, 3–4; and Amazigh-Tuareg relationship, 97; and Arab Spring 2.0, 3; and associational activism, 150–151; and Berber identity, 7; compromise on official languages, 29; and constitutional reforms in Algeria, 39; context of social protest in, 125–127; and Democracy Spring activism, 125; and discrimination against Amazigh population, 119; distribution of Amazigh-speaking groups, 8; human insecurity in rural areas, 135–139; and Imider protests, 139–143; independence, 9, 11; indigenous languages of, 7; influence of Islamist movements, 2, 9, 125, 133–134, 154–155; legacy of colonialism in, 127–129; and Mohamed VI era, 129–131; responses to Arab Spring protests, 2, 22, 131–135; responses to constitutional reforms, 151–153; response to Amazigh activism, 13–14; and Rifian *Hirak*, 143–150; and scope of Amazigh identity movement, 17, 19; and scope of Arab Spring, 1; Tamazight-speaking peoples of, 6; Tunisia contrasted with, 125
Moukhlis, Mouha, 135–136
Mouvement National de l'Azawad (MNA), 99
Mouvement National de Libération de l'Azawad (MNLA), 87–89, 91, 99–103, 104

Mouvement Populaire (MP), 136, 153, 155
Movement for Amazigh Culture, 68
Movement for Autonomy of the Mzab, 44
Movement for Kabyle Self-Determination (MAK), 29–30, 32–37, 41, 52–53, 88
Movement for the Autonomy of the Rif (MAR), 145–146
Movement for Unity and Jihad in West Africa, 100
Movement of Rural Landless Workers, 141
Movement on Road 96 Imider, 140
Mubarak, Husni, 1, 47
Mukhtar, Omar al-, 67
music and poetry: and Algeria's Imazighen, 25; and Amazigh activism in Libya, 65–66; and Amazigh-Tuareg relationship, 96–97; "Fi Bladi Dalmouni" (song), 190n3; and Imazighen of Libya, 61; and origins of Arab Spring, 16; and Tinariwen, 94–96; and Tunisian Amazigh culture, 121–123, 124
Muslim Brotherhood, 2, 55, 74
Mzab Valley: and Algeria's Imazighen, 23–25; Amazigh-speaking regions in, *42*; and distribution of Amazigh-speaking groups, *8*; ethnic tensions, 35; and Kabylian activism in, 41–45; Mzabi-Ibadi community, 23, 58; and scope of Amazigh identity movement, 17, 158

Nadrani, Mohammed, 146
Nafusa region (Libya), *8*, 58–61, 64, 66–67, 72, 82–83, 85, 122
naming practices, 119, 150
Nasser, Gamal Abdel, 10, 57, 110
National Assembly (Algeria), 28
National Council of Languages and Culture, 154
National Council of Languages and of Moroccan Culture, 132
National Council of Moroccan Languages and Culture, 152

National Democratic Institute, 82
National Dialogue Quartet (Tunisia), 115
National Federation of Amazigh Associations (FNAA), 150, 151
National Front for the Salvation of Libya, 61, 73
national holidays, 40, 73, 134. *See also* Yennayer (Amazigh New Year)
nationalism and national identity, 6, 9–14, 62, 69–71, 84, 129. *See also* ethnonationalism
National Liberation Army, 64
National Pact (Tunisia), 93, 111
National Transitional Council (NTC), 55, 64, 67–71
National Union of Popular Forces, 148
Nefzi, Samir, 120, 121
neoliberalism, 138–139
Nettl, J. P., 56
Niger, *8*, 16, 55, 79, 91, 98, 104
Nigeria, *8*
Nobel Peace Prize, 115
nomadic cultures, 43, 58, 90, 109
Norland, Richard, 83
North Africa, 4. *See also specific countries*
North Atlantic Treaty Organization (NATO), 55, 65

Official Gazette, 151–152
official languages: and Algerian elections, 27–28; and Amazigh activism in Libya, 84–85; and Azawad autonomy movement, 87; and colonial legacy in Tunisia, 110; and constitutional reforms in Algeria, 39–40, 52; and constitutional reforms in Libya, 68, 70, 72–73, 76–78, 83; and constitutional reforms in Morocco, 132–133, 134, 151, 157; and Imazighen of Libya, 57, 62; and independence era, 11; and Republic of Azawad, 87; and Rifian autonomy movement, 146; and scope of Amazigh identity movement, 17, 19; Tamazight in Tunisia, 114
oil and gas resources, 43, 46, 51, 56–57, 65, 75
Omrani, Fatma al-, 81

Organic Law (Morocco), 19, 40, 132, 151–152, 154, 157
Organisation Commune des Régions Sahariennes, 90
Organization of African Unity, 98
Othmani, Saad Eddine El, 133, 134, 152
Ottoman legacy in North Africa, 7, 67, 109, 163n9
Oufkir, Mohamed, 129
Oulhaj, Lahcen, 132
Oussedik, Fatma, 32, 44
Ouyahia, Ahmed, 47

pan-Amazigh discourses and institutions, 6, 69, 98–99. *See also specific organization names*
pan-Arabism, 10, 57, 110
Parti de la Justice et du Développement (PJD), 133–134, 151
Parti de l'Authenticité et de la Modernité (PAM), 153
Parti Démocrate Amazigh Marocain (PDAM), 153
Parti du Progres et du Socialisme (PPS), 153
Pföestl, Eva, 73, 134
Plateforme pour le Front d'Action Politique Amazigh, 153
political opportunity theory, 141
political prisoners, 48, 80, 138
politicization of collective Kabyle identity, 25
polygamy, 110
Popular Movement for the Liberation of Azawad (MPLA), 93
populism, 149
Pouessel, Stéphanie, 110, 124
poverty, 135, 140, 141
Prague Spring, 25
Projet pour un état Kabyle (Project for a Kabyle State), 32–35, 33
Provisional Government of Kabylia (GPK; "Anavad"), 30, 37

Qaddafi, Muammar: and Arab Spring protests, 1, 21, 55, 85; coup and authoritarian rule, 56–57, 84; and Ima-

zighen of Libya, 58, 60–63; and independence era, 10; influence in North Africa, 94; and origin of Azawad autonomy movement, 99; overthrow and death of, 55, 65, 159; political prisoners of, 80; refugees from, in Tunisia, 116; and scope of Amazigh identity movement, 17
Qaddafi, Sayf al-Islam, 62, 63
Qatar, 56
Qayrawan, Tunisia, 108
Qur'an, 73, 102. *See also* Islam and Islamism

Rabita Shamal Ifriqiya (North African League), 61
Ramadan, 140
Rasmussen, Susan, 96
Rassemblement National des Indépendants (RNI), 153
Rassemblement pour la Culture et la Démocratie (RCD), 23, 26, 32, 35, 44, 120
Rassemblement pour la Kabylie (RPK), 37
refugees, 64–65, 94
regionalization, 145–146, 155
religious rights, 61, 84
Reporters sans Frontieres, 48
representation, 33. *See also* democracy and democratic reforms
Republic of the Rif, 144–147
Reseau National Amazigh pour la Citoyennete´, 131
resource mobilization theories, 141
Revolution of Dignity, 3
Revolution of Freedom and Dignity, 106
Rif region and culture: and Amazigh activism in Morocco, 131–132, 195n88; anticolonial background, 143–144; and distribution of Amazigh-speaking groups, *8*; and French colonial legacy, 127–129; and independence era, 14; Mohamad VI's visit to, 130; and prospects for future confrontation, 156; regional autonomy movement, 145–150; Rifian Republic flag,

146; and scope of Amazigh identity movement, 3–6, 19, 158, 160
The Rights to Land and Natural Resources in the Countries of Tamazgha (conference), 138
Riqdalin, Libya, 72
Roberts, Hugh, 22, 39, 167n18
Rossi-Doria, Daniele, 134, 137
Roughi, Ramzi, 11
Royal Institute of Amazigh Culture (IRCAM), 116, 130, 151, 154
rule of law, 26. *See also* constitutional reforms; democracy and democratic reforms
rural-urban divide, 134–139
Russia, 56, 79, 163n9
Ryser, Sarah, 139

Sadi, Saïd, 23, 155
Sadiki, Larbi, 3
Saharan oases, *8*
Sahel region, 18
Salafism, 34, 41, 43, 70, 82, 102, 104, 148
Saleh, Layla, 3
Salih, Ali Abdallah, 1
San Remo conference, 163n9
Sanusi religious order, 56
Sarraj, Fayez El-, 75, 77
Saudi Arabia, 2
scalar dilemma, 137
sculpture, 97
secularism: and Algeria's Imazighen, 23; and Azawad autonomy movement, 87–88, 89; and constitutional reforms in Libya, 68, 70; and democratic political dynamics, 2; and Kabyle activism in Algeria, 26, 32–34; and Rifian autonomy movement, 148, 149; and scope of Amazigh identity movement, 18, 159; and Tunisian politics, 110, 115
self-defense groups, 43–44
Sellal, Abdelmalek, 38, 47
Senegal, *8*
"severely endangered languages," 112
sexual violence, 80–81
Sfax, Tunisia, 122

Shari`a law, 71, 127
Shoshenq I, 58
silver mining, 139–140, 158
Silverstein, Paul, 137
Sisi, Abd al-Fatah al-, 55
Siwa oasis, 7, *8*, 11, 16
Smith, Anthony, 10, 146
smuggling, 90, 93
social activism, 150–151
social contract, 35
social media, 5, 48, 50, 131, 160
Songhays, 101
soulaliyate women's movement, 139
Soummam Valley, 32, 169n38
South Sudan, 88
"stateness," 56
Stevens, Christopher, 72
strikes, 25, 28
student activism, 14, 25, 27–28, 50, 137–138, 140, 150
Suárez Collado, Angela, 145–146
Sudan, 3, *8*
Sufism, 34, 109
Supreme Council for the Amazigh of Libya, 73
Supreme Council of the Arabic Language, 40
Supreme Fatwa Committee, 82
Sykes-Picot agreement, 163n9
Syria, 1, 2, 22–23, 57

Tabbou, Karim, 48–49, 173n92
Tajmaat, 33
"Takrust" ("The Knot," or "The Problem"), 121
Tamashek/Tamaheq language, 58, 93
Tamaynut ("New") association, 137
Tamazgha, 5, 11, *12*, 17, 58, 88, 97, 98, 113–115, 140
Tamazight language: and Algeria's Imazighen, 26, 28–29; and Berber collective identity, 11; and constitutional reforms in Libya, 68–74, 76–78; degrees of fluency in Morocco, 165n21; and French colonialism in Tunisia, 109; and Imazighen of Libya, 57, 61–62; in Morocco, *128*; as official language, 39; and political conflict in Libya, 79, 80, 81–83; and the Republic of Azawad, 87; and scope of Amazigh identity movement, 4; and Tuareg culture, 89
Tamazight Women's Movement (TWM), 80–81
Tamunt ("Unity") Party, 153
Tanekra, 92–93, 94
Taoujout Association for the Preservation of Amazigh Villages, 109
Tarifit language, 146
Tashelhit-speaking tribes, 127
Tataouine Province, Tunisia, 65, 116
Tawalt ("Word") website, 62–63
Tawja, Moha, 141, 143
Tebboune, Abdelmadjid, 47, 48
Tebu (people and language), 57, *59*, 67, 74–75, 77–78, 80–83
Temoust ("Identity"), 98
terrorism, 23, 29–30, 93–94, 130
teshumura, 92
Thawrat al-Ibtisam ("Smile Revolution"), 46
Tifinagh script, 52, 64, 66, 72, 83–84, 97, 119, 122
Tilmatine, Mohand, 34, 52, 167n13
Tinariwen, 94–96, 97
TIRA Research & Studies, 81
Tlemcani, Rachid, 31
Tocqueville, Alexis de, 74
Touré, Amadou Toumani, 99, 100
Transparency Index, 31
Transparency International, 21
Traroé, Moussa, 93
tribal identities, 60. *See also* ethnicity and ethnic tensions
Tripoli, Libya, 61, 70–71
Tripoli House of Representatives, 83
Tripolitanian Republic, 67
Tuaregs: and Algeria's Imazighen, 23; and Amazigh activism in Libya, 67; and Amazigh identity, 96–97; and Amazigh movement prior to Arab Spring, 15–16; and Azawad autonomy movement, 87–89, 99–103, 104; and "Azawagh" identity, 182n1; and background of conflict in Mali,

89–94; and constitutional reforms in Libya, 75, 77; and demographics of Libya, 58; and distribution of Amazigh-speaking groups, *8*; and ethnic groups of Libya, *59*; and Imazighen of Libya, 57; and indigenous Tamazight-speaking peoples, 6; and Kabyle-Amazigh dimension of the *Hirak*, 50; and Libyan civil society, 82; migrant populations in Libya, 55; music and poetry of, 92, 94–96, 96–97; and pan-Amazigh institutions, 98–99; and scope of Amazigh identity movement, 4, 18, 158; Tuareg language, 78, 79, 89; and women's rights movements, 80

Tumzabt dialect, 41

Tunisia: and the Akal party, 120–121; and Amazigh political identity, 4; Amazigh population of, 105–106, 107, 111–115; Amazigh-speaking groups of, *8*; and Arab Spring protests, 1, 2, 63, 105; and Azawad autonomy movement, 90; context of Amazigh politics, 108–111; independence, 9, 10; indigenous Tamazight-speaking peoples, 6; influence of Islamist movements, 2; influence on Algerian politics, 22; Libya contrasted with, 55; and origins of Amazigh identity movement, 4; post-Ben Ali political landscape, 105–108, 115–119, 123; promotion of Amazigh culture, 121–123, 124; and scope of Amazigh identity movement, 17–19; and "stateness," 56

Turkey, 56, 61, 79, 109

2030 Agenda for Sustainable Development (UN), 81

Twitter, 48

tyranny of the majority, 74

"Ulaç Smah" ("No Forgiveness"), 16

Umadi, Mohamed (Madghis), 62–63

unemployment, 21–22, 92, 126

Union Démocratique et Sociale (UDS), 173n92

United Arab Emirates (UAE), 56, 79

United Nations (UN): and Amazigh activism in Tunisia, 116, 123; and associational activism in Morocco, 151; and Azawad autonomy movement, 89; Charter, 100; Committee on Economic, Social, and Cultural Rights, 118; Committee on the Elimination of Racial Discrimination (CERD), 58, 113–115, 118–119; and constitutional reforms in Morocco, 152; Declaration on the Rights of Indigenous Peoples, 5, 33, 77, 100–101, 138, 158; Human Development Index, 21, 125, 135; and human insecurity in Morocco, 138–139; Human Rights Commission, 117, 119; and human rights issues in Algeria, 44–45; International Day of Indigenous Peoples, 75; intervention in Libya, 55–56, 78, 85; and Kabylia autonomy movement, 30; Office for the Coordination of Humanitarian Affairs, 64; Office of Human Rights, 118; and pan-Amazigh institutions, 98, 160; Permanent Forum on Indigenous Issues, 138; and scope of Amazigh identity movement, 18; Security Council, 80–81, 103; Special Representative on the Rights of Indigenous Peoples, 44; sustainable development agenda, 81; Universal Declaration of Human Rights, 33, 113; World Heritage Sites, 43

United Nations Educational, Scientific and Cultural Organization (UNESCO), 43, 112

United States Embassy (Benghazi), 72

Universal Declaration of Human Rights, 33, 113

US Agency for International Development (USAID), 82

U Salet Idnegh Tefsut ("Together We Raise Up Spring"), 61

US Department of State, 34

Volpi, Frederic, 3

voter turnout, 48, 51

Wahhabism, 35–36, 37
water resources, 61, 72–73, 92, 135–136, 138–143, 150, 158
Wehrey, Frederick, 34, 65
Westernization, 154
Western Sahara, *8*, 145
Wikileaks, 126
Wilayat Béjaïa, Algeria, 32, 51
Wilayat Tizi Ouzou, Algeria, 51
women's rights, 80–81, 123, 130, 139. *See also* gender norms
Workers' Party (Algeria), 47
World Amazigh Assembly, 16
World Amazigh Congress: and Amazigh activism in Libya, 64, 66; and Amazigh activism in Tunisia, 112, 116, 118; and Azawad autonomy movement, 88; and Benkhalifa, 79; and constitutional reforms in Libya, 69, 71, 73; Djerba meeting, 106; establishment of, 98, 155; and human insecurity in Morocco, 138; and human rights issues in Algeria, 44–45; and Imazighen of Libya, 63; and Kabyle-Amazigh dimension of the *Hirak*, 49; and origins of Arab Spring, 16; Tataouine meeting, 116
World Factbook (CIA), 58, 89
Wouerghemma confederation, 109, 111

"Years of Lead," 11, 146–147
Yemen, 1, 2
Yennayer (Amazigh New Year), 16, 40–41, 66, 73, 79, 134, 170n64
Young Turk revolution, 67

Zafzafi, Nasser, 147–150
Zagora "thirst" protests, 136, 158
Zawiya oil refinery, 65
Zawiya University, 84
zawouiyat, 109
Zaytouna College, 110
Zenaga, *8*
Ziani, Silya, 121, 149, 160
Zintan Arabs, 64
Zoubir, Yahia, 31
Zuwara region, Libya, *8*, 58, 72, 79, 85